# The Blue Square Method

Duncan MacPherson and Chris Jeppesen

Second Edition

All materials copyright 2022 Blue Square Apps

ISBN: 9780968440193

Discover other titles by Duncan and Chris:

The Advisor Playbook

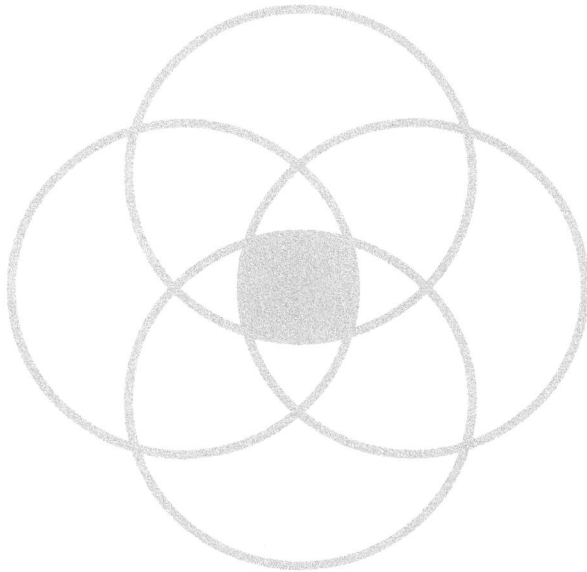

# Table of Contents

# Acknowledgments

We would like to thank the many clients who've collaborated with us over the years as they embraced our approach, added their own customizations and shared their results with us. Crowd-sourcing this mindset and these best practices has been incredibly gratifying. We'd also like to thank our team members and colleagues who have made countless observations and contributions while providing invaluable insights that have reinforced our philosophy and process.

Project Management and Fulfillment by Michael Lane

Edited by Michael Lane and Terry Gronbeck-Jones

*Note: Before using any social media, message apps, etc. mentioned in the following, check with your compliance department.*

# Foreword

The Blue Square Venn diagram on our cover may look familiar to you, if you're familiar with the Japanese concept of ikigai. The word is a compound of the kanji for "life" and "meaning" and the concept – generally believed to have originated in Okinawa – roughly translates to "what you live for" i.e. your reason for being.

Ikigai reflects a state of self-actualization (something Maslow with his hierarchy of needs would understand immediately) and, in a general sense, keys off the intersection of the answers to these questions:

- What do you love doing?

- What are you good at? What are your talents and skills?

- What does the world need? What problems can you uniquely solve?

- What can you be rewarded for, both financially and emotionally?


This premise is ideal to apply as one begins their career path, but it is not only applicable early in life. As your life progresses, the Blue Square serves as a gentle reminder for what matters - sometimes prompting you to make a mid-course correction to offset the unconscious drifting that can occur while living a busy and multi-faceted life. A high achiever is never sure how many gears they will shift through or how many chapters they'll flip through in their lifetime. In many ways, it's the pursuit that is the achievement, not the arrival at a destination or the attainment of a specific result.

In a broader sense, each person's ikigai is unique to them, and when you've reached the center of the overlap, your mental state reaches balance and a sense of peace. By aligning your skills, talents and purpose with the world, you propel yourself towards self-actualization. That alignment is an organic one, too. You don't have to force yourself into an "ikigai-ready" position. You'll naturally click into the place you were always meant to be, and that is what it means to become the best version of yourself, personally and professionally.

To paraphrase Hemingway, the goal is not to be superior to another person. The goal is to be superior to your former self. That is exactly why we compiled this book - both for you, the reader, and for us as we write.

To put it succinctly - once you meld your talent and interest in what you love doing, apply it to what the world needs and for which the world rewards you. Do that, and you have defined your ikigai and have reached your own Blue Square.

Look closely at the center of the Blue Square icon. Within that bullseye, you'll note our tribute to the pyramid from Maslow's hierarchy of needs, and we want you to focus intently on the summit – self-actualization. This is what we want all of our clients to work toward. The outside components of the image quantify the aspirations they have and what we want for them. We want our clients to truly love what they do. In fact, some are so enthralled that it seems they would actually pay to do what they do. They love it that much. It isn't a job. It never feels like work. That is very fulfilling to us.

Your process drives enterprise value, so everything you do has to be process-driven rather than solely skill-based. Over the years we've developed and refined a process that our clients can adopt, customize and deploy to create an impactful client experience. Process creates consistency. Process drives enterprise value. Enterprise value matters. Every business should be built to be sold for maximum value and include a 'torch' that the acquirer can grab hold of to keep the momentum going.

When that liquidity event arrives, we don't want your enterprise value to be tied only to your technical ability, the size of your business and its core elements. Your enterprise value is reinforced by your processes that continuously convert clients to referral-generating advocates. We want your primary new revenue stream to be client acquisition through advocacy. That's monetizing rather than transacting, and that's a goal that is elusive to many.

Along the way, we don't want your achievements to be just measurable, they should be meaningful, too. There can be an anticlimax to strictly quantitative productivity. We want your success to be panoramic and all-encompassing. This last point brings us to the four overlaps surrounding the Blue Square - these four elements are more qualitative.

Gratitude is one. Appreciating what you have while you aspire to what you want. Reaching for the next level but taking nothing for granted. Kurt Vonnegut was right when he wrote, "Enjoy the little things in life, because one day you'll look back and realize they were the big things."

Second is a sense of Purpose, seeing your work as a calling. You don't have to do it, you get to do it, and that mindset creates unstoppable self-motivation.

Fulfillment ultimately means that your business serves your life, not the other way around. It liberates you to pursue other interests along the way. You're not a one-trick workaholic pony. Business is a means to an end.

Finally, you have Balance. This includes work/life balance but goes much deeper in terms of finding your sweet-spot between contentment and ambition.

That's the Blue Square. Hopefully our book ignites a blue flame of intention, conviction and execution for you as you move towards your personal and professional goals.

This book picks up where our previous effort, *The Advisor Playbook*, left off. Six years came and went between it and *The Blue Square Method*. Our clients became six years wiser and moved six years further down their path. Our interactions and shared experiences helped shape and elevate our approach. The needs and aspirations of our clients evolved and market forces became more turbulent, all of which has prompted us to keep refining, optimizing and innovating in real time. Jim Bowen, a titan in the world of commerce and arguably the biggest supporter of the fee-for-service professional community, likes to say "As we go through time together." That speaks volumes about what it means to continually grow with and collaborate with clients rather than to occasionally transact with them.

# Chapter 1:

## *The Blue Square: True North*

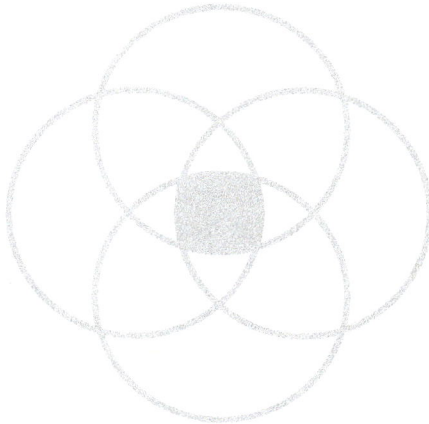

The Blue Square Method was written for the successful fee-for-service professional who has reached or is approaching a fork in the road in their personal and professional life. Life is good today, business is steady and you have every reason to be content while riding your momentum, but perhaps contentment in-and-of-itself was never the goal? You appreciate what you have, but you aspire to something more. We're not talking about just more money and quantitative success. We're also referring to qualitative success: Amplifying your sense of gratitude, purpose, balance and fulfillment.

This chapter is called True North because we want you to look down the road and get crystal clear on your trajectory and the beacon you are heading toward. Stephen Covey suggested that we "begin with the end in mind" and to "keep climbing the ladder, but be sure it's leaning against the right wall." We want your day-to-day to be aligned with your clearly defined aspirations, especially now, when the world has gotten noisier, less predictable, and the velocity of change has intensified. Those external factors can distract you, cloud your thinking and nudge you off course. Throw in a disruptive and once-in-a-lifetime *force majeure* and we can fall into a reactive trance, sleepwalking our way forward. We don't want you to fall for the head-fake that life can throw at you. We want to remind you that you can achieve panoramic success on your terms despite the fluctuations in the world around you. Bottom line, change can create consequences, but so can the status quo.

This is especially important for a fee-for-service professional. You're not selling tangible items, nor do you have a brick-and-mortar business in the traditional sense. You think for a living. You provide solutions within a fee-for-service business. We will refer to fee-for-service throughout this book as F4S to constantly reinforce that your sector is unique and becoming increasingly commoditized every day. Every sector is under siege to varying degrees, but F4S professionals have more headwind and friction than most. We believe that, with the proper preparation, this environment can be a tremendous opportunity to achieve professional contrast so that you can elevate and differentiate yourself.

Part of the True North beacon can be found in The Blue Square Method icon. The Blue Square in the center of the four-circle Venn diagram is the bullseye every enlightened F4S professional aims for, perhaps not always deliberately, but at least subconsciously. In the outer rings you'll find the professional benefits: You love what you do, which gives you sustained energy to be consistently productive; you've developed a proprietary process that drives your enterprise value; you consistently convert clients into referral-generating advocates; and you are monetizing on your business fully and completely.

To paraphrase legendary thought leader Jim Rohn, it's not just what you earn that matters, it's who you become that counts.

This brings us to the inner rings closer to the Blue Square. It's not just what our approach is but also what it does. Next level achievement activates your sense of gratitude and appreciation for what you have. It galvanizes your sense of purpose, it governs your decisions and conduct so that you maintain balance and it fuels your sense of personal and professional fulfillment. When ambition is fueled by contentment, when you take nothing for granted, when you savor your wins, when you stay true to your convictions and when you are aware of the legacy you are building in real time, you have a business that serves your life rather than the other way around. When you take care of yourself physically, socially, spiritually and intellectually, you find another gear of effectiveness. You realize that you are the keystone to the success of your team and your clients, but you also understand that their happiness can't come at your expense. You take care of them by taking impeccable care of yourself. You realize that you can't pour from an empty cup and yet, over time, the cup gets bigger and so, too, does the amount of value you bring to the world.

## All Roads Lead to Conversion and Convergence

Practically speaking, a big part of your True North is a fixation on conversion and convergence – they are the ultimate goals of a F4S professional. Let's first look at conversion.

We've been talking about this for many years but it's never been more important to growth than right now - your understanding that your primary addressable audience is right under your nose.

Conversion reminds us that you have three types of clients. There are customers who occasionally transact with you, clients who empower you fully while also endorsing you to others, and the advocates who are the dream clients. They are a joy to work with and they consistently introduce new people to you. In this book you will discover our philosophy and process to enable you to go back to all of your existing relationships and reintroduce yourself - to reframe your value and impact to help them see the merit of becoming a totally engaged, fully empowering, referral-generating advocate.

Don't get us wrong. Customers are fine. They move the needle, but they don't empower you fully. They also do business with somebody else that they could be doing with you. Your relationship with a customer is a transaction. They also tend to come with a bit more hassle factor as well as a fleeting ROI. As you read further you may determine, after reframing existing customers, that in time you will no longer bring on some new customers because you decide that a relationship with a specific prospect can be flawed in many ways.

You may decide to allocate existing customers who don't convert to a different service model that liberates you to work with more deserving and more profitable clients. You may determine that you are doing your existing non-converting customers a disservice by keeping them and you may delegate them to someone else or respectfully disassociate all together. After all, if they won't fully take your advice, perhaps it would be better to introduce them to someone whose advice they will take?

There is a self-fulfilling component to this mindset in that, when you do have the conversation with customers about the merit of becoming a totally engaged client, many will respond favorably while a few do not. Some customers will tell you that it didn't occur to them that they should empower you fully. It was not intentional. Some customers will prefer the status quo and choose to not engage with you fully. At that point you have to decide what to do with them and how your rules of engagement will change going forward.

The beauty of clients is that they don't dabble. They see your value. They don't say, "I'm not putting all my eggs in one basket" because they don't think of you as a basket. They think of you as someone who liberates them to go live their lives. You've got the goods and they know it, and what's great is that, in a referable moment, clients will wave your flag. They'll sing your praises and, with great intentions, they endorse you. Here is the thing about endorsements, though - they often have the lasting value of a Red Bull. A client tells a friend to call you and that endorsement goes to the friend's head to die. Have you ever had a client ask you, "Hey, did my friend call you?" But they never called?

The endorsement was undermined by the Law of Diminishing Intent and had the longevity of a wind-up toy.

Advocates don't endorse. They take action and they introduce people to you. Clients can bring people they know to the red-zone, advocates bring them into the end-zone. They are the people who call you up and say, "Hey, you've got to do me a favor. My friend is going through some issues right now and I outlined your process and told him I'd make an introduction. I know you're busy, but do me a favor and talk to him."

Does it get much better than that? Advocates are the ultimate asset. They increase in value over time and they pay dividends in the form of new client acquisition through introductions. They are the ultimate profit center and recurring revenue stream. Let's increase the frequency of that happening.

It's not uncommon for a typical F4S professional with 200 relationships to have 50 customers, 140 clients and 10 advocates. What would it look like if, in the next 18 months, you had 50 advocates? How would that impact the quality of your growth? As a friend of ours would say, "the fish start to jump in the boat."

## Math Wins

If you received six referrals in the last 12 months, you were probably talked about and endorsed 30 times. It's about a five-to-one ratio between endorsement and introduction. Closing that gap is not only where the lowest-hanging fruit lives, but your growth model elevates you from transacting – trading time for money and pumping up a leaky tire – to a more predictable, efficient and durable approach. With advocates, you're not selling something, you're building something. Like owning a home versus renting, you're building equity along with pride in ownership. Basic customer and client acquisition through various marketing strategies alone is practical but can be anticlimactic because it's a transaction without any lasting, long term benefits. Before you know it, the rent is due, meaning you have to go out and find more clients. Advocate conversion, on the other hand, means that you are consistently being found by new clients. When you nurture advocacy conversion in your business, you look back on the old client acquisition model and realize that it was more costly and there was far more friction. There are few things more rewarding than cracking the conversion code - not convincing new people, but instead working with people who are already convinced and showing them why, to whom and how to convince others. We are going to walk you through that proven process throughout this book.

You probably have a handful of advocates now who are simply predisposed to the role – it's their nature to be a rainmaker. You can nurture that predisposition for a larger group. It's engineered. It's by design. You can master the art of activating advocacy. Teach clients how to create awareness for your professional contrast, so they know what to say. It's not just that they are good messengers, but that they are also equipped with the messaging.

When a friend asks for an endorsement, imagine if a client replied with "The thing I love about my relationship is the consistency of the communication. Everything is scheduled and process driven and nothing falls through the cracks." Or if they were to ask, "Have you done a gap and exposure analysis so that you know exactly where you stand? I can make an introduction if you like."

Messaging like this can enhance a triggering event for someone who is on the verge but still undecided. The friend asks themselves, "Why do I keep accepting my current mediocre experience?" Which then prompts them to ask your client, "How can I meet your advisor?" As advocates, they are not just singing your praises to friends, they are using your IP and language to tip them over.

## The Power of Convergence

Convergence occurs when you don't think of your enterprise as a practice or a book of business, but rather as an actual business. Every investment of effort you make creates consistency in the client experience, opens up scalable growth opportunities and drives enterprise value. You do this by getting all of your value out of your head and documented in a proprietary playbook. You take your technical ability, your full array of deliverables and every aspect of your client experience and you transform it into an intellectual property. While you may have a talented team, if their procedures reside in their heads, then they simply have good qualities, skills and intentions. Those are not proprietary to your enterprise. It's essential to have talented people on your team, but we want you to de-personalize your value, meaning that clients appreciate the practice and the process as much as they appreciate your people. This stage is a powerful next step because it creates order and lowers uncertainty and complexity. It has been proven time and time again that complexity is the silent killer of growth and sustainability because it causes your business to lose traction and spin its wheels. Process is the antidote to complexity because everything has been thought through, taken out of your head and documented. It's as strong as the practice that creates muscle-memory in sports.

Before we delve deeper, let us point out that throughout this book we hope to prompt you to assess your past, present and future more significantly and panoramically than you ever have before. Taking a moment to savor and evaluate all aspects of your journey can activate appreciation and clarity.

A Quero Apache Prayer offers a pleasant nudge, "Looking behind I am filled with gratitude. Looking forward I am filled with vision. Looking upwards I am filled with strength and looking within I discover peace."

## Rein*vennt* Yourself

By putting conversion and convergence front and center, you are already elevating yourself in terms of awareness. This chapter is ultimately designed to not only brighten your beacon and amplify its magnetic pull, but also to be a precursor to the Strategic Planning section that can be found later in the book. For now, we just want you to be clear on where you are, how you got there, and where you're going. Success is incremental but it's also directional. To that end, we've provided four Venn diagrams that will prompt you to assess your approach, recalibrate, and galvanize your planning strategy.

### Your Progression

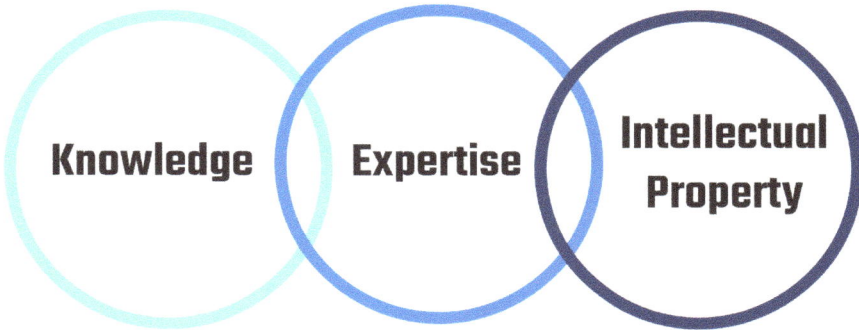

**Knowledge**　　**Expertise**　　**Intellectual Property**

### The Enterprise Value Drivers

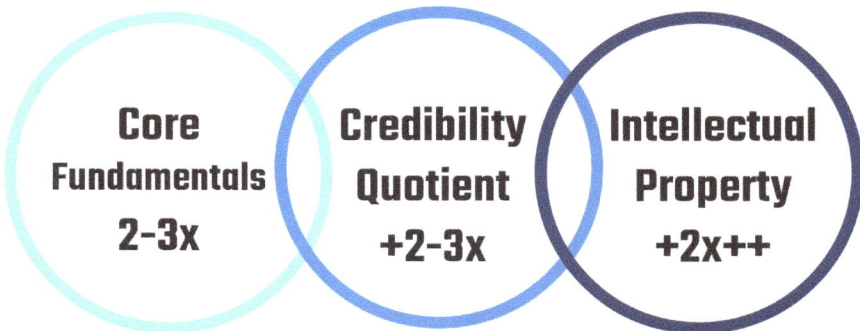

**Core Fundamentals 2-3x**　　**Credibility Quotient +2-3x**　　**Intellectual Property +2x++**

## Growing Up-Market

**Level Up**

**Brand within a Brand**

**All In**

## Re-Imagine Growth

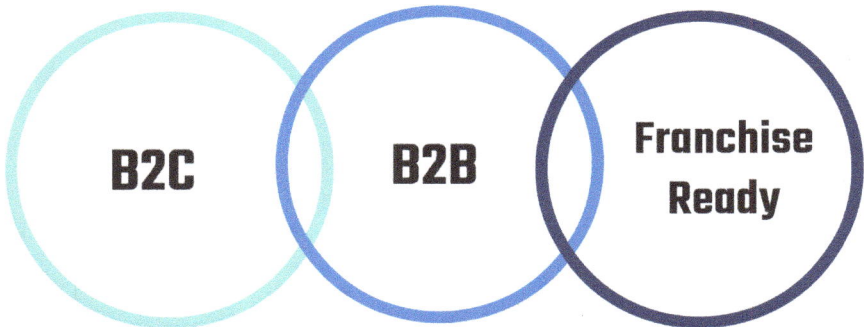

**B2C**

**B2B**

**Franchise Ready**

## KEIPing Ahead of the Joneses

Undoubtedly you can relate to this vital commonality we see amongst top F4S professionals. They don't rest on their core competency. They build on it. The best in the fee-for-service space are relentlessly striving to land in the perfect intersection between professional contrast and professional scarcity. In the early days, arriving at this nexus was a subconscious pursuit that was fueled more by personal standards than anything else – mediocrity was unacceptable. Eventually, differentiating from the pack and ensuring people were drawn to their unique value became more deliberate. As their frame of reference grew more acute, the lens they used to view their achievements became stronger – fueled by reputational equity, personal fulfillment and the need for plateau avoidance. They realize limitations are self-imposed, not driven by external forces, and that excellence is not a form of natural selection, it is by design.

## Your Progression

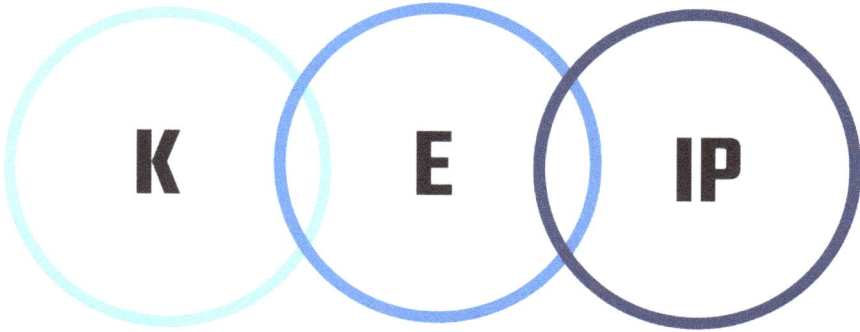

## Never Forget Where You Came From

Think of your own 'professional contrast progression'. In your formative years, you tried to put distance between yourself and competitors by emphasizing your technical ability and core competency. Your designations, credentials, continuing education, work ethic, judgment and integrity were more than enough to make you fee-worthy. At that time you were part of the Knowledge Economy.

As the world woke up and tried to catch up, you made the shift to the Expertise Economy. Your sector started to show signs of commoditization and fee-compression, so you began to place more emphasis on the client experience using best practices, and more emphasis on the client relationship by being a goals-based professional. You started being more deliberate about the kind of client you were ideally suited for so you could focus on the relationship directionally in terms of where the client's evolving needs were heading in the future. You took a team approach by adding bench strength to your roster. This evolution from broadcasting to narrowcasting elevated you from a generalist to a more coveted specialist. This was an evolution from being a technician capable of delivering solutions to a business owner capable of building a meaningful enterprise. Consider the difference between an architect who can create masterful blueprints, and an entrepreneur who can also run a successful architectural business.

## Keep Going

You're now entering - or have already entered - the next frontier: the Intellectual Property economy. You're becoming process-driven in everything you do. You're branding your practice and process to ensure clients appreciate them as much as your people.

You're constantly adding to and refining your proprietary playbook of best practices and standard operating procedures. You're establishing a Value Added Support Team (VAST) – as opposed to calling them COIs - and engaging them into your process. You're constantly working on yourself personally and professionally to be positioned as a thought-leader and subject matter expert along with providing a proprietary array of deliverables that are yours and exclusively available to your clients. People can only get this degree of value from your business.

Consider the impact that has on your professional scarcity. You want people to be drawn to you and to feel they belong to something special. This is where you carefully curate an approach, an experience and an environment that ensures the world perceives you as a more exclusive community - and the ideal client wants in.

The best place to start with respect to an IP mindset is what we refer to as Always ON.

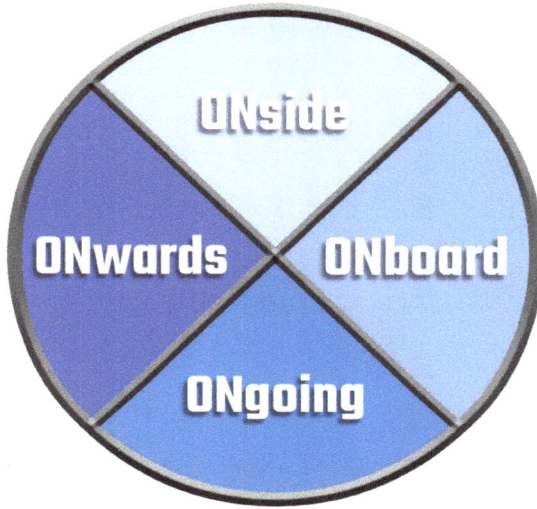

## Always ON

This book was inspired by our many interactions with successful F4S professionals as well as many highly respected leaders in the world of personal and professional development. Jim Rohn urged us to "work harder ON yourself than you do on anything else." Michael Gerber, the author of The E-Myth opened our eyes to the distinction between working IN a business and working ON a business. A great place to activate convergence in your business is to use our Always On framework and structure to create an initial placeholder for the four key quadrants that relate to your most important best practices. This simple exercise of professionalizing and standardizing the most essential procedures can put you on a path to an enhanced client experience and consistent advocacy.

You may have noticed that the word "on" was highlighted within the words conversion and convergence earlier in this chapter. This wasn't just word-play. This is a deliberate, intentional and laser-focused initiative that is built into your mindset, actions and team meetings.

As we shift to this and many more actionable items, understand that all of this will be outlined in detail throughout this book and supplemented with tools at thebluesquaremethod.com/implementation-resources.

### ONside

Think about your current process when you make an initial contact with a prospective client. Let's say an advocate or strategic partner calls to inform you that they want to introduce someone to you. What happens the moment you end the call? How many steps are there in your current process to thank the rainmaker, connect with the prospective client, engage with them so that they can contrast you to others and so you can both determine if there is an alignment of interests and a good fit? For most F4S professionals, there are about eight to 10 steps in the ONside process. Each step needs to be defined and documented fully in order to be deployed consistently.

### ONboard

After your fit process, you bring the prospective client to the moment of truth where they opt in and there is a signing ceremony. How many steps are there in your process to transition them over to you, onboard them and fast track them to advocate status? In our world there are commonly between 10 and 12 steps. This is especially important when you consider that you are at a very high level of referability early in a relationship, primarily because your value is so fresh - especially relative to the provider they just left in order to join you.

### ONgoing

Now that they are a client, how many steps are there in your 12-month client experience to build a firewall around that relationship? How many steps in that process to competitor-proof them, and with that to ensure they continually empower you fully as their life unfolds and needs evolve, not to mention ensuring consistent advocacy? At a minimum, you may have a 12/4/2 model that includes 12 proactive touches, four scheduled phone calls and two face-to-face or virtual meetings throughout the year above and beyond reactive service issues. That is a solid baseline. As you build out further, you may define a service model and matrix tied to the classification of the client, where your most deserving clients receive an even more robust experience. As you will see, for AAA PLUS clients, your service model may include as many as 34 ongoing touches throughout the year. Whatever the case may be, it needs to be defined.

## ONwards

This quadrant speaks to your mindset as an enlightened F4S professional and the culture of your enterprise. It's not promissory on the performance of your solutions *per se,* but focuses more on your client experience – what it means to be your client - especially when something dramatic happens to them. When a critical life event, milestone or moment of truth occurs in your client's life, how do you respond to, recognize and pay tribute to it? The only constant in life is change. Your client's life could be chugging along beautifully and POW, there is a lightning strike. It could be an illness, divorce or setback. It could be a breakthrough or accomplishment. Either way, the event disrupts the status quo and may turn calm into chaos. It could also potentially reveal an array of new needs. How do you respond to that? How do you get out in front of that?

Define your code-of-conduct. Itemize some examples and empower your team with an ability to respond so that moments of truth never go unrecognized. These opportunities can define a relationship and open up the referral floodgates.

There is a reason that there is an X separating the four quadrants. This is the starting point to give your enterprise the proverbial X factor – an energy that's hard for a client to put their finger on, but it is palpable and appreciated, nonetheless. There is a reason why the Always ON icon resembles the face of a clock, too. The moment your team starts documenting, refining and optimizing everything you do, the business starts running like a Swiss watch, whether or not you are there. Your enterprise isn't at the mercy of maverick talent and you don't have to always be present for your business to be productive.

## What Do They Trust?

Something powerful occurs when you embrace conversion and convergence in your business. Not only do you fully liberate yourself from the grind of transacting, everyone you interact with perceives and describes you more persuasively. Today, when given the opportunity, potential influencers and advocates probably tell their friends that they trust you. That's great, but what does that mean, and isn't it a given, anyway? Yes, it's crucial that clients trust your technical ability and competency and yes, it's essential that they trust your integrity and decorum - but again those are the qualities, skills and intentions of a person. You are increasingly at the risk of commoditization. When the world starts to also appreciate your practice and your process, the professional contrast that builds predisposition for advocacy grows dramatically.

Call them evangelists, raving fans or cheerleaders - the bottom line is people start going out of their way to introduce people to you. Make no mistake, we will never trivialize your qualities, skills and intentions as a person - just remember, those aren't proprietary. Your best practices and your panoramic process are. As a result, because of increased advocacy, you are essentially making money while you sleep.

## Now Jump Ahead to the End

There are many benefits to evolving your business from just having clients "trust you" to having an IP-driven enterprise. Growth is consistent, the client experience is consistent, your team is stable, and hassle factor is reduced, among other things. Just as importantly, every investment of effort – like forced savings – gets plowed into your enterprise value. Yes, you want a business that is built to last, potentially through another generation or even further, but you also want to build a business to be eventually sold for maximum value. Many business owners park that goal in the back of their mind as something they'll revisit later on when it's closer to go-time. We're asking you to consider it now.

There are three key drivers that impact enterprise value. Consider where you are and how well built out yours is right now. This is your life's work and probably your biggest asset – so let's get it right.

## Enterprise Value Drivers

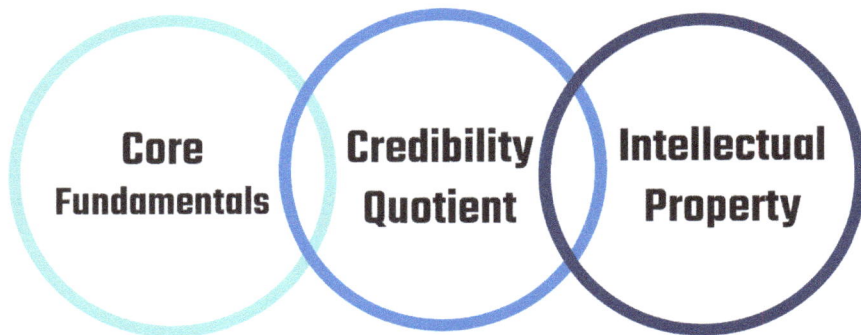

**Core Fundamentals**   **Credibility Quotient**   **Intellectual Property**

Your Core Fundamentals are primarily quantitative, relating to EBITDA, recurring revenue streams and predictable profit centers. These are obvious and generally contribute to a 2 or 3 x multiple.

More subtle is your Credibility Quotient. Are your books squeaky clean or is there some hair on your back office? Are there any skeletons lurking or indications of things falling through the cracks? Is your HR taken seriously, especially around redundancy and continuity? Is your business process-driven - meaning it's not dependent exclusively on talent? Do you know your metrics around demography, referral genealogy and revenue per client? In this era, especially relative to others who have neglected this, you're adding approximately 2 to 3x on your valuation.

And then there is the kicker, the qualitative yet unmistakably proprietary IP. You are fully built out with a documented and standardized process-driven business. You can pinpoint how you have addressed "the four -ables", a predictable, sustainable, duplicable and scalable business, and it's not just in your operations. The client-facing aspects of your process are demonstrably appreciated by clients and impactful on business performance. This has been shown to add between 2 to as much as 5x or more to your enterprise value. When you combine the Quantitative with the Qualitative panoramically, you have the ultimate Q+ business asset.

As with many offers that you will consider, the value proposition comes down to time and money. When the day comes, your goal is to shorten the amount of time it takes for someone to vet the intrinsic value of the business - and in the process turn the tables so that the buyer becomes aware of how valuable your business is and strives to convince you they are the right buyer. You want the amount of money they are prepared to pay you to be on your terms and fully maximized.

## In the Meantime

Let's assume that you are mindful of the factors that contribute to an exit and liquidity event, but you have no intention of selling in the foreseeable future. Until then, perhaps you're in the mode of looking at fresh perspectives when it comes to your approach to growth? This is a fascinating study that needs to be considered and might bring you to a fork in the road; do you remain with the status quo or do you re-imagine your growth model?

## Growing Up-Market

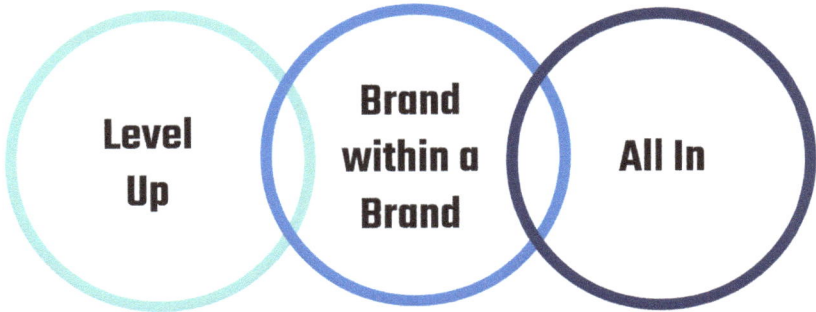

**Level Up** · **Brand within a Brand** · **All In**

Perhaps you've been in a serious growth mode. You've been attracting new clients with a wide array of needs to be addressed along with a smattering of legacy holdings and issues. Along with that, the complexity of solutions, regulatory issues, competitive and other external forces all prompted you to put your head down and execute. Now, when you pop your head up and survey the situation, it was almost like you were in a time warp.

Caught in a growth tractor beam - meaning here you are and you're not even entirely sure how you got here – it just happened and was a bit of a blur. That approach is not sustainable going forward. You're putting your ideal life in the cross hairs if you don't make some adjustments.

The first stepping stone is to consider growing down. Again, this is just a primer to consider, we address this in far more detail later on - especially when we talk about time auditing in the Gap section – and we'll show you some ways to create more efficiency. For now, if you and your team find yourself reactively firefighting instead of proactively driving your business, the writing might be on the wall to look closely at your capacity. How and with whom do you allocate your time? This is an essential first step towards professional scarcity that is low in its complexity yet very foundational. It allows you to show the world you are evolving but with minimal disruption. It also allows you to reflect and assess if this progression is right for you after you've tested the water. It begins by creating an ideal client profile and sticking to it without deviation so that you can start to grow up-market.

It continues by automating and outsourcing as many of the commoditized aspects of your overall deliverables as possible. It then involves allocating less complex clients to a protégé on your team. It is enhanced by growing down - by disassociating from clients that will never truly be a good fit. As this progresses, you start to re-frame existing long-term clients so that any amnesia for your value is addressed and their appreciation for that value is rejuvenated and expanded to include your people, practice and process.

Once you're on the other side of that – growing down to grow further up-market by managing fewer relationships and more complex needs – you may ignite another level of ambition where you want to build out a brand within a brand. This means you create a "Gold Desk" for your top 50 relationships and allocate your 250 other clients to another person on your team within the same practice and using the same process. It's not a hand-off. Your B and C clients can become an associate's A clients and you provide oversight, accountability and support - but not at the expense of your top clients.

They will appreciate your freed-up bandwidth and with that comes a rejuvenated sense that they can never outgrow you as their needs become more complex. Legacy clients who've been with you forever don't feel offended that you've outgrown them. You reintroduce yourself to the top 20% of your clients, informing them that you and your team will be raising the bar to get out in front of their evolving needs.

Shorn of the bells and whistles, a Lexus is not dramatically superior to a Toyota, but the buying and service experience is. There is a cachet to the brand and there is a sense that you are treated better by owning the car, not because of the car itself. A shinier showroom, a more comfortable service area with snacks and a cappuccino machine and a more responsive staff are all designed to create a vibe that proclaims that you have arrived.

The 'brand within a brand' model is just right for most F4S professionals who are re-imagining their approach to growth. A select few, though, go all-in and create a Multi-Family Office deliverable where they create a concierge level, all-encompassing depth and breadth model that considers every possible deliverable that is process-driven, all under one roof. "All in" means you have 25 to 40 clients – and that's it. Your reframing and future pacing approach will awaken sleeping giants who will not only never feel like they've outgrown you as their needs evolve, but will also become advocates for people like themselves. Again, we get into this in detail throughout this book. We consider the unintended consequences that comes from concentration risk and we discuss the upside of deeper engagement and advocacy that can come from this approach.

Building an enterprise that is driven by quality people, a solid array of best practices and a well-defined, proprietary process brings you to the fourth Venn diagram.

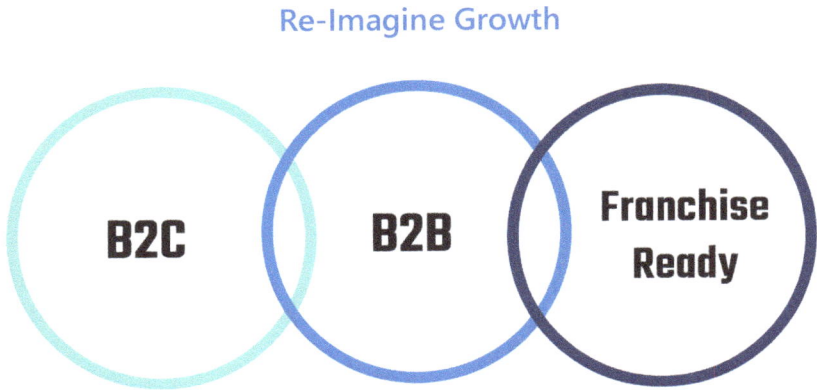

## Re-Imagine Growth

B2C  B2B  **Franchise Ready**

The culmination of all of your work might crescendo in a business-to-client enterprise, one that grows organically. Or it might fire up your ambition to add a business-to-business growth model that positions you to also buy a business and unlock immediate growth as you absorb it, and then subsequent growth in a second wave through uncovered untapped opportunities. Ironically, the litmus test before you consider that choice is to ask yourself these two questions: "Am I obsolete?" (Meaning my business is not dependent on me being there), and "could I sell my business for maximum value quickly because it's a best-in-class enterprise?" If the answers are "yes" and you have the appetite and clear expectations, you are ready to go shopping. As a further proof of concept through the B2C and B2B growth plan, after you've successfully acquired one, you can keep going.

## Franchise Readiness – The Next Frontier

An Always On approach to conversion and convergence propels you down a path where you can eventually pivot from a strictly organic B-to-C growth model to a scalable B-to-B growth model. It enables you to buy an undervalued business from a retiring competitor or colleague. You can attract protégés who have plateaued because of the friction of the world, who can draft in behind your process and replicate your outcomes without being left to their own devices.

Consider demographic forces. How many people in your sector are three to five years away from an exit and have no continuity or succession plan? How many professionals are tired and vulnerable and are looking for a way out as daunting market forces amp up?

Yes, they want to monetize through a liquidity event as their careers wind down, but they also want their clients to be left in good hands. You can become their succession plan and secure their legacy by elevating the client experience through the transition.

They can exit quickly or ride into the sunset gradually with complete anticipation and fulfillment. The study of demography is fascinating and any time you can harness this powerful force, it's like adding a booster rocket to the supply and demand dynamic. As an example, did you know that in Japan there are more people over 80 years old than under 10? Demographic shifts and trends are going to create some spectacular opportunities the world over. Harness this, locally at first, but remember that geographic limitations are removed if you are a process-driven professional. The tighter your process, the more the entire world becomes your oyster.

Franchise-readiness can provide scalable growth with additional protégés, too. Consider the younger people in your sector who are trying to break through, but because of the many headwinds they are starting to wonder if they will be viable five years from now. Without reinventing the wheel they can adopt, master and deploy your proprietary best practices to unlock a vein of gold that was dormant within their business, while liberating themselves to focus on what they enjoy doing - and you both can participate in that lift. As a financial professional client of ours who has cracked this code would say, "Why would I bring on another 100 clients when I could bring on one advisor with 100 clients?"

While some or all of this might resonate with you, something might be nagging in the back of your mind. Something along the lines of "I work hard enough as it is and I don't really want to work any harder, and frankly there isn't enough time in the day to do this." Or perhaps you're concerned about disrupting your current model? Remember, we're not trying to change you. We just want to expand your thinking and prompt you to feel motivated to refine and optimize what you do without worrying about unintended consequences and collateral damage. Remember: Most limitations are self-imposed. There is a process to achieve both consistent organic and scalable growth and they are interconnected through conversion and convergence without compromising your values, personal health and wellness or work-life balance. We get it. If you're a parent we know that you've got about 18 summers with your kids and those 18 years will come and go very quickly. We want you to cherish that time as you flourish professionally. We've seen where, in an attempt to grow, the wake of disruption on the home front has been colossal.

Remember that old saying - you're only as happy as your least-happy child - but you can have it all. You might not be able have it all at once, but your trajectory aims you and your momentum can incrementally compound, moving you to a personal and professional inflection point.

The epiphany occurs when you realize that, while others are winging it, you can achieve a personal and professional breakthrough by deploying a proven process-based approach. Consider the Japanese word "kaizen" which literally means 'improvement', but look deeper, specifically at the word Zen (good). Zen is a 'good' place to be. Improvement requires change, but change can be good - and by change we're talking about personal and professional refinement and optimization.

Sure, when you stir the pot hiccups and speed bumps can occur. *Jevon's Paradox* states that an increased-efficiency solution to a problem can eventually create a new problem and unintended consequences, but that is acceptable and manageable. There is a greater benefit that comes from never getting locked in the status quo and never being complacent or prone to inertia confidence. Be mindful of the powerful force of entropy. Understand that nothing improves because it is neglected.

## Ultimate Balance - Qualitative and Quantitative Results

There is an art and science to working ON yourself and ON your business. We've experienced first-hand that you can learn a lot from reading a book. You can learn even more from writing one. The exercise of creating something is powerful. It forces you to dig deep and study a subject in a more meaningful way, and that knowledge can be retained. It takes you to an experiential reality rather than a theoretical one. Coaches are notoriously "often wrong but never in doubt". By that we mean, they have confidence in their ideas and strategies that are both timely and timeless, and they can have immense persuasive impact, but they too can be lacking in customization and implementation longevity. Square peg, meet round hole. We spent the past several years playing at a high level - interacting with some of the most accomplished F4S professionals in existence - and extracted those observations, shaped it all into this book and expanded our relevance in the process.

So much so that we've resigned ourselves to the point that, if we are the only people who read this book, it will have been worthwhile. Consolidating our thoughts in a structured manner will make us better coaches. Creating something changes you more than simply transacting services. Your movement toward the Blue Square will reveal something in you, too.

We highlighted the Q in the Blue Square Method icon because we noticed a trend over the last few years in many of our interactions with our clients. As we mentioned, their aspirations have evolved over the years, especially recently. They started sharing more collaborative experiences with other F4S service providers and we started being included in those conversations, expanding our views. With those changes, our clients changed. Not that they needed to change, but the maturity, the panoramic view on what success means, the deeper appreciation for what life has to offer, has been impressive. We noticed that, in a typical 45-minute consultation, as much of the conversation revolved around the Qualitative personal progress being made as it did around Quantitative results in the business. What you strive to earn professionally must be book-ended by what you achieve personally. As an analogy, having a nice car doesn't make you a good driver. You need the skills. You need the mileage. You need to look at the entire picture. In business, the goal is to be the complete package. It became evident that our clients had a heightened awareness that every decision they made had to be aligned with their sense of purpose. It is no longer just about making a living and financial security, but also an aspiration to do the right thing and see what we are capable of. Wisdom is knowing the correct path to take. Integrity is taking that path. It becomes axiomatic. Our clients strive for complete congruency to achieve real and personal fulfillment. Gandhi said it best: "Happiness is when what you think, what you say, and what you do are in harmony." As you progress through this book, you'll notice a lot of insight from others because many people in the past have said it better than we ever could - more specifically, more efficiently and with brevity. This is part of the recipe for making people think. Again, we're not trying to change you, nor are we trying to tell you how to live your life. Our words, along with the words of historical figures and the profound insights passed along by our clients, have been invested into this book to help you move in the direction of your own personal Blue Square.

Again, the concept of the Blue Square is inspired by ikigai - the Japanese approach to understand our reason for being. Among other things, it reminds you of the ongoing necessity for having a 'True North'. It provides you with a beacon to see past hurdles, distractions and setbacks without straying from what's important.

Just as the Inuit, the indigenous people in the far North, use an inuksuk to guide them, and just as sailors in the past would use a lighthouse and the stars to get their bearings, personal and professional achievement is as much about trajectory as it is about destination. Like every journey, we need mile markers to ensure we're on track, and as the pace and complexity increases we have to be aware of where inertia is taking us. Just like progressing in your car through fog, though you can only see 100 yards in front of you as you are travel, the destination is never in doubt. You know what's beyond the fog and you move in that direction, making continuous adjustments to stay on track.

## The Perils of the Status Quo

Because top performers are busy, some tend to drift into patterns and either put off or forget to work on themselves. When it comes to change, some are reluctant because they feel that disruption is risky. Keep in mind, the best are forever improving but rarely swinging for the fences. World class golfer Justin Rose has a great mindset. He would say "I don't try to find one thing and improve it by 10%, I want to find 10 things I can improve by 1%".

He is a serious student and has immense respect for his coaches. He knows that his swing coach could never beat him at a round of golf but he finds the coach's insights and observations to be invaluable. The key is, he doesn't just work on his game. He also focuses on stretching, meditation, nutrition, strength, critical thinking, mental toughness, endurance and many other "soft skills" - all of which contribute in small but meaningful ways.

Part of this exercise is to help you self-assess. You're either coasting, cresting or climbing. Coasting means you're set in your ways and potentially on a collision course with obsolescence. Cresting means you're still growing but you haven't gotten out in front of your capacity issues and you're therefore on a collision course with a plateau. Climbing means that you're constantly refining and tweaking – the clay remains soft – and that requires humility. Undoubtedly you are confident, but those with the highest level of ability often have the highest level of humility, too. Which is why they have such a high appreciation for relevant insight and value.

If you've ever watched the *Tour de France,* you know that most of the cyclists look pretty comparable on the flats. You start to see who put in the work as they hit the mountains, because a few pull away from the peloton. What's interesting is that the preparation, innovation and effort isn't just revealed when you're peddling up your business mountain. Watch the YouTube video of Michael Guerra as he stops peddling and lays out flat after the apex of a mountain and glides past everyone with zero effort expended. It can be counterintuitive to innovate even when there is no friction. Headwinds can be revealing, but so can tailwinds.

With that in mind, and to validate that your vision and mindset are aligned with our philosophy and process, allow us to itemize the drivers that contribute to your ability to move towards your own Blue Square:

You love what you do - you often feel like the luckiest person on earth because you get paid to do something that isn't always a grind - and rarely even feels like work. You are tired at the end of the day but it's a fatigue that comes from accomplishment. Just like exercise, when you expend energy you create more of it.

Your process drives enterprise value - the goal of every business owner is to build something that lasts and, eventually, to sell it. Like forced savings, your efforts are deposits into that equity and intellectual property. The bricks are your solutions, your proprietary process is the mortar that holds it all together, creating beauty and durability.

You convert clients to advocates - you consistently attract new clients rather than having to chase them. Your phone rings and your email fills with people reaching out asking you to meet people in their inner circle. Advocates don't just want to see you succeed, they are also advocates for the people they care about and they go out of their way to make introductions.

**You are monetizing fully** - advocacy and IP create recurring revenue and multiple income streams. Your enterprise value grows incrementally and then exponentially. Like a jet at cruising altitude, your friction is reduced. You start to take more time off and become even more productive while expending less effort.

**Gratitude** - you take nothing for granted as you embrace the yin and yang of life. Adversity serves you, it doesn't hurt you. You realize that you need the cold to appreciate the warm. You need the dark to appreciate the light. You savor success fully and completely because you know that only a small percentage of people are afforded the opportunities in life that you have earned.

**Purpose** - you enjoy an enviable level of meaning and purpose because you know that your value is appreciated. Your influence is impactful and you cast a substantial and positive shadow over the many people you interact with. There is no dread and no regret because you achieve your results through the service of others, never at the expense of others.

**Balance** - you are unwavering in your pursuit of work-life balance. By extension, you balance your appreciation for what you already have with your aspirations for what you still hope to achieve. You master the balance of cause and effect, putting as much emphasis on solid activity as you do on measurable productivity. Keep in mind - being in balance is interconnected with your sense of belonging. A massive part of your own happiness stems from the degree that other people are happy to see you and that you are a part of their life. Being present, not preoccupied or distracted, in your interactions with others contributes to that.

**Fulfillment** - you constantly rejuvenate yourself because you find meaning in your impact and reach. You're not obsessed with work because you know that it is always a means to the end of discovering who you are. You are at peace because you understand what you can control, you understand external dependencies, and you understand what is completely out of your control.

Balance your opportunistic and capitalistic ambitions with your personal pursuits of unlimited potential. Yes, there is always a bull market somewhere and we want you to find it, but when you're not just focused on market forces but also on your personal forces, you magnetically attract everything you could hope for. Keep in mind, it's been estimated that 100 billion people have lived on planet Earth with close to eight billion alive as you read this. There's a good chance that 90% of them would do anything for your worst day. Be at peace as you go forward, know that you're worthy of self-actualization and do everything you can to share your wisdom and good fortune.

Now that you are acquainted with our motivations around why we created this book, we hope that you are developing some expectations around why reading the rest would be a good investment of your time. You can approach it with an à la carte mindset, taking one or two things that have an impact, or, as one client would say, 'getting a phrase that pays.' Perhaps a minor adjustment where you simply turn the dial a bit. So take what you need. If you pay for two hours on a parking meter but you end up only needing 40 minutes, you're not obligated to stay. On the other end of the spectrum, you may work all the way through this book, highlighting a dozen or more applicable strategies. Either way, we ask that you fixate on implementation. Inspiration and motivation are important but they can fade.

The *Law of Diminishing Intent* can affect a F4S professional more than anyone because of the abstract nature of your business. It's not uncommon to get lost in the no-man's land between intent and implement. There is an interlude between intention and implementation and the degree of self-motivation you possess is often the bridge.

Being at peace with mistakes, overcoming adversity and striving for the best version of yourself is good for the soul. As you know, life goes by fast. It's just a blink. We all want to get to a point where we're aware of living a life that's fulfilled. The essence of Zen is that we could live to be 100 or it could all be over tomorrow. We can take nothing for granted and must use hindsight to serve us, not haunt us. We'll feel gratified if this activates you to reach a little further, try a little harder, and if it disrupts any complacency that slows your self-actualization goal. Artists will tell you that a work of art is never completed, it's abandoned, which means that we come to the end of the road and move on to something else. We'll conclude this chapter with two great quotes about life, mortality and the pursuit of happiness. Robert Louis Stevenson said, "Don't judge each day by the harvest you reap but by the seeds that you plant." CS Lewis said, "You don't have a soul, you are a soul. You have a body." Whatever form of spirituality you believe in, there has to be good energy and karma in those sentiments.

# The Blue Square Method

# Chapter 2:

## *The Origins*

Indulge us as we give you a bit of our back story so that you have a sense for what you've gotten yourself into. It's not uncommon for readers to skip through the introductory chapters in a book to avoid the preamble and get right to the gold. You're putting some serious skin in the game here. A book like this requires a significant investment of time, not only to read but to consider how to apply what you sift out that is relevant to you. To that end, this chapter is designed to help you identify an alignment of interests; that what you aspire to achieve is aligned with our expertise and approach.

For years we've reminded people that, contrary to the old cliché, time is not money – time is more valuable than money. You can earn more money but you can't earn more time. It's the one thing we all have a finite amount of. We wrote this book with the intention that this be a wise time investment and that you would see an ROI.

This quick tangent is relevant because it will give you a window into our mindset. If you are anything like us, you've probably invested some of your time teaching younger people about the power of capitalism. Wealth creation is the best antidote to poverty. In the chapter 13, The Torch, we touch on the importance of relaying sound advice to the protégés in your life. It's common for younger people to be idealistic and susceptible to romantic notions of socialism. You know the expression: "If you aren't a liberal in your 20s, you have no heart. If you aren't a conservative in your 30s, you have no brain." Part of the mentor protégé dynamic is to try to accelerate one's awareness of the immutable truths of personal responsibility, merit, self-motivation and unwavering integrity – key elements to pure, ethical and compassionate capitalism.

A gentle reminder: Capitalism is a ladder we climb. Socialism is when someone lowers down a rope and offers to pull you up – and they can stop pulling any time they choose - which sounds a little risky. With a ladder, you get to ascend upwards and each rung is a stepping stone. The bottom rung is minimum wage. The more value we bring to the marketplace the more rungs we climb. It might not be perfect but "what the market will bear" is a pretty solid premise for the most part. The prime minister of Canada earns about $350 per hour. The President of The United States is compensated with about $450 per hour.

We have clients whose time is valued at well over $1000 per hour – each and every business hour! (Is there a top rung, and if so is it an illusion or a self-imposed limitation?)

The point is this: By being here you are temporarily taking yourself away from your earning ability, and we know why you made that decision. We're reminded of many enlightened leaders like Abraham Lincoln who suggested that if you have six hours to cut down a tree, you should invest a big chunk of that time sharpening your ax. Of course, some people feel they are so busy chopping that they don't have time to stop and visit the sharpening station, and that is where diminishing returns are born and a plateau of productivity will appear.

Moving along, let us outline how our business development approach was shaped, how our panoramic process was developed and refined and how it all will relate to you. Our intention is for you to see the merit in investing your time - not just to read this book, but to take action and translate these ideas into results. You've undoubtedly read many books, attended many conferences and seminars and probably even hired coaches and consultants along the way for the purposes of unlocking another level of productivity and efficiency. Undoubtedly the investment of that time was a mixed bag of good results and misfires. Those investments that didn't pay off probably occurred because you weren't able to implement for whatever reason. The value of reading this book will begin to make itself evident when you've finished. Like a meaningful conversation with a friend that activates self-assessment on an issue, the value of the advice lasts long after the conversation takes place. We want the same to be true here. When you finish you will come to a moment of truth. You will either feel validated that our approach aligns with how you see the world and that you were doing many things properly already, or it may trigger a nagging feeling in your mind that you have some unmet needs that should be addressed. If that occurs, pounce immediately! Don't let your intent to address those issues diminish. At a minimum, set a goal to make a list of six to eight adjustments you feel are relevant and take action. Again, there's probably nothing wrong with your business - nothing's broken, we're not trying to fix something or repair damage. You just have a few gaps. Addressing one or two will help to a degree but in-and-of-themselves won't be profound. In contrast, cumulatively getting clarity on six to eight and addressing them in a reasonable period of time can unlock another level of effectiveness. Much like using a stud-finder during a home repair project, sliding it along the wall until it lights up – not guessing with trial and error - we want you to have that same level of confidence in your ability to find those gaps and address them.

Here's where things get good. You won't need to reinvent the wheel when it comes to implementation. At thebluesquaremethod.com/implementation-resources, we will put the odds in your favor by providing resources you can deploy quickly and predictably.

Which brings us to another important point. We've both been referred to as being thought leaders in this field, and we appreciate that, but we don't want to radiate a sense that we are lecturing or highlighting faults. John Locke said it well; "It's one thing to show a man that he is in error and another to put him in possession of the truth." We have immense humility in every interaction we have with our clients. Our approach is accretive, collaborative and designed for execution.

A big part of our insight and judgment comes from our own personal and professional growth as fueled by our clients. They have taught us as much or more than we have taught them. Between the two authors of this book, we have in excess of 50 years of experience working directly with professionals in the F4S space. We've experienced countless engagements revealing untapped opportunities and overlooked vulnerabilities, and unlocking professionals' full potential both personally and professionally. It's not one year of experience 50 times. It has been an ascending progression that has built on itself through periods of calm, moderate fluctuations and intense volatility. As time passes, needs evolve, philosophies evolve, and market conditions evolve. There is an incremental and cumulative benefit from those many years of experience. The Blue Square Method is not rooted in a theoretical construct nor is any of it on trial. This has been time-tested by some incredibly effective people. We've been saying for years that the people who respect and adopt our approach the most actually need it the least. These people are already considered the best of the best and, fortunately, they've provided confirmation that our approach works. Additionally, the willingness of our clients to show us how they have tweaked, customized and expanded on our methodology has been telling, as sharing results that were achieved goes far beyond a proof-of-concept.

The primary reason we mention this is to instill confidence so that you will feel compelled to take action. The interesting dynamic about coaching and consulting is that it really does fuel each person's motivation. There is a reciprocal energy where giving starts the receiving process. It's synergistic and it adds fuel to one of the most important drivers in business - self motivation.

There is a profound difference between doing something because of compliance and obligation and doing something because of deeply seated desire. One of the many examples we've seen that personifies the human spirit in terms of self-motivation comes from the world of athletics. A gentleman from Kenya named Julius Yego decided that he wanted to become an Olympian.

He chose the javelin as his preferred sport. The problem was, he didn't know how to throw a javelin properly. In fact, he didn't even have a javelin, let alone a coach to show him how. As the story goes, he fashioned himself a javelin and taught himself how to throw it by watching YouTube videos. In time he ended up becoming the best javelin thrower in Africa. He then went on to success in the Commonwealth games and then went to the Olympics in Brazil and won a silver medal. He earned the nickname Mr. YouTube. It's tough to argue with the fact that the self-motivated auto-didactic achiever is probably the most authentic there is.

While that is a nice story, how does it apply to you? If you think about your credentials and the time you've invested into your core competency, nobody wanted your success more than you did. You were highly motivated. Here is your next opportunity. Apply the same level of motivation, importance and effort to practice management and relationship management as you do to your technical ability. This will unlock another level of progress. Yes, you're (1) managing the quality and impact of the core deliverables you provide, you're also (2) managing a business that creates a client experience and you're (3) managing how clients perceive and describe you to others. Dial all three of those numbers into the combination and the vault will open.

Here's one more piece to help confirm if this book is a good fit for you. It's not just that our clients verified and enhanced our process by closing the feedback loop and sharing their meaningful and measurable results with us. A pattern started developing in about 2008, where an increasingly large group of our clients started looking at their respective business successes more deeply and as a means to an end, not as the end itself. You'll remember there was a pretty substantial headwind in 2008 and while many F4S professionals were struggling to survive and get through it, many of our clients saw that period as an opportunity to thrive both in business and in life – they were getting from it. It's something that repeated in the early 2020s and will occur again. The point is, it was counterintuitive at the time but makes perfect sense in hindsight that a personal and professional renaissance can occur coming out of a disruption. There's always going to be opportunity for those who find it, and there is a self-fulfilling prophecy that comes from optimism - a mindset that says "I'll see it when I truly believe it."

In addition to all of that, many of our clients started thinking differently about the world and their lives in terms of meaning, purpose, and relevance – the things that matter. This revealed another level of personal and professional growth for all of us. As we continued going up-market we realized that, in most of our consultations, about 20% of the exchange revolved around the tactical, strategic and quantifiable impact. The other 80% revolved around the philosophical, the spiritual and the qualitative impact. It became apparent that our interactions focused on WHY success mattered as much as HOW to succeed. It occurred to us that the why fuels the how.

As these patterns emerged and our clients became more enlightened, our consultations started connecting the why with the how across the board. It wasn't just how to get more referrals, it was also about why a client should refer. It wasn't just about how to refine and deploy an onboarding process, but also why it creates professional contrast.

Don't misinterpret this. Our clients wanted to make more money and be more productive and efficient, and drive the value of their business higher. It's not as if there was an emptiness in any of that as an achievement. They simply pushed to add more meaning to their success. Our consultations often shifted to discussing how to engage their team more fully to achieve these breakthroughs. Our clients started to decline bringing on new clients that weren't aligned with their ideal client profile and even started disassociating from clients who weren't a good fit, respectfully right-sizing their client base. As one of our graduates so eloquently put it, "Life is too short to have a crappy client."

Our clients started taking more time off to charge their batteries and restore liberation and order in their lives. They became obsessed with guarding their time. They became unwavering and relentless in terms of their goals and convictions and it all started taking on a more all-encompassing and integrated feel.

As this expanded theme got more traction it revealed something in us, too. It forced us not just to raise our game in terms of relevance to our clients but also to look inward at ourselves. Were we walking the talk? Being consistent and congruent in how we conducted ourselves? As a coach and consultant, every time you engage a client on a module or deliverable, you get to hear yourself as well as hearing the many different reactions and input. As we started encouraging deeper conversations, two trends emerged; the first being the importance of the Socratic Method and goal-setting.

The Socratic Method is a fascinating study that reminds us that good questions are the route to a good answer and that many issues or two or three questions deep. This ensured that we weren't going through the motions reciting plug-and-play concepts. It also ensured that we avoided the echo chamber of confirmation bias. We listened more intently. Our clients listened more intently, too.

We started going deeper into the goal-setting process, instead of skimming the surface. Early in our interactions, we wanted everyone involved to get crystal clear on the why. This is an early stage in the goal-setting process and especially important because not everyone is formal about setting goals. There are people who succeed without writing out their goals, but even then it's not like they shot an arrow and drew a bullseye around where it landed. They had a destination and outcome in their minds and achieved it – we just wanted to be more deliberate and intentional by getting it out of their heads and uncovering the core motivators.

There are three questions that we often use to kick start that process:

1. *Are you today where you said you would be five years ago?* As you can imagine, some said yes, others said they got close and a few said they fell short. The irony is that the answers revealed more about the gratitude the client had in their life rather than if their outcomes aligned with their ambitions. It also often revealed silver linings that came from disruptions and overcoming setbacks.

2. *What does nirvana look like for you in the next five years?* This was the first step in investing the past into the future by creating an all-encompassing wish list of aspirations for the future while appreciation for the present was still fresh.

3. *Why is all of this so important to you?* Here is where the conversation went deeper. We could feel it. The energy was palpable and we could sense the forces of self-motivation emerge, the resolve to overcome adversity and friction, and the real balance of being mindful of the cause-and-effect reality that impacts achievement.

A big part of our engagement process included assigning an accountability partner to get into the weeds with our clients, once we established an alignment and fit during the initial goals and gap analysis consultation. As our clients rolled up their sleeves and got down to work, it became apparent that not only did they stay motivated, their motivation grew with each consultation in the incremental and sequential approach.

They didn't dread the calls with the accountability partner and they didn't postpone or reschedule appointments because the process started "looking like work". Nor did they approach each consultation half-heartedly. They stayed clear on the why and they wanted to learn the how. Which again brings us to the three-circle Venn diagram you see below. The first circle is where you are, the third circle is where you want to be, and in the middle is the interlude – the space between. Without self-motivation this can be a no-man's land where intent diminishes. Self-motivation and clarity of action are the bridge.

Intention    Diminishing Intent    Implementation

The second inflection point came even closer to home. This is where The Blue Square Method found another gear. It wasn't just our clients that forced us to think things through - to constantly scrutinize and elevate our process - it was also conversations with our kids. Both of us have kids that are of an age where decisions are bigger and so are the potential rewards and consequences. While our clients are pretty far down the path of success, our kids were just hitting the on-ramp. Because of this, each of us had powerful and fulfilling conversations with our respective progeny. We're going to get into this theme more thoroughly at the end of the book in the chapter called The Torch, which is dedicated to leadership, continuity and succession and the lost art of giving and receiving advice. For now, let's give you a primer to make this last connection. If you are a parent or a favorite uncle, aunt or mentor and a child approaches you directly or indirectly asking for some guidance, especially on a career path, it's pretty common to invest your own experiences into the conversation - and in our case the experiences of some of our clients.

When a child is trying to figure out what they want to do when they grow up, you might be compelled to start by saying, "Do something you love and you will never work a day in your life," along with other sound bites to round out the pep talk. For both of us, when we started going deeper in helping our kids on the verge of some of their first big decisions, we found ourselves drilling down below the basic talking points and core beliefs and into our philosophy and playbook that we applied to our clients. It was here that our Blue Square icon was born. As we mentioned, the four circle diagram is an ikigai – a Japanese visualization for our reason for being that helps us take a balanced approach to life by considering four questions:

1. What is your passion?

2. What are you good at?

3. What does the world need?

4. How can you get compensated?

During our interactions with our respective kids, the ikigai symbol made its way into the exchanges unintentionally. Before we even knew that it was an ikigai, we were drawn to it, because of its simplicity and because the focus on money was at the bottom – everything on top cascaded down to compensation rather than the other way around.

For many young people, financial stability is the first thing they focus on which can contribute to some anticlimax or regret down the road. Before we go further, if you're thinking even remotely that this is a bit of an esoteric or mystical approach to life, let's just address that right now – we are capitalists through and through and we want our clients to monetize fully – but through a purposeful and panoramic approach.

It's hard not to agree with that, even though that approach can take more time. It is validated by many accomplished people. If you read *Good to Great* by Jim Collins, you know that he asks some excellent questions in that book, such as:

1. What can you be the best in the world at?

2. What drives your economic engine?

3. What are you deeply passionate about?

*Good to Great* was among the fastest selling business books of all time and yet look at the symmetry. He is essentially saying, "Deliver more value, make more money and have more fun." It's virtually the same, but slightly different if you believe that the order matters.

As we became more acquainted with the ikigai premise in our interactions with our kids, we witnessed first-hand how the protégé can teach the mentor. It was a mirror for us. We started easing this into our consultations. We added more structure to the why and how dynamic by highlighting the importance of doing what you love, focusing more on process and IP, imagining the full potential of a relationship with advocates and believing that achieving full monetization with multiple income streams – literally financial independence where your money makes more money than you do, leading to a work-optional lifestyle - was attainable. We blended that as the conversation moved closer to the core of The Blue Square with deeper discussions about gratitude, purpose, fulfillment and balance becoming even more impactful – for all of us!

### Achievement 360

Since that discovery, the lift for us, our kids, our clients and team members has been immense. There is a multiplier of energy that goes beyond 1+1=3. We've all learned a little more about ourselves, how to see past adversity, how to avoid self-sabotage and cognitive dissonance and keep chugging towards the ultimate goal of every enlightened F4S professional – again, what Maslow perfectly described as self-actualization – the best version of us - our own personal Blue Square.

### Duncan's Journey

It was completely accidental that I became a consultant, coach and speaker on best practices for F4S professionals. In the early 90s I had a marketing company and a couple of my friends, who happened to be financial advisors, asked me for some ideas on business development and client acquisition. I knew virtually nothing about their space at the time, but I had some awareness for client acquisition, so I gave them some ideas. Fortunately, the ideas made an impact and soon after, my friends started waving my flag. In time, my phone started ringing. Being a coach became a bit of a hobby and started consuming more and more of my time. I became fascinated with the uniqueness of the fee-for-service space and started taking it more seriously. As my client base grew, so too did the invitations to speak at conferences and I thought, "There is a there, there."

A year or two passed, but I still had one foot on the boat and one foot on the dock – I wasn't fully committed until a turning point while I was on Vancouver Island doing business unrelated to the consulting field. I'll never forget it. I rented a brand new Mazda Miata to zip around in with the top down so that I could soak up the beauty of Victoria and Nanaimo. I purchased the new Pearl Jam CD to listen to as well as a couple of books on tape. Yes, I had a Sony Walkman attached to my belt right beside my fanny pack – no judging, they were very practical.

The first cassette was *The E-Myth* by Michael Gerber, the now legendary book on entrepreneurship. I heard him say there is a difference between working in your business and working on your business. He used the analogy of the difference between being a good baker and running a successful bakery – one has technical ability, the other is actually running a business. At that point I thought of myself as an entrepreneur. I never wanted to "get a job," I always wanted to create a job – and create fulfilling jobs for others too. (On a side note, some consider the word entrepreneur to be French for someone working at home in their underwear – making for a very odd casual Friday if you think about it). At any rate, for me, Gerber's distinction really expanded my thinking.

The second cassette was *Think and Grow Rich* by Napoleon Hill. A classic that required extensive research, and today it's still a timeless and essential read, especially for young adults. In that book, Hill said, "Thoughts are things. We are what we think about." He was ahead of his time, but he was really referring to the self-fulfilling power of the *Law of Attraction* – you can manifest your reality by how you think and what you visualize, but I heard something different.

A F4S professional thinks for a living. You're not selling a tangible thing, you are promoting services that address an immediate need, or you are promoting the promise of a positive outcome in the future. That can be abstract. It can be transactional. It is becoming increasingly more commoditized with fee compression. There can be external dependencies and delayed gratification.

My takeaway was, how can a F4S professional transform their thoughts into a thing? For example, if you are a financial professional and you tell the world that you "help people achieve their financial goals," what does that mean? How much more powerful would it be to say that you are "a financial professional and you've developed and refined a process that helps your clients achieve their financial goals?" You see, now it's a thing. It's like a handle to grab onto that makes your value more conceptual.

As I got rolling, I started speaking at various events for estate planning attorneys, forensic accountants, property and casualty insurance firms, life and health insurance firms, mortgage brokers, real estate agents, financial planners and consultants, to name a few. As different as each sector was, there were many similarities, too.

A lightbulb went off when I read Harry Beckwith's bestselling book *Selling the Invisible* outlining how to grow a service-based business. It occurred to me that your value should be bought, not sold. Services and solutions are not something you should sell, it should all be positioned as relationship-driven and something a client buys into. They're not buying a product from you, they're buying into your process. Now obviously his book couldn't be called Buying the Invisible (or could it?) At any rate, it was at that point I made the decision to go all-in as a consultant, coach and speaker for fee-for-service professionals, but I still had a lot to learn. It was around that time my reading and consumption of information and ideas became insatiable. A standout was Jim Rohn's simple little book *The Seasons of Life*, where he eloquently made sense of the ebb and flow of life and the peaks and valleys of success. That helped give more perspective and proportion to my pursuits, as well as more awareness for market conditions and the dichotomy of the strength and fragility of the economy. He also made me think long and hard about the dynamic between free will and God's will.

Jim Rohn also encouraged me to start buying a new journal at the beginning of each year. I'd spend 20 bucks or so on an empty book and spend all year filling it up with observations and ideas, hoping that by the end of the year that book would be worth at least 20 bucks. Today those journals are invaluable to me.

Slowly but surely, I arrived here, along with Chris and a great team, deploying actionable proven strategies and a turnkey process that enables our clients to achieve consistent client acquisition and create an impeccable client experience while achieving liberation and order in their personal lives. I realize my 30-year overnight success story is more interesting to me than you, but I enjoyed writing it out and reliving it.

I was telling my kids recently that, as we've gone further up-market, the demand for speaking has increased and fortunately with the advent of digital platforms, my capacity has also increased. My wife and kids are still a little surprised that someone would pay to hear me talk, whether in-person or online, and they're still not convinced that anyone listens. I explained to them that you're only a guru if you live more than 100 miles from the client, even if the presentation is virtual.

I've told them that I've traveled well over three million miles – equivalent to going to moon and back six times. I've spent the equivalent of four years of my life in hotel rooms. (Which explains why often when I get home and have a shower, when I'm done, I throw the towels into the bathtub – they're still there later, that's the only difference.) Like many people, I'm guilty of doing virtual presentations with a suit jacket up-top and shorts and sandals down-low.

I'm only relaying all of this to you because the mileage and experience that has gone into this book is unrivaled. I don't pretend to have the Midas touch. I've made many mistakes and errors in judgment, but they all served me, eventually. I've internalized the mantra *"success is never final and failure never fatal. It is courage that counts."* Michael Gerber will echo that. He wrote another book called *The Power Point*, describing how he reacted when he was on the brink of failure. It's an incredible paradox that someone would consider taking business advice from someone who almost failed in business, but the wisdom that comes from that experience is incredible. It's not something you learn in a simulator. The scar tissue that forms after overcoming adversity can be invaluable to someone else.

Some of my favorite books are about overcoming, rather than being overcome by setbacks, injustice and misfortune. *The Gulag Archipelago* by Aleksandr Solzhenitsyn, *The Razor's Edge* by Somerset Maugham, *Les Miserables* by Victor Hugo, *Atlas Shrugged* by Ayn Rand and *The Count of Monte Cristo* by Alexandre Dumas are some of the best personal achievement books ever written, speaking profoundly of heroes who confronted some of the darkness of the human experience. We develop perspective, proportion, and humility by struggling. We learn the dynamic and mystery of how God's will interacts with our free will. In *The Count of Monte Cristo*, the main character Dantes says, "We need to know what it feels like to die to really appreciate what it feels like to live."

As I get older, I'm at peace with my mistakes because I know they were honest and I know that they were necessary. I joke with my wife that I do have a lot of mileage, which prompts her to point out that they are mostly "city miles." She has said that I'm always right eventually – it just takes more time than expected. (She has told me that I am the smartest kid in summer school on more than one occasion.) We've been through some highs and lows as all couples and families have. I am surprised that, at one particularly bleak point, she didn't hand me the book of matches – (remember back in the day when they had other career options like Small Engine Repair and Hotel Management printed on the matchbook cover?) – but she is enlightened and knows full well that those struggles give life more meaning. Bruce Cockburn said it best, "You have to kick at the darkness until it bleeds daylight."

Tenacity and overcoming adversity breed resilience and humility. If any of this book resonates with you, just know that it's a blend of personal experience and countless interactions with some of the best people in your field. I'll paraphrase Thomas Carlyle, "Everyone is my superior in that I may learn from him or her." I say that because I may be considered an authority, and yes I am confident in what I do, but there is zero self-importance or arrogance in these pages. I've had a few eureka moments and cracked the code in a few areas, but it really is a composite of interactions with great people. That said, we don't get truly rich by what we possess, but by what we can do without. I can do without sanctimony. Thomas Sowell, an epic philosopher, says, "Morality is being hard on yourself and easy on others. Sanctimoniousness is being easy on yourself and hard on others."

I say that because I'm sure you always consider the source before you act on anyone's advice. You probably don't like being lectured by athletes about geopolitics or on life skills by a celebrity, but everyone is a teacher, to either validate your beliefs and conduct, or to introduce you to ideas at the right time.

Over the years I've expanded my sources of inspiration and insight in the spirit of being a perpetual protégé. Adler, Maslow, Jung and many others who have studied achievement confirm that humility opens us up to more opportunity. The clay stays soft, we don't believe our own hype and gifts of insight seem to drop into our lap. When my youngest son started taking golf more seriously, I would drive him to his lessons and I would sit in the waiting room checking emails. Over time, I noticed the sound of the shots in his lane sounding better. I started listening to his interactions and internalizing some of the tenets passed along by his coach. I started applying some of the concepts in my own game and seeing results. Nothing else changed. I didn't practice more, I didn't play more, but I got better just being a fly on the wall - almost by osmosis. It reminds me of the (possibly apocryphal) story of Captain Jack Sands, the Vietnam POW who played golf every day in his mind – and visualizing the entire experience, teeing the ball, the clothes he wore, pulling out the pin and every shot he hit was perfect. After his release, and having not played actual golf for years, he proceeded to play the best round of his life.

In addition to being a serious student, I'm also fortunate in that I've been surrounded by some incredibly successful people over the years, but not just in terms of financial success. Some of the most balanced capitalists I've met possess all of the most admirable qualities I can only hope that my kids will emulate, let alone myself.

I've seen an entrepreneur give up his first class seat on a plane to a senior who was struggling with mobility and sit way in the back - in a middle seat - with a contented smile on his face.

I've seen an entrepreneur buy lunch for a soldier standing in line behind him at a food court.

I've seen an entrepreneur hand a coffee and bagel to a homeless man shivering on the sidewalk – and stand there for 10 minutes talking to and encouraging him.

I've seen an entrepreneur buy a used car for a new employee whose car broke down on his way to work – his first day of work – who then walked the three miles to work and still arrived on time.

On it goes. Quiet, unassuming kindness and benevolence without any expectation for praise or recognition. Kahlil Gibran said it well, "The smallest act of kindness is worth more than the greatest intention."

We're all busy and we all have good intentions, but seizing the moment and taking action – being mindful of our habits, rituals and actions - creates incredible energy. As a dad, I know they're watching. We all want our kids to be kind, do no harm, embrace the golden rule, be confident and thrive. Some of that is learned because of our actions, most of it is learned experientially. I remember when my oldest son realized he was a small fish in a very big pond. Some doubts about worthiness started creeping in. I just reminded him that ultimately, they're all small ponds. Just prior to that we were at Niagara Falls, marveling at its power and size. Soon after, I showed him a picture of Niagara Falls from space. It's pretty small from up there. It's a form of forced perspective, the illusion that something looks small but is actually big. Perhaps you've had your picture taken in front of The Eiffel Tower in Paris and it looks like you're pinching it between your fingers, or perhaps you are trying to straighten up the Leaning Tower of Pisa in Italy? With faith, confidence and proportion you can help a protégé take what seems to be a big problem and make it smaller and more manageable.

We teach our kids to know the difference between right and wrong, the difference between making money and having money, the difference between confidence and arrogance, the difference between fun and folly, the difference between being self-conscious and being self-aware, to knowing that if you're not early, you're late, and so on.

I'm only telling you this because I'm an open book, I'm a serious student and I'm a serial entrepreneur. I want what's best for you and I sincerely hope there is something in this book that moves you to taking action. There is a lot of credibility in these pages, but just as important, there is immense authenticity as well.

## Chris' Journey

"You were born to do this!" At least that's what I remember many people telling me throughout my life. Looking back on it, it was clear that they saw something even before I did. I can remember being barely 10 years old and grabbing the first adult looking book from my dad's bookshelf in his office. It was Zig Ziglar's *Secrets to Closing the Sale*. I started reading it, first out of curiosity, but quickly it grabbed hold of me and activated a genuine interest in success. That set me on a journey to understand what it was that drove people to succeed and then keep going further to be the best of the best within their given profession. A few years later in junior high, I was a Boy Scout and we had the opportunity to sell fruit door-to-door as a fundraiser. Then it was coupon books and then pretty much every other fundraiser you can imagine. I was pretty good but what struck me was how much I enjoyed the conversations with a variety of different personalities I met along the way.

In high school, I graduated to telemarketing and earned more in a few hours after class than friends that were working 20 to 30 hours with part time jobs. That's when it begin to hit me that not only did I enjoy it, but the world seemed to value those with the ability to communicate a given message and create a result. After high school, I volunteered for a two-year mission for my church in a foreign language overseas. I knocked on doors for roughly six hours a day, five to six days a week, for two straight years. This was an opportunity to learn, through trial and error, what it meant to communicate. My focus shifted from trying to make a sale to building relationships, earning trust and genuinely helping people help themselves. As I look back on it, those were two of the most fulfilling and impactful years of my life. At the time, I didn't appreciate how formative that experience was in shaping my approach to interacting with others and how foundational it would be on my career.

Entering college, I was drawn to law, but the cost was prohibitive in terms of both time and money. There was urgency, because I also met the woman I was going to marry, and starting a family was a priority that prompted me to think about getting something that would propel me to a real job. As graduation approached, I saw an advertisement for becoming a stock broker outside the counselor's office. I had an uncle that was a stock broker and he seemed to be doing well and was perhaps the wealthiest of any of my relatives, so I set up an interview to meet with the branch manager. Not knowing anything about being a stock broker, I set myself up for what is still one of the funniest experiences of my professional career. In the interview, the manager said, "Sell me a stock." I knew nothing about stocks but fortunately, I had glanced at a brochure in the waiting room promoting the stock symbol GTE.

So, armed with that deep knowledge, I suggested that he buy GTE stock because pretty much everywhere you look, you'll see a refrigerator, a stove, a microwave oven and in fact, virtually every appliance out there will have a GTE name on it. At this point, the branch manager started laughing and then respectfully wondered if I didn't mean GE. To which I replied, yes you might be right, that was probably a brochure for GE. We had a good laugh, he extended me an offer and I was on my way to a career on the retail side of wealth management. I enjoyed it, had fair amount of success and learned a lot about how to interact with and bring value to my clients.

A couple of years later I was recruited out of retail and into the wholesale space by a company known at the time as Nike Securities but today is known as First Trust Portfolios. I was now marketing to stock brokers and other financial professionals, and combined the insights learned in my earlier years along with expertise around managed money solutions. As of this writing, 25 years have passed and throughout that passage of time I witnessed a growing appetite for best practices around client experience, efficiency and growth. The First Trust environment afforded me the opportunity to meet with some of the most successful financial professionals across multiple platforms. This gave me a window into the commonalities of the very best. I began to refine and share these best practices with others. My capabilities grew stronger, the appetite for success stories and actionable strategies grew larger, and before long our company created a position and a department for me to do that full-time. Today that department has evolved into The Advisor Consulting Group, where we meet with thousands of top teams and solo practitioners to deliver and continue to uncover the best practices in the areas of wealth management, practice management and relationship management. It has also afforded me a front row seat on how fee-for-service professionals from a variety of sectors interact with each other to elevate the client experience and professionally differentiate themselves from the pack.

*The Blue Square Method* is a very important book for me, primarily because it allowed us to invest many interactions with successful professionals into an intuitive and actionable resource. It's been crafted in a way that will remind you to look not just on what you're accomplishing professionally, but also on who you are becoming personally. It's meaningful to interact with people who arrive at a point where they are aware of how we are impacting the people we work with and serve. In my view, that is a big part of what leaving a legacy means.

Speaking of legacy, poetry was a passion instilled in me by my father. We passed many an afternoon together memorizing poems and trying to recite them back to each other to see who would be able to do it without a mistake. I can remember one specific poem to this day that still impacts me greatly. Written by Saxon White Kessinger, the poem was titled *The Indispensable Man*. A quick excerpt:

> *Take a bucket and fill it with water,*
> *Put your hand in it up to the wrist,*
> *Pull it out and the hole that's remaining*
> *Is a measure of how you'll be missed.*
>
> *You can splash all you wish when you enter,*
> *You may stir up the water galore,*
> *But stop and you'll find that in no time*
> *It looks quite the same as before.*

The moral of this quaint example is to do the best that you can and be proud of yourself, but remember there is no indispensable man. It's with this humility that we tackle the great task of sharing how others have overcome and excelled in their professional lives in ways that I believe would leave a positive mark on those they came in contact with. It's with this spirit that we hope to have a small impact on a decision of yours that is adjusted by something that you've read in *The Blue Square Method*.

# The Blue Square Method

# Chapter 3:

## *An Enlightened Philosophy*

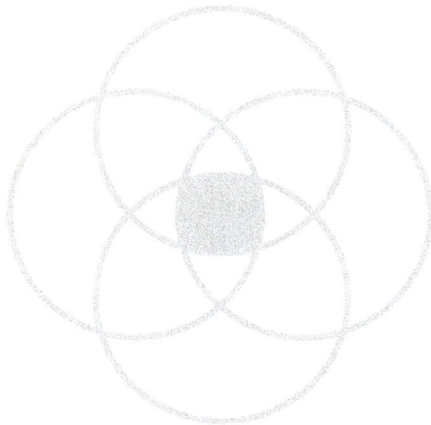

In the first two chapters we went into detail explaining how our approach is not based on a theoretical construct, but instead is designed for implementation at a high level. So why do we need an entire chapter dedicated to our philosophy? Isn't it time to stop 'talking about talking about' things and get down to business? We are, in fact, on the verge of outlining the best practices of top F4S professionals, but we need to fully define the distinctions of the mindset that separates the best from the rest. After all, it's not just what they think, but also how they think that matters. Hence the reference to the mindset of top fee-for-service professionals in the subtitle of this book. It's not just that they conduct themselves differently, they also think differently. Their worldview is different.

There is an old saying, "Those who can't do, teach, and those who can't teach, teach teachers." The gist of that humorous maxim is that it can be impressive to hear from someone who has mastered ideas as an academic, but the shine comes off the penny when you realize that it's only knowledge they are relaying, without the benefit of actual experience or results. To grow, you ideally want to discover who has already figured things out so you don't have to reinvent the wheel. Some of the most impressive figures in history have combined the power of thought and action, giving them outstanding credibility. Booker T. Washington comes to mind, especially when you consider the era in which he thrived, the friction he had to overcome and the longevity of his impact over the years. Do a quick search of his best quotes to get inside his head. One of his best was, "A lie doesn't become truth, wrong doesn't become right and evil doesn't become good because it's accepted by the majority." That's a bold statement and a reflection on how he lived his life. He also said, "I have learned that success is to be measured not so much by the position that one has reached in life as by the obstacles which he has had to overcome while trying to succeed." He opened our eyes to the distinction between getting a job and creating a job, which is the very essence of entrepreneurship. He is in elite company when it comes to driving home the importance of a sound philosophy on life to supplement your technical ability and work ethic.

You know the expression 'never meet your heroes'? Perhaps you've met a celebrity, professional athlete or political figure and realized quickly that they were far less impressive in person. Aside from their public accomplishments, when you pull back the curtain with a personal encounter you sometimes find that the individual doesn't rise to your expectations. The exceptions are people who actually get more impressive after you meet them; more interesting long after the initial impression. It's generally because of how they are wired, their philosophy, the way they see the world and their understatement. It's an X factor in many ways, but impactful.

## You Can't Count Everything That Counts

We've come to truly appreciate the spirit of McNamara's Fallacy, though we may challenge the notion that if you can't measure something, you can't manage it, in some cases. In business, we can't live solely by the metrics, especially as a fee-for-service professional. No matter how thinly you slice it, there are always two sides – in this case we mean the measurable and the meaningful. A singer can have a great voice but lack stage presence. An athlete can be a thoroughbred of physical ability but a menace in the locker room. The most successful owners of engineering firms are not necessarily the best engineers on the team. This chapter is more about the qualitative aspects of success which contribute immensely to the quantitative. Ultimately, your philosophy governs your decisions and actions. If your creed is that you always strive to add value and find the multiplier in all relationships, you are already in elite company. How you are wired and how you see the world in terms of integrity and synergy – always striving for fairness in outcomes, an alignment of interests and a coincidence of needs – is key. Every prospective client you interact with wants something; either to replace a solution that has become inadequate or to address an unmet need. In Adam Smith's *The Wealth of Nations*, written in 1776, he described the 'invisible hand' theory which, in this context, means that the pursuit of your self-interest in the marketplace does not need to come at the expense of someone else. When your code-of-conduct states that you will do no harm, you power up a magnetism that attracts those whose interests align with yours. It's palpable when you interact with someone and you realize that they are trying to achieve something through the service they provide. They don't chase. They don't press. They don't over-promise. From a practical perspective, this approach to productivity is not always conducive to instant gratification, but the impact on durable reputational equity and sustainable results is unquestionable.

It probably wouldn't occur to you to operate in any other way, but looking down the road, let's talk about why this is even more important in the future. First, the more technology creeps into our lives, the more the human touch matters to some people. We say "some people" because the ideal client will be drawn to a relationship that is supported by technology, not led by it. Too much tech in the client experience creates a vacuum – a void that can only be filled by human interaction. Technology does make many things more efficient and convenient, but it's missing the human connection. Artificial Intelligence is incredible in many ways and is a powerful force, but the one thing AI will never have is EI, emotional intelligence. There is a huge opportunity to create professional contrast and carve out a niche for the right addressable market.

Moore's Law stated that the capacity of an integrated circuit doubles in power every 24 months. Since 1975 that prediction has held, with a few exceptions. What does technology look like in the next 10 years? When you consider that a robot has already cracked a safe that was considered impenetrable by a human, just as the Deep Blue computer completely dominated Gary Kasparov in chess, you realize that this is getting real.

Among many other disruptions, AI is putting the middle man under siege. As a F4S professional, you've felt fee-compression fueled as much by technology as by competitive forces, both locally and globally. Many wonder about their long term viability because of commoditization. Hundreds of years ago, the *coureurs des bois* in Quebec used to be a wholesale conduit of furs between the trappers and the European buyers. Nothing was proprietary to them, and as logistics improved, they became obsolete. Commoditization, fueled by technology, is sweeping the world. Watch a YouTube video to see a robot assembling a building frame of cinder blocks with incredible speed and precision and you will see how technology is changing the world. Speaking of video, does it boggle your mind that Blockbuster had a chance to buy Netflix for a song not so long ago? Blockbuster dominated video distribution in North America with thousands of brick-and-mortar locations. They had a good run but the writing was on the wall. They had nothing proprietary. They were the *coureurs des bois* of video products. Their biggest profit center was late fees. "Let's punish our customers" was not a sustainable model. Often, the popular new releases were unavailable, too – talk about a pattern of letdown. Which always prompts the question in someone's mind; "is there a better way?"

Netflix came along and initially offered the gift of time. Their model was a little horse-and-buggy in that they would mail you a DVD. You didn't have to get in your car to pick up or drop off. You got what you wanted and there were no late fees, but they always said they would stream and create their own content in time. Then they cratered under the weight of their growth. Blockbuster was advised to snap them up, but their view was, "Hey we'll put up kiosks and rent movies in grocery stores!" Poof. They're gone, and today Netflix represents 15% of Internet traffic. We're not saying we love the Netflix model – it has its issues – but symbolically, is there a better example of what complacency and commoditization does? Yellow Pages might argue with us regarding the impact of Google, and taxis with respect to Uber, but you get the picture on a macro level. How about on a micro level? A radiologist can have an X-ray sent to her over the Internet and give an opinion from her iPad without coming to the hospital. That's great! But that also means they can send the same X-ray to a radiologist in India and get as good an assessment for a fraction of the price. Robo lawyers, accountants, advisors and consultants are growing exponentially. It's Darwinian, but not in terms of survival of the fittest: It's who can adapt.

## Our Philosophy about Change

All of that brings us to an important layer of the enlightened philosophy, and that is how you view change. You must be a serious student. The clay must remain soft - which means you have to be constantly open to both learning and unlearning. As a client once said, "I'm hiring you because I've found that it's tough to grow in a comfort zone."

Alvin Toffler, author of *Future Shock*, wrote about what he called "The New Illiterate," which has nothing to do with the ability to read or write, but rather the inability to break old patterns, learn, relearn and unlearn. Not being set in your ways and defending it with, "we've always done it this way" ensures that you will constantly refine and optimize your current approach while being open to expanding it. We rationalize to ourselves that there is more risk associated with change than with the status quo, but in real life that isn't always the case. It's understandable that people can be resistant to change and skeptical of new ideas because they've been burned before. As Mark Twain said, "It's easier to fool someone than it is to convince them they've been fooled." The key with change is that it happen on your terms. You're not forced into it reluctantly and through necessity, you crave it to prevent complacency. Socrates referenced that mindset when he said that the highest form of human excellence is to continually question yourself and others.

It's vital that your philosophical position is consistent in terms of ethics, and when it comes to personal and professional growth, you have immense humility because you don't have all the answers. You will never be a victim of your own confirmation bias or cognitive dissonance, but you will have unwavering confidence in your value and worthiness.

## Our Philosophy about Selling

When it comes to client acquisition and business development, the most enlightened philosophy is that of stewardship, not salesmanship. Salesmanship asks a client to buy something, chasing them with closing techniques and trying to convince them to take action. Stewardship asks a client to buy into something, attracting them with a process-driven, win-win approach, and letting them come to their own conclusions – convincing themselves with reason and self-motivation.

## Why is this so important?

In the world of transactional one-off encounters, salesmanship is used to drive business and capture a buyer's fleeting enthusiasm before their intent diminishes, but you're not selling a car. This is not a transaction. Your value must be bought, not sold. Salesmanship seeped into the F4S world as a way to drive business. At conferences, language like "You eat what you kill," "You're a hunter gathering assets," "Squeeze more juice out of the orange to gain more wallet share," "Increase your net-new households," "Open up new accounts" and "You have to drive production," became common. The problem is, that kind of jargon is from the lexicon of the coin-operated brokers of the world.

If we are in a consultation and our client uses any language of salesmanship, we point to an empty chair in the office and say, "Imagine your best client is sitting right there. Would you talk about sales tactics? Would you be proud if they described you to a friend as being a great salesperson?" Open kitchens in restaurants are popular because you can see what is going on. It's a beehive of activity. There are flames, hustling staff, screaming chefs, plates dropping and intense aromas – and there it all is. It creates a vibe and they're proud of what they do and how they do it. There is nothing behind the curtain to wonder about – it's all completely transparent. We're asking you to be an open kitchen, too.

If you've ever been on the receiving end of salesmanship of any kind - a telemarketer, a door-to-door canvasser, a contrived time-share rep or a high-octane cell-phone salesperson - you've felt the discomfort of the intrusiveness and pressure. It's natural to have an aversion to being sold because if feels like something is being done to you. Many people develop a sales immunity over time – and as a buyer, it poisons the well because trust is undermined and sometimes permanently shattered. It's even worse if you've felt the anti-climax and buyer's remorse that creeps in after a sales encounter that prompted an impulsive decision. Clearly this isn't a new concept. *Caveat Emptor* is a Latin warning, which tells you something about how long this has been a thing. The lessor known *Caveat Venditor* stated that the seller has implied responsibility when they sell something – it had better deliver what was promised. Stewardship and a transparent two-way vetting process removes any concern about mutually implied risk. It's all about fit, not about a one-sided win.

There are no closing techniques, tips on overcoming objections, selling tactics or secrets to persuasion in this book. In fact, when you bring on a new client, it isn't considered a 'close' - it's an engagement. You're not opening an account, you're establishing a relationship with a path to advocacy. You could hand this book to your best client, tell them this is how you roll and be proud as a peacock.

The best way to start a relationship is through a fit process, not a sales process. You're not trying to convince a prospective client to take action, you're trying to activate professional contrast and let them come to their own conclusion that your combination of people, practice and process is an upgrade from their current situation - or any other option. Ironically, it is common that using a fit process will prompt a prospective client to try to close you – they interrupt you halfway through the meeting saying, "You know what, I've heard enough. I just want to get started." You're not convincing them, they are trying to convince you there is a good fit. You've undoubtedly had that happen before. The stars just lined up beautifully. It was the perfect synchronicity of professional scarcity and professional contrast. You projected no pressure or need and yet you were able to convey that no one else was better suited for the client. The point is, that can be engineered – it's by design, not by luck or by chance.

For obvious reasons, a client who engages with you due to fit is far more predisposed to becoming an advocate. Why? Because of the ultimate incentive that comes with advocacy. Charlie Munger, Warren Buffet's right-hand man, said it well: "Show me the incentive and I'll show you the outcome." The incentive of advocacy is that the client is an advocate of their friend, not just you.

They feel they are doing that friend a disservice by not introducing them to you. They know you will appreciate the new business, but that isn't the only incentive. The advocate knows how the introduction will reflect on them and how their friend will benefit, and let's be honest, a consultant is far more referable than a salesperson.

## Our Philosophy about Trust

A successful F4S professional understands that trust is the lifeblood of meaningful long term relationships, but if trust is so important, let's expand on this and consider for a moment what it is specifically that your clients trust.

When we ask our F4S clients to list specific things that their clients trust, we usually hear things like professionalism, integrity, knowledge, confidentiality, fiduciary responsibility and the like. All of which are important – but those are the qualities, skills and intentions of person – they are not proprietary assets of your practice and process. There was a time they were enough, but today they are a minimum requirement. Today, we want your clients to have as much trust for the proprietary aspects as they do for you as a person and your people. That's the paradox of true entrepreneurship.

The people are not the only factor – the practice and the client experience it creates, as well as the process and the client's appreciation for how it puts all the pieces together for them – that's the total package.

## Welcome to the C-Suite of Trust

As a business owner or team leader you wear a lot of hats, but consider how an enlightened philosophy and approach creates accelerated trust - through contrast initially - and then develops into durable trust over the long haul. The five Cs of the C-Suite can help define your route.

**Your Credentials** – depending on your role and core competency, this is you being a Chief Investment Officer, Chief Financial Officer or Chief Fulfillment Officer. This is ultimately promissory on the performance of your technical ability. This is you being a good baker. The next four speak to you running a good bakery.

**Your Consistency** – this is you being the Chief Executive Officer with an overall mandate that promises a panoramic client experience that balances proactive and reactive service to create real dependability.

**Your Congruency** – this is you being the Chief Operations Officer that is promissory on expectations being set and met. No over-promise, under-deliver. Zero anti-climax. You go out of your way to anticipate needs and exceed expectations. You do what you say. Some refer to their COO as a Concierge of Operations to make the role and responsibility even more client-centered.

**Your Chemistry** – this is you being the Chief Information Officer, specifically around the goals, nuances and unique objectives of your clients. It's promissory on caring about what each client cares about, treating everything they tell you about their aspirations as an invaluable intellectual property and investing that information into the rest of the relationship.

**Your Communication** – if the first four make you referable, being the Chief Branding Officer converts referability into actual referrals. This is you being a sound messenger and blending it with compelling messaging that resonates with clients. It removes the mystery of your value, creates professional contrast and ultimately is promissory of clarity. You and your team can verbalize it so that clients can internalize the messaging and then socialize your value to others as persuasive advocates.

As a package, the complexity of roles in the C-Suite may seem ominous, but the point is to broaden your mindset to be more intentional and process-driven about every aspect of your approach. The result is that you become dramatically more attractive than anyone else vying for those client engagements, while building a resilient, limitless business. Among many other benefits, this approach is like laying out a tripwire to prevent unwanted intrusions by outside forces that try to derail your momentum.

## Our Philosophy about Referrals

As you will see throughout this book, we will never suggest that you ask for referrals. We've seen it all. Common variants are: "Who else do you know?" or "I get paid in three ways" or "I'm trying to grow my business" and all the other nonsense that a) doesn't work and b) makes you look needy. You can't pitch the idea of a referral as a favor you are asking of a client, but you can position it as service you are providing to a client. That distinction is massive and we will outline it comprehensively in subsequent chapters.

## Our Philosophy about Growth

When you get started in business, you'll take just about anyone on as a client so you can pin your first dollar earned on the wall. As you get rolling, you begin to be more selective and deliberate about who you engage with. Once you get traction, you have to shift your attention to the most important vein of gold there is – organic growth from within your inner circle. Your need for marketing techniques for client acquisition shifts entirely to relationship management for the sake of conversion. Then you set it and forget it. By that we mean you have to have constructive tunnel vision. Don't get seduced by the sales pitches around marketing tactics to feed your pipeline with strangers. Nurture existing client and strategic partner relationships and activate the advocacy magnet.

Then, in the spirit of planning, you need to be aware of *Littles Law*. This simply states that cracks start to emerge and things tend to break down as you approach your natural capacity – in this case your client count. It's like the red-line on a car. You have to get out in front of that to achieve plateau avoidance. Then, as counterintuitive as it may sound, you may need to grow-down in order to grow further up-market. This is where the 80/20 rule and professional scarcity gets even more intensely implemented. We'll cover that in the reframing chapter.

The serendipity is that the two-for-one special on mastering organic growth lets you then shift to scalable growth. We also have an entire chapter dedicated to those practices, but for now, the point is to have a rational and methodical philosophy about growth.

## Our Philosophy about Legacy

In the spirit of building something rather than selling something, one of the many things you are building is a legacy in real time. A legacy is something that people primarily look back on, but being mindful of it as you are developing one creates a special energy. One of the best quotes we've ever encountered on legacy is this, "Society grows great when old men plant trees in whose shade they know they will never sit." That speaks to the gathering momentum that is generated by a vision and code-of-conduct that culminates in an admired legacy. Artists aren't often fully appreciated until they've passed, but the most unique tend to be remembered longer. Business professionals tend to be respected once they've hit their stride and then their impact fades, but that isn't really the incentive, is it? The goal is to be a beacon that inspires others, regardless of the time frame.

While you are building your business, also be creating and innovating a better way and striving for your own personal version of the Blue Square. Mowry Young, a F4S professional who personifies a client-centered approach, would say it this way: "Success and failure can be memorable, but what matters is how you live your life." When you ponder your own version of the blended concept of *cui bono* – who benefits - and *pro bono* - for the benefit of others - you can move to the purest form of capitalism.

There is a good chance that you have second and third generation clients today. Very few people in business can say that. The multi-generational F4S professional sees it all, from married to buried, as one of our clients likes to say. They get invited to weddings, retirement parties, funerals and so much more in between. They get asked for advice beyond their core competency. Have you ever had a client ask you if you know a good marriage counselor or a parenting coach? Your role comes with a huge sense of fulfillment and responsibility that is shaping your legacy as you read this.

Of course, there is your humanity, integrity and ethics. Joseph L. Badaracco asks in his book *Questions of Character*, how flexible is your moral code? Few things impact legacy more than your own answer to that question. We've heard stories about people in their youth who were ambitious and confident, and less enlightened about this until later in life, when they became a bit wiser about the power of humility, empathy and decorum. Again, it doesn't always contribute to instant results, but everything matters, and eventually some things matter more.

We've all seen movies and read stories about a criminal enterprise that used silver or lead as their incentive to get a result. We've all read stories about people who, in a moment of weakness, sold out to reach for the ring. We've all encountered a sales enterprise that is driven by commissions as the primary incentive, and eventually to everyone's detriment. A professional enterprise that uses self-actualization and legacy as its fuel will remove any limits to growth potential without any collateral damage along the way.

From a different perspective, look at some of the tumultuous outcomes of legacy building. Watch the video of Archie Williams, who, after being found to be wrongly incarcerated for 37 years, was released and performed on *America's Got Talent* and knocked everyone's socks off. What advice would he give on legacy? Read Nikola Tesla's letter to his mother. He was arguably one of the biggest contributors to humanity and yet he wrote "All the years I have spent in the service of mankind brought me nothing but insults and humiliation." Have a chat with him about legacy.

Or the next time you look at Van Gogh's *Starry Night* and read about his troubles and torments, only to see that his painting is worth in excess of 100 million dollars, today. It's all very perplexing, but probably designed to help prevent us from sleepwalking through our own journey.

## Our Philosophy about Success and Adversity

When we reach for any form of achievement, there are two possible outcomes – success or failure. How we embrace both will have a huge impact on how we see the world, and how much meaning we give to our outcomes.

Success and setbacks are both revealing and both have their share of external dependencies. One of the greatest gifts a human receives is free will and the ability to pursue happiness and fulfillment. But our free will is still at the mercy of God's will, and sometimes to the free will of those we interact with, who may have their own conflicting agendas. Sometimes, outcomes feel like destiny, at other times they feel like a curse.

We hope that your philosophy includes embracing adversity. We get it. Adversity is only cool after you've overcome it. It can stink while you're in it, but it shapes us. This is not an absolute and there are exceptions to every rule, but there can be real meaning found in the friction of life. There is an old saying that A students work for B students at companies founded by C students. Early in life, nothing came easy for the C students, but they didn't feel a sense of victim-hood. A resolve was born and they simply asked more from themselves than from the world. A good poker player will never ask for a better hand. They know that every conceivable hand has won a big pot somewhere in the world. They instead take ownership and simply ask themselves to become a better player with better judgment. When in doubt, when you're in the thick of it, just remind yourself, "I'm standing on a planet that is floating in space." It might just interrupt your dwelling on the minutiae of your problems and reset you in a direction of resolve and faith.

## Your Philosophy about People

It has often been said, "Have faith in people, but lock your car."

We all have to deal with people on our team, in our supply chain and within our client base. With that in mind, make the study of people part of your lifelong pursuit. This includes the study of history and what societies have endured, overcome or succumbed to. It's a great tribute to the past and a great investment in yourself.

Take some time to think about how you think – especially about the people you interact with. The study of philosophy and human nature can add tremendously to your professional prowess. Socrates, Plato, Aristotle, Nietzsche, Adler, Freud, Jung and Maslow, to name a few, all made immense contributions – not all of it accurate but virtually all of it valuable.

Gary Klein, author of *The Power of Intuition*, urges us to 'embrace our sixth sense.' Some might consider that a spiritual force, Klein considers it a learned skill. Some elements are surely innate, while other aspects can be discovered, understood and put to use in our interactions.

Part of that journey forces us to be mindful about our environment. Everyone you meet will either be a fountain of optimism or a drain of negativity, to varying degrees. Some people have optimism for the future, others perpetually dwell on the past, while others are somewhere in between. All people create an energy, some of which you will be drawn to and some of which you will be allergic to. Some relationships need to be dropped like a hot biscuit. Others need to be nurtured.

Be mindful and conscious of all of them. In Qigong (cheegong), you learn about life energy, and the belief is that there isn't bad energy in your life, but there is energy that doesn't belong in your life. So let it move out and move along to where it belongs so that you can restore balance and harmony in your life.

## Your Team

It's important to be deliberate, intentional and unwavering with the clients you choose to surround yourself with. It's just as important with the members of your team. There is an accretive, collaborative array of benefits that come with the right philosophy.

One client of ours used to hire based entirely on experience and technical ability, but had a bit of a revolving door when it came to retaining talent. He was just checking boxes and throwing bodies at problems, resulting in a lot of collateral damage. His vetting mindset drifted to "hire a clown, expect a circus." Being of Scottish descent, we appealed to the concept of tartan – the plaid fabric with many different colored threads woven through it. The point was to look at the mosaic of the team, but also to get granular on each component. Talent, in-and-of-itself, is a currency that can fluctuate in value over time. We would suggest that your vetting process to attract great talent, and your ongoing culture to keep it, have a philosophical component to complement the technical. You need to keep an open mind here. As political columnist and author PJ O'Rourke said, "C students will open a restaurant and A students will write the review."

From an enterprise perspective, ensure that all team members embrace best practices and process, meaning that nothing resides solely in the heads of your people. Remove any mystery. Define roles, responsibilities and expectations. Embrace the Rule of Three, which states that everything anyone does three or more times, and which has three or more steps, is documented. It creates an intellectual property that has intrinsic value and also liberates the team to elevate themselves. It's counterintuitive in that, when everything is documented, individuals can become obsolete – meaning if they depart, they can be replaced quickly. Faces can change on the team, but the clearly defined roles do not. However, the real outcome is that you are creating an environment that they won't want to leave, because they aren't plateauing as a person. You are liberating everyone to grow and maintain relevance and even indispensability, but in a good way. We have an entire section dedicated to team dynamics later on, but for now, we just want to emphasize our philosophy on leadership.

Leadership is about empowering and liberating a team to see what it brings out in everyone. You may have heard of the fascinating (and hopefully true) phenomena that an alpha wolf will lead from behind. When moving, the front of the pack is apparently made up of the youngest, in the middle are the oldest – they determine the pace – and then trailing behind are the strongest of the group. There is no need for bravado or an obvious show of strength. Even if this is only the stuff of legend, it's still something we should consider ourselves.

Surround yourself with good people, empower them to strive for excellence, and hold them accountable to building enterprise value, and you will create loyalty among some and reveal a lack of fit in others. Incentivize for quantitative performance and offer discretionary rewards for qualitative performance, too. No matter how much we talk about best practices and processes, people are essential.

## Get Grounded

With technology, people are tempted to always be putting information into their brains – much of which doesn't stick because it's random noise instead of meaningful signals. Detach from the noise and embrace Gaia, the mythical goddess of earth, a.k.a. "Mother Nature." Golfers and tennis players, among other athletes, will tell you their power comes from the ground up. They push intentionally from the earth to harness all the power in their entire body – not just the arms.

Discover the full spectrum of teachers in every area of knowledge you pursue. When it comes to health, you can learn about the benefits of holistic medicine from the controversial Alfredo Bowman and work all the way across to modern medicine derived from science and research – and the entire spectrum plays a role. Fortify your body. Amplify your natural immunity. Add longevity to your life with stretching, meditation and other pursuits that pay tribute to your panoramic good fortune.

We have to seek counsel, learn to sift out the dross through due diligence, and keep searching for answers, but nature is waiting to show you miracles every day. If you've ever seen a bubble floating in the cold and freeze before your eyes – you have witnessed an art form. Look at a monarch butterfly, and realize that, with its migration from Mexico, by the time it reached you it went through a generational metamorphosis seven times – and then heads back to return to the same tree. It's easy to get lost in work because you love what you do.

Just don't lose yourself. You're not going to die at your desk. You run the business, but it does not run you. Get centered. Schedule your getaways. Regroup with your core philosophy and restore your purpose. As part of your gentle reboot, consider the one thing you can go the least amount of time without – oxygen. You take over twenty thousand breaths a day without a second thought. It's automatic, yet you'd miss it pretty quickly if it was gone. Take 10 intentional deep breaths. Inhale some essential oil to draw in the elements of the earth to activate your awareness for gratitude, purpose, balance and fulfillment. An enlightened philosophy needs the fuel of awareness and validation which will help guide you to solid decisions and enhanced professional contrast.

# Chapter 4:

*Getting Clear on Your Gaps*

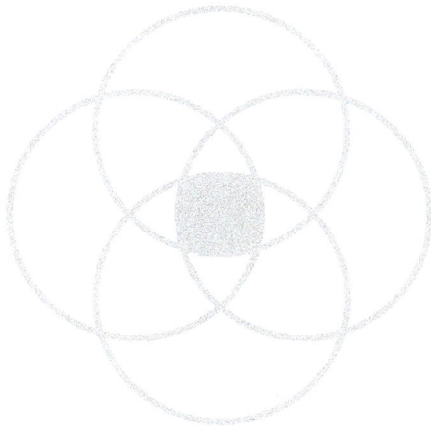

Hopefully your sleeves are rolled up, you've got a fresh set of highlighters and a thick pad of multicolored Post-it tabs ready, because we are going to move into some heavier lifting. In this chapter we pop the hood on your business to gain clarity on the specific actions you can take to unlock another level of productivity and efficiency. We follow the identical format that we use with a consulting client engaged in the early stages of our process. We approach it this way because virtually all of our clients come to us with more issues around breaking through a plateau than in addressing specific problems. It's not that they have fires they are trying put out, or mistakes they are trying to remedy – they have a good business but they want to be more deliberate and intentional around preempting future growth ceilings and insulating themselves from possible lightning strikes. They are also mindful that they are approaching or have hit a self-imposed limitation and, in their current model, they have simply run out of hours in the day.

This gap format also ensures that we aren't trying to apply a one-size-fits-all approach. There are universal principles, but a custom plan is not off-the-shelf. There has to be a diagnostic methodology to not only reveal the addressable issues, but also to help determine if there is a good fit in terms of how to take action going forward.

As you can see from the icon below, there are four quadrants to our model. This is a more panoramic approach than a SWOT analysis because, again, our clients typically already have a good grasp on their strengths, weaknesses, opportunities and threats. This is designed to clear up what the next level looks like and how to get there, while fine tuning their own trajectory towards the Blue Square.

As you do with your clients, the first step is to get clear on specific goals – personally and professionally - to galvanize the 'why' even further. Like any attempt to climb a summit, the effort can get intense and the needs more complex the higher you go. The beacon you establish for yourself creates a force that helps you avoid distractions or fall victim to subconscious drift.

The next step is to get crystal clear on specific gaps that you need to address. We generally set a goal of identifying six to eight gaps that can be dealt with in 90 to 120 days. Addressing one gap by itself generally won't lead to a breakthrough, but as a composite, addressing six to eight can cumulatively be profound, and be mindful of the progress paradox – addressing six to eight can reveal another six to eight.

The rubber hits the road when you shift from a mindset of "intent" to "implement" to hold yourself accountable. This is the launch pad where you look closely at how you allocate time, how you will disrupt your patterns to find another gear, and how you will engage others. This is the Rubicon few cross after a plateau. This ensures you don't drift into a state of contentment or complacency, but instead balance appreciation for what you have, along with aspiration for what you want.

Lastly, you will assess your progress. This is where you will identify specific Key Performance Indicators (KPI) that are both meaningful and measurable. As you know by now, we want you to make both quantitative and qualitative progress.

The beauty of the four quadrants is that we always know where we are in our engagements with consulting clients, and so do they. It's not a sporadic series of pep talks and Band-Aids, but rather an incremental progression that also includes a feedback loop. As we are professionalizing and standardizing the enterprise, it helps everyone be patient with outcomes, trust the plan and be at peace with things we can't control. Yes, we want to move the needle and drive the business forward, but focusing on cause and effect allows us to methodically move forward without impatiently dwelling only on results. This creates durability in the business and pleasant surprises instead of letdowns. Our consulting clients also have access to a Practice Management Index (PMI) that they can use in the future to keep a finger on the pulse of their business.

The exercise of identifying six to eight gaps also forces you into a mindset where you and your team buy into the constant refinement and optimization of your current approach. It's rarely a dramatic adjustment that is required, but more often a subtle twisting of the knobs to tune in a clearer signal (at the risk of dating ourselves with an analogue analogy in a digital era). It also ensures you aren't looking for pixie dust, quick fixes, silver bullets or magic wands. Individual ideas, à la carte or spot-coaching, where you implement one stand-alone strategy, can offer a temporary impact, but have a tendency to unravel and fade in time.

## Goals – a Deeper Dive

If you reflect on the initial three questions we posed earlier (Are you today where you said you were going to be five years ago? What does nirvana look like for you in the next five years? Why is that so important to you?), you kick-start the goal-setting process. Just the exercise of thinking it through is beneficial. Syncing that up with the ikigai questions can take you a bit further. Let us round it out with our deeper dive W5 goal-setting process so that you can galvanize your vision to paper. If you have followed our work over the years, you might have been exposed to this in the past, however, we find that it's quite common that someone doesn't take actual action on it until later on, when their awareness for plateau avoidance is more acute. So here we go.

W5 is not unlike the method journalists use to assess a story and reveal key points. Framed in five questions, we've seen clients use personalized variations themselves, for their team members, with their clients and even with their kids to help design and navigate the future.

## What

The first question is "what." What are you grateful for? It is powerful to invest your past into the future, if for no other reason than to activate a level of gratitude for what you've already accomplished in life. It's a good idea to take a moment to savor our achievements and good fortune so that we don't take things for granted. This allows us to tune out the noise, smell the roses and to add meaning to the things we hope to achieve going forward. This brings us to quite possibly the most concise concept we've ever seen to summarize human aspiration – Maslow's hierarchy of needs:

**Self-actualization**
desire to become the most that one can be

**Esteem**
respect, self-esteem, status, recognition, strength, freedom

**Love and belonging**
friendship, intimacy, family, sense of connection

**Safety needs**
personal security, employment, resources, health, property

**Physiological needs**
air, water, food, shelter, sleep, clothing, reproduction

# Maslow's hierarchy of needs

Now if you are like us, you were probably exposed to this many years ago, but perhaps it didn't impact you as much as it might today – primarily because you are further down the path in life and opening up a broader definition of your idea of success.

Maslow identified the five progressions to human aspiration. It's good to know where we are and where we are going.

The first step is **survival**. When a person becomes self-aware, their survival instinct kicks in and they focus on the necessities of life. We'll assume you have that box checked but there is some good karma that comes from acknowledging that for a big percentage of people on planet Earth, survival is every day.

If you've traveled the world, you've seen first-hand what that looks like. There was a time, in Manila in the Philippines, a country of absolutely beautiful people, you might have seen Smokey Mountain – a community of thousands of people fighting to survive each day. It got its name from the constantly burning landfill on which it was built. Imagine what survival looked like during the annual rainy season. Our ability to travel was recently disrupted, but remember that it's estimated that 80% of people on planet earth have never been on an airplane. Many things have come pretty easily for us.

The point of the first question is to dig deep to activate another level of personal gratitude. We are often so fortunate that we get lulled into a state where we unknowingly take things for granted. If you have ever seen the video of a baby - born deaf - who was fitted for a device to help her hear, and you saw her face when she actually hears the words coming from her mother's lips, you feel the universe nudging you. Not to feel guilty that you didn't give hearing a second thought, but to appreciate something that just came automatically to you. If you ever saw a teenager born colorblind, fitted with glasses to give him a sense of color, you feel his energy and euphoria. The universe wants us to be happy, but real happiness is in understanding that some people appreciate things that we tend to take for granted. There is a video circulating of a horse named Peyo that is escorted into a hospital in France to walk the halls to find people who he feels would benefit from his presence. Without any suggestion, Peyo picks a room and simply stands beside a patient. Even though it's on video you can see the energy in the room. We mention this because Peyo represents something that is hard to understand, but easy to appreciate when it comes to paying tribute to the direct blessings in our life, and the indirect clues that there are many things to appreciate in life that are yet undiscovered. Survival for many can seem like a Gordian knot, and for others things seem to come easily and effortlessly. Let's acknowledge that just for a moment.

The next step in Maslow's Hierarchy is **security**. This shift occurs when we have our basic survival needs under control. Again, food insecurity is a reality for roughly a billion people every day. Owning a home seems impossibly elusive for some. Retiring comfortably even more so. For those of us who aren't perpetually worried about treading water in life, appreciating our security creates a humility that fuels us. When you consider that as much as 50% of the western developed first world couldn't miss a single paycheck without being in serious trouble, you get a sense for how meaningful that is.

From there we become mindful of and work toward the concept of **belonging**. This is where we not only feel appreciated and loved but also that we matter to others. We cast an important shadow on people in our circle. There is a nurture-nature dynamic to belonging – unconditional love is a real thing but relationships with depth and breadth require investments of time and effort. Those of us who are fortunate to be afforded the opportunity to proactively nurture relationships in life have achieved something very special. In a broader sense, being mindful of this reminds you that your team wants to belong to something. Your clients want to belong to something. It's a 'safe harbor' mindset. How you leave them feeling after an interaction is the ultimate measure of success.

Do they feel safe, taken care of and insulated from external forces? Do they feel enlightened and optimistic? Awareness of this hard-wired need makes you more deliberate in engineering this for yourself and everyone you impact.

Then, aspiration gets even more interesting. The next step, **esteem**, is where we start to understand the difference between what we achieve in life and who we become as a person. Money becomes a means to an end. That's not to say that you can't reach deep levels of personal esteem without money – there are many examples in history of people who have – but money can help liberate us to reach another level of enlightenment and achievement.

Esteem helps us study the human experience further, to make sense of things and give meaning to the good, the bad and the ugly. This often comes later in life as we gain more experience and wisdom. Considering that 200 years ago the average lifespan was closer to 40, you start to realize that having a little more runway is a massive blessing on its own. When you consider the last 200 years, you are tempted to acknowledge the people who blazed trails for us. Two hundred years ago it took about five months to walk from Miami to Los Angeles. A few years later if you were lucky enough to have a horse, you could cut that down to five weeks. A few years later, if you could afford a train ticket you could make the trip in five days, and it wasn't long after that you could jump in a plane and touch down in five hours. In a short span of time, the human experience changed radically. If you know anything about the velocity of change with technology as governed by Moore's Law, you realize that breakthroughs have been achieved in many other areas, too.

Finally, and something we will keep alluding to, the achievement of esteem is the gateway to the highest aspiration, **self-actualization**, attaining the best version of ourselves. There are many layers and meanings to this, all of which are very personal. It lines up perfectly with the Blue Square of both qualitative and quantitative success, but it goes deeper.

Self-actualization not only gives meaning to our own success, it helps us fully appreciate the achievements of others. Legendary singer-songwriter Gord Downie said, "We are what we lack." Some people have envy and even resentment of others because they are only focusing on the attainment of 'success' rather than on the process and what it took to become a success.

Self-actualization also helps govern our aspirations and aligns them with our purpose. This goes beyond fashioning a moral compass. It's about the integrity of balancing service to others along with service to self. One of the most powerful stories of this is Nicholas Winton, a gentleman who saved hundreds of children from the horrors of World War II, putting himself in extreme danger in the process, but he did it because he felt that's what he was called to do, and he expected no fanfare or accolades. Fifty years later, and without his knowledge, a large group of the survivors arranged an event where they surprised him with a tremendous outpouring of appreciation and love. The look on his face was priceless.

That was a pretty exhaustive outline on the importance of gratitude on the goal-setting process. Let's pick back up with W5 and shift from focusing on the past and present to looking into the future. The next question is "where" - where do you see yourself in the future?

## Where

Admittedly, some people find this exercise to be somewhat cosmic or mystical. Others feel they are at a stage in their lives where they are beyond this. Ultimately, you live by the rules you set. We believe this exercise is timeless. Dizzy Gillespie performed a great song called *When I'm Too Old to Dream*, but you are never too old. It's never too late to create a wish list of things you want to achieve, places you want to go and items you'd like to acquire. There is something self-fulfilling about writing 10 things down and looking at them. This exercise helps to make the aspirations real and conceptual, and also makes them attainable. In the great book *The Art of Racing in the Rain* by Garth Stein, he wrote "The car follows where the eyes are looking." The best way to prompt you to draw out a Wish List (a great Pearl Jam song btw) of 10 or more meaningful goals is to frame them in FORM. Write out the acronym vertically and start populating your Family, Occupation, Recreation and Money goals. You activate something when you take this simple step and it is integral in fashioning your ideal life.

### When

From there, the next question is "when". When do you hope to achieve the goals on that wish list? Casually give each an approximate time line. It's not that the timeline is etched in stone, but it should help you sift through your planning based on importance and urgency.

Some goals will be short-term, others mid- or long-term. Others may remain open-ended. It's an exercise to turn the lens to create more focus and clarity, not to make an etched-in-stone blueprint. It also tempers expectations to revisit cause and effect yet again. As always, the enlightened are at peace with the 'when', yet unrelenting on the 'where'.

### Why

The shift to meaning and purpose is activated further by asking yourself "why". Why is all of this so important to you? Carl Jung said that the privilege of a lifetime is to become who we truly are. Getting clear on the why propels us, not just to the how, but also who. Peter Drucker asked Jack Welch, "If you weren't already in this business, would you enter it today?" That had more of a technical and practical meaning, but you can ask yourself a version of that question when you are in the "why and how" dynamic.

### Who

That leads to the heaviest question to close the loop on the goal-setting exercise, "who". Who do I need to become to make all of this happen? For outcomes to change, sometimes we have to change. It's not always an easy proposition. Sure, some things are gradual yet inevitable – we just need time for things to compound. For other aspirations, some disruption is needed. Our mindset and thinking needs to expand, limiting beliefs need to be shattered and self-doubt needs to be overcome. Charles Hardy, in his book *The Age of Unreason*, stated that, in his era, most people worked 47 hours a week for 47 months of the year for 47 years of their life to achieve the goal of retirement. He also identified that it was possible that one of his children could achieve that within 37. There are constructs and norms that we can choose to comply with or choose to not have define our lives. W5 is simply designed to expand our thinking around what is possible, while at the same time being aware of unintended consequences, collateral damage and the costs associated with reaching further benchmarks.

Po Bronson in his book *What Should I Do with My Life?* Wrote that, first, we must be honest with ourselves and others, and then discover and maximize our strengths and talents. A F4S professional can often work in isolation and be infected by cognitive dissonance. Self-sabotage can prevent us from acting, or derail us mid-journey. Anaïs Nin said, "We don't see things as they are. We see things as we are."

Cognitive dissonance occurs when a belief we hold is challenged by new information, but we choose to preserve our original idea or position despite the evidence. Cognitive dissonance is not much of an ally for self-actualization. Objectivity is undermined because our former-self is essentially holding our future-self back.

Khalil Gibran wrote, "God said Love thy enemy and I obeyed him and loved myself." Reach for self-actualization, be patient with the pace, and at peace with the outcome. When you are the recipient of good luck, or God's touch as some would call it, acknowledge it by looking up and saying "That was you." When you achieve a goal, savor the process as much as you do the accomplishment. Anne Frank wondered why people would bring flowers to a grave site to pay tribute to someone who died more often than give flowers to someone who was still alive. The average person has 15 to 20 perfect days a year. Those who strive for self-actualization are certain to attain more.

## The Bridge from Goals to Gaps

Once you take a balanced approach to writing out both your personal and professional goals, a shift must happen to create a blueprint to bring those aspirations to life. Keep in mind that we're not referring to an exhaustive and time-consuming plan, but more of a road map for your trajectory going forward. Your progression is fluid and dynamic, not theoretical or static. The term *"Quo Vadis"* translates to "Where are You Going?" This takes into consideration that there is a difference between a plan and planning. A document that outlines your aspirations is important, but connecting it to a relevant planning approach as you deploy and execute the plan takes into account the reality of life.

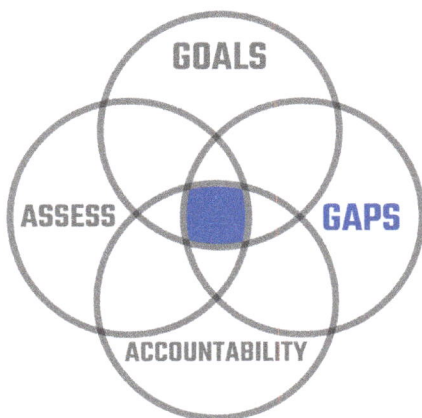

GOALS

ASSESS

GAPS

ACCOUNTABILITY

Captain Obvious would probably remind us that both business and personal life have many uncertainties and external dependencies. We all occasionally step on a rake and make errors in judgment, just as none of us are immune to occasional lightning strikes. Every driver assumes mutually implied risks that we'll stay in our lane, respect the yellow line, and stay in control. This exercise reminds us that as we reach, we must keep perspective and proportion around what we can control and what we cannot.

W5 is a good high-level approach to identify goals, but is has to be bookended with a strategy for implementation. Many of our clients have adopted and customized a version as part of their goals-based planning approach with their own clients. You may want to consider expanding the exercise and connect it to your gap analysis and planning approach to balance out your personal and professional goals. SOPA is an acronym that speaks to both Strategic Objectives and Personal Aspirations and helps you go deeper. Remember, this is an exercise rather than an exact science and builds on the premise that you are identifying and addressing specific gaps in an established business, rather than identifying problems to fix or damage to repair. That is a positive mindset, of course, and it pays tribute to the fact that you have built a solid foundation, but now is the time to identify the necessary adjustments that can propel a business forward. Again, the goal is to never plateau and avoid entropy while balancing contentment with ambition.

As mentioned, we generally set an expectation with our clients that it is reasonable to identify the six to eight gaps that they can address in 90-ish days. Several small adjustments are generally more sustainable than one dramatic one. Which brings a lot of credence to Justin Rose's mindset of 10x1% versus 1x10% we described earlier.

But where are these gaps? Some are self-evident and some have to be sifted out and revealed. This is a very simple exercise for connecting your goals to specific actions going forward. At your next State of the Enterprise meeting, use this quick list as an agenda to ask yourself and your team these questions to bridge your past into your future.

1.   What have we accomplished that is meaningful and measurable over the previous year?

Take a moment to slow life down and tune out some of the noise so that you can savor your wins.

2. What remains outstanding?

Be specific on the items that you didn't get over the finish line and carry them forward to sustain momentum.

3. What needs to be added?

Reflect on ideas you discovered, unmet needs that appeared, and embrace the paradox that, as soon as you address six to eight gaps, six to eight new ones emerge. It might feel like shoveling the driveway while it's still snowing, but it is progress.

4. What needs to be re-imagined?

For tasks that didn't quite play out as expected or weren't executed flawlessly and could be refined and optimized.

5. What needs to be removed?

The truth will set you free, but first it might tick you off! Perhaps there are things (or people) you have outgrown, or things you need to let go of to open up room for something new and improved.

Self-awareness and clarity are the benefits of this exercise. Just getting you thinking critically and rationally can fuel gratitude, optimism and motivation. It also ensures that you don't get complacent or faked out by setbacks or external factors. Like a baseball pitcher who loses his fastball, but adjusts and evolves to stay in the game, you strengthen your vision to the point where you can almost see around corners and believe in your ability even more than you do currently.

Growth is fluid and dynamic but not accidental. There are shooting stars that come out of the blocks quickly and then fade and then there are steady burners that keep on trucking, and both are valuable teachers.

With that in mind, consider applying your own version of the 'innovation adoption' life-cycle to your own life and enterprise. When you think of a new idea or technology that comes on the scene, it is adopted in waves - by a few initially and the masses over time. Some of our most successful clients have a philosophy of "I've never met an idea I didn't like." Ultimately what that means is they are always looking for new and innovative ways to do things – and sometimes they over-commit and overreach during the learning process. They attend events, read books and talk to peers, vacuuming up ideas and actively stirring the pot when it comes to identifying innovative ways to do things more effectively.

## Where do you place yourself?

1. Innovators – they are always out in front, but not to a fault. They are deliberately not set in their ways.

2. Early Adopters – a part of their due diligence is interpreting the feedback of innovators and deciding if the idea is a good fit.

3. Early Majority – a concept reaches a tipping point of acceptance and is now safe to be considered.

4. Late Majority – a concept becomes popular and this groups feels they are conspicuous if they don't embrace it.

5. Laggards – those who are resigned to accepting an idea even if they're not fully bought into its benefits.

The point is to know yourself and your business. As one client who found another gear of enthusiasm and ambition said, "I've still got some gas in the tank and I want to finish strong. I can't expect better results if I don't find ways to get better." At the same time, the pendulum can't swing all the way over to the point that you're abandoning the tried and true. There is a sweet spot.

## All Gaps Exist in These Three Areas

We often look at growth potential being a combination lock with three numbers. Dial all three in and you have a breakthrough. Dial in just one or two, and you will plateau.

1. TACC Management – this is your Technical Ability and Core Competency.

2. Practice Management – this drives your client experience, efficiency and enterprise value.

3. Relationship Management – this impacts how you are perceived and described by people.

## Gaps in Your TACC Management Process

Undoubtedly you are a serious student when it comes to your technical ability. Professional development is an ongoing pursuit - and not just for CE credits and compliance reasons - but also because of your personal standards of excellence.

There was a time when your core competency was enough. You could hang out your shingle and the world would beat a path to your door. Today it is a minimum requirement. For many F4S Professionals, they go deep into their core skills and also look at the deliverables they are providing to identify efficiencies and activate professional contrast. One example is in the distinction between being a generalist and being a specialist. Do you have too many households or clients to serve? Do you have too many holdings or products to keep track of properly? Have you diluted your brand by offering too many individual solutions versus building them into a panoramic, all-encompassing and proprietary process?

Clients can become numb to complexity. Your value proposition has to be clear and intuitive. The goal is to constantly find ways to decommoditize your value, so that clients focus on what you are worth rather than what you cost. We'll talk more about the concepts of right-sizing clients and reallocating clients to more suitable models throughout this book. The point is to expand your thinking beyond the way your competitors view themselves and deliver their solutions.

Robert Fleming created one of the original mutual funds in Dundee, Scotland, where smaller investors could pool their money and take advantage of safety in numbers and buying power. In Dundee, Nebraska, Warren Buffet, regarded by some as one of the shrewdest investors, bought companies and made investments that he liked, but kept his number of core holdings to a manageable number of about 25. Think of your enterprise. Are you as happy about client number 250 as you were about client number 25? Are you as excited about holding 50 as you are about holding five? It's common to cobble together a mass of clients over time and a vast array of solutions, but does that type of growth cost you more than it gets you? Streamlining can be liberating in terms of hassle factor, but also in focus, efficiency and growth potential. Growth is for vanity, profit and progress are for sanity. We will connect these dots specifically in quadrant three and the reframing chapter.

We're moving on for now, because if you are like most of the F4S professionals we've worked with, there are few, if any, gaps in your technical ability. It's the second and third numbers in the combination where we see more issues.

## Gaps in Your Practice Management Process

Your technical ability is a foundation to build on. It's promissory on an outcome and the performance of your core deliverables, and you don't want to be living and dying strictly by that sword.

Practice management is promissory on a client experience – it represents what it means to be your client over the lifetime of the relationship. Professional contrast can start with your technical ability but it is amplified by your commitment to practice management. It's the difference between being a good dentist and running a thriving dental practice.

The goal is to depersonalize your client relationships - not to downplay your personal contributions, but to enhance their appreciation for your bench strength, your practice and your process. If they can trust all of that as much as they trust you, the person, you are poised for something special.

If you think back to the Always ON concept, practice management means that there is a place holder for everything. All interactions have been thought out. You live and thrive by *The Rule of Three* - anything you do three or more times, and that has three or more steps, is documented and put into your proprietary playbook and procedures manual, aligned with your organizational and structural chart and assigned to your client classification service matrix and model. No one on your team operates out of their head or heart. They don't wing it. Roles and responsibilities are clearly defined. This is the distinction between client service and a client experience. Good client service is an intention and a reaction to an issue – it says you are a good person and that you care. A good client experience is deliberately engineered, proprietary and scalable. It's anticipatory and over-delivers on expectations, not just because the bar is low when it comes to competitors, but because overall, in business today, client expectations have been beaten down by mediocrity. A client experience is not at the mercy of maverick talent or undermined by someone having a bad day. It is your culture brought to life by process. When you consider everything we went through in 2020, there is a tremendous opportunity to put distance between yourself and competitors because of your client experience, fueled by best practices.

A client experience activates professional contrast, helping elevate you above the pack. It creates a sense of belonging. Clients feel they belong to something special. It generates advocacy because it makes you referable. It makes your enterprise more valuable because your process is an intrinsic asset.

At this point you might be saying, OK this is starting to sound like work. Relax. You do not have to reinvent this wheel. We have the tools and templates you'll need to create a critical path and chassis. It all starts with this checklist:

- Create an org chart of roles and responsibilities.

- Create a playbook documenting your operation based on the Rule of Three.

- Create an ideal client profile defining who you are suited for.

- Create a service matrix and model to set expectations and create contrast.

You'll have access to these resources and more at thebluesquaremethod.com/implementation-resources.

If you embark on this path, you will populate your list of gaps and address them easily to position yourself for more efficiency, consistency and productivity.

When you dial in the first and second numbers by identifying and addressing some of those gaps, you are not only doing preventative maintenance on your business and relationships, you are creating predisposition for advocacy. Your clients and strategic partners start to sense that you're not just good at your TACC deliverables - there is something else present they've rarely, if ever, seen. They are on the verge of becoming a brand ambassador. They feel compelled to share how they admire your process, but is their advocacy perhaps getting lost between endorsement and introduction? As we said in The C-Suite (chapter 3), there are many referable F4S professionals who don't get the quality or quantity of referrals they could be getting, and that comes down to dialing in the third number.

## Gaps in Your Relationship Management Process

Relationship management encompasses how you manage the world's perception of you and how people describe you to others. You're not just managing the performance of your core competency, you are managing a business and you are managing people. You have to be as deliberate, intentional and process-driven with numbers two and three as you are with number one. The branding chapter of this book will enable you to bring that to life.

This goes beyond your "bedside manner". You are developing a branding strategy that takes all of your qualities, skills and intentions and makes you stand out. It starts with your ability to articulate your value, so that if you have a team of seven, each of those seven messengers represents your value with one message – not seven that are made up on the spot. How you all verbalize that value, so that clients can internalize it and then socialize it to others, has to be reinforced by everyone.

This is professional contrast intensified. The beauty is that, not only is this where most of the gaps exist in a F4S business, they are also among the easiest to address. The next chapter is dedicated entirely to developing and deploying a scalable branding strategy quickly and predictably. That chapter moves the needle fastest and taps into the lowest hanging fruit that awaits you.

The goal with branding is to demystify your value so that everyone who interacts with you understands and appreciates your value fully and completely. You can communicate and demonstrate your value, differentiate your value and capitalize on your value. When you consider the productivity spectrum, starting with maintenance for what you have, all the way to attracting what you want, addressing the gaps in relationship management might shock you in terms of the degree of impact it has.

## Accountability

Once you get your goals crystallized on paper and identify the gaps you'll need to address to achieve those goals, your blueprint starts to come together. As you know, many plans have been created that never saw the light of day or weren't acted upon. You could e-mail your plan to 50 of your closest competitors without a worry in the world, because the chances are that nobody would do anything with it. Many people are locked in the status quo, talking a good game about change but reverting to their deeply-rooted habits, rituals and inertia confidence.

As Jim Rohn pointed out, it's easy to change. The problem is, it's much easier not to. Millions of people ordered P90X from a late night infomercial, and while some achieved great results, many more simply took comfort in placing the order and then holding the package when it arrived, hoping that through osmosis a GI Joe physique would emerge. Many of those who did take action poured it on for a solid 30 days and got results, and then, for whatever reason, stopped. Maybe they got a cold and that derailed their ability to form a pattern? Maybe they went on vacation, or maybe they just didn't give it enough time to become an ingrained habit and ritual. Discipline compounds. Neglect compounds. Both take time to incrementally create a result. Achieving a tipping point, taking it to critical mass and realizing sustainable outcomes is the goal that eludes many.

Coincidentally, if you read *The Tipping Point* by Malcom Gladwell, you know all about how mastery is achieved in a pursuit after toiling away at it for at least 10,000 hours. It stands to reason that to make anything a habit, it would require an investment of a few hundred hours at a minimum.

## It's About Time

One of the biggest factors conspiring against change is time. For many of us, there doesn't seem to be enough time - but is that true? Time is the one thing we all have the same amount of. A key distinction is moving beyond a mindset of time management to time allocation. How do you allocate your investments of effort?

When many people max out and realize that something has to give, often the first action they take is to work longer hours, start prioritizing and or delegating tasks and even reassigning clients. That's a good start, but often superficial and unsustainable. Ultimately, we don't want you to work harder than you already are. Ideally, we'd like to see you expend a little less effort while seeing better returns. So let's go deeper. Do an audit of a typical week in your life. With one of our clients, we revealed that he worked 45 hours in one week. During that period, he invested five hours with the 20% of his clients who generated 80% of his business, but he spent 40 hours reacting to the 80% of his clients who generated 20% of his business. Is it any wonder that his business plateaued and he "ran out" of time? Further, the top 20% were less demanding and more respectful, while the bottom 80% were needier and less appreciative. What does that time allocation model look like after 12 months?

Socrates, a man considerably ahead of his time, said the secret to change is to focus your energy not on fighting the old but on building the new. What has happened up to this point is history. You can learn from it but you can't change it. Instead let's focus on making some adjustments going forward.

The following are best practices of top F4S professionals:

**Find the Time** – Book a recurring meeting with yourself for an hour every day to work ON your business and yourself. Rather than just reacting to your schedule of appointments and tasks, and then using whatever is left over on "other things", deliberately allocate a slot from, say, 3 to 4 pm every day to tune out the world and stop letting the business run you. Run the business. View this appointment with as much importance as any other meeting with a client and show this initiative off to the world. At the end of your voicemail greeting add this message: "I return voice mail messages received between 3 and 4pm every day, if your matter is urgent during that time, please contact (your client service associate)."

On the bottom of emails, put the same message. You can give your top clients your cell phone and tell them they can text you directly, or give them access to an automated calendar scheduling function (again, only for the 20%) if there is something urgent. The bottom line is this: Tell the world that you value and guard your time.

Unless and until you do, nobody else will. You will find that people will start respecting your time more and your productivity will increase. You may even have people commenting on the initiative and inform you that they are now doing the same thing or at least considering it.

You can go one step further. Many of our clients will block off Monday to work on their business with team meetings, professional development, and various other aspects of enterprise refinement. They will carve out four client, prospective client and strategic partner meeting slots for Tuesday, Wednesday and Thursday at 9am, 11am, 2pm and 4pm, and that's it. Those are the 12 slots in a given week people have access to. The lead will also schedule occasional breakfast, lunch or dinner meetings to round things out. Finally, Friday is reserved for proactive relationship management – primarily activities like a call rotation, email correspondence, card writing, milestone recognition and the like. The staff protect this structure, and the reactive "drop-everything" mode is completely abandoned. Some initially feel this approach is too rigid, but those who adopt, customize and deploy it swear by it.

If you agree that time is more valuable than money, apply a version of Warren Buffett's advice. He says that you should save your money first and spend what's left, rather than spend your money and save what's left – because often there is nothing left. To paraphrase Hemingway again, success tends to build gradually and then suddenly. Incrementalism and compounding are unstoppable forces.

We'll outline a reliable team meeting scheduling matrix in the teams section that has proven to be a winner.

**Take the Time** – Again, the best way to take care of your business, your clients and your growth potential is to take impeccable care of yourself. You can't pour from an empty cup. We've seen F4S professionals strive to take care of everybody and everything around them, but it came at their own expense. Self-sacrifice does not breed respect; self-interest does. So in that hour-a-day, or whatever model you adopt, charge up your batteries, pay tribute to the temple (your mental and physical health) and slow life down a little.

## The Rule of 10

Think of the things you can go the least amount of time without. We talked about oxygen earlier - those breaths you take every day without a second thought. Schedule a daily energy-builder so that you take 10 deep intentional breaths, focusing deliberately on the inhalation and exhalation. Go a step further and keep some essential oil nearby, open the lid and inhale deeply.

Pour yourself a 10-ounce glass of the purest water, and don't just consume it, savor it slowly and feel it nourish you. Master those 10 simple stretching exercises. Stand up and pay tribute to your mobility. It's another form of getting grounded. Legendary tennis player Pete Sampras used to work on his leg strength as much as his arms because he knew he drew his power from the ground up.

Put a little extra into your time spent. If you go for a brisk 10 minute walk, add 10 sets of 10 lunges. It takes no more time but soon you will feel your core and legs getting stronger and your energy increasing.

It doesn't take much and these simple investments into yourself will compound, but they have to be scheduled and deliberate. You reach a point where the natural decline of age is chipping away at you. Push it back, and then keep going. If you like golf, but your game has started to resemble landscaping due to neglect, schedule some time to go hit some balls. If you like tennis but your game has eroded until it looks like you're swatting flies, work on your game. If you bought a ukulele in Hawaii five years ago and never unzipped the case, download an app and take 10 minutes in your office (with the door closed, initially). Carve out the time.

Many of our clients are competitive, and these practices are intended to compete with the procrastination that blocks your own untapped potential. You can embrace the energy of legendary baseball player Brooks Robinson's stern advice: "If you're not practicing, somebody else is, somewhere, and he'll be ready to take your job." If you're not elevating, you're stagnating. Sometimes the competitor is unknown but lurking and we have to constantly be vigilant.

If we are at the mercy of time, and we don't schedule time for renewal to restore ourselves, there are unintended consequences. We start cheating, trying to buy time. For many, the microwave oven has been a major time saver, but is the cure worse than the disease? Have you ever seen how plants grow using water that has been microwaved, versus distilled water or even regular tap water?

**In the Meantime** - It is natural to find ourselves at a point of introspection where we not only focus on what could be, but also what could have been. Hindsight is a gift on many levels. We all strive to make better decisions in the future, and judgment from experiential learning contributes to that. Good decisions come from strong positions rooted in wisdom. Optimism can sometimes propel us to overreach, or try to put 10 pounds in a five-pound bag, so to speak. Skepticism can prevent us from taking action. It's a tremendous self-study. Another fascinating study is to read stories of people who, at the end of their lives, were asked if they had any regrets. In no specific order, here are some of the most common answers:

*I wish I:*

Took better care of myself

Took a few more risks

Said I love you more often

Was less concerned about the opinions of others

Many also talked about benevolence. Giving of yourself can happen in two forms, monetarily and as time. Giving of either, especially to someone where there is no expectation it will be repaid, is both pure and rejuvenating. That investment actually amplifies the appreciation for your own time and achievements.

**Make the Time** – We have encouraged many of our clients to put an hourglass in their office as a symbol of time. Not to show its limitations but rather to envision popping the lid and pouring in more sand. That notion is great, but how do you do that, practically? Start with looking at how you allocate time to clients.

As we discussed earlier, you have clients who deserve you and clients who need you, but as you can see from the icon below, there is also a group called the movable middle.

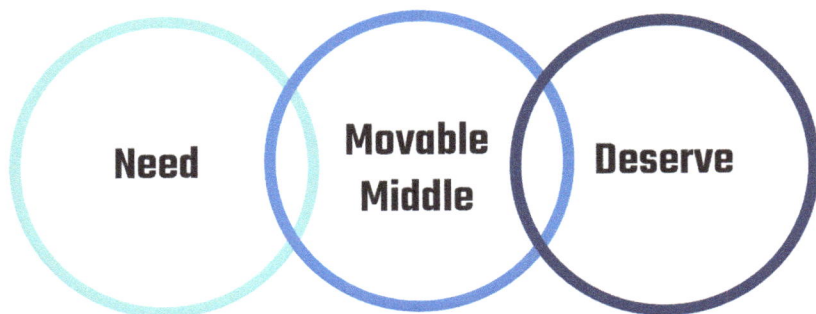

These are not perfect clients, but they have potential. Is there a chance that you are spending time with people who need you at the expense of the potential of the movable middle? Let alone the most deserving? Going forward, resist the temptation of bringing on clients that have no reasonable path to being ideal.

It's easy to get into the reaction trance of grinding out deliverables for clients who need you because it feels like growth and it moves the needle on paper, but how many more of the needy clients would you have to attract to replace a deserving client that you lose? Did the movable middle plateau or defect because they were neglected as well?

The question is, can you reduce the time expended on clients who need you to liberate yourself to invest more time with the most deserving clients and those relationships with the most upside? Perhaps a Skype meeting to replace an in-person meeting? A silver lining of the bizarre period that kicked off in 2020 when everything went virtual, is that many clients enjoyed the virtual meetings and asked to continue them. Perhaps a protégé was positioned to work with the 80%, moving them along the path to potentially progress through to the 20%. Again, the protégé is a different person, but they rely on the same practice and process that you do, so in many ways that allocation is an upgrade. We'll touch more on that in the reframing chapter, and as you will see in the branding section, when clients have a relationship with a practice and a process, it is less dependent on the person. The assignment to a protégé can feel like an upgrade rather than a hand-off. You are adding not just technology, but time. We're in an era where high tech combined with high touch can benefit everyone. A one-to-many approach with some can enhance your 1-to-1 approach with others.

When you consider your addressable audiences, you aspire to loyalty and advocacy from the deserving, future empowerment from the movable middle, and a respectful "in the meantime" approach with those who need you.

It's not unlike when Toyota introduced Lexus. They were tired of losing customers who felt they outgrew a Camry and decided to upgrade to an Audi or BMW. So Toyota invented a competitor. Lexus also helped sell more Toyotas. A Camry salesperson would highlight some of the tech from Lexus that made it into a Toyota and the Toyota customer would see that as a value-add.

If scale and refinement is not the entire answer for addressing your client allocation issues, rightsizing may be appropriate. We'll discuss respectful rightsizing more in the reframing chapter, but take a page from Vilfredo Pareto - the creator of the Pareto Principle, popularized today as the 80/20 rule. He identified that 80% of the tomatoes come from 20% of the vines and sometimes the counterintuitive concept of pruning – reducing the overall size of the harvest to increase its quality – is the answer.

## Hindsight is 80/20

The point of this is to remind you that often no good deed goes unpunished. We've seen it too many times. An F4S professional spends too much time with an 80% client that needs them and ends up losing a client in the 20% as a result. You don't want to win a race to the bottom.

## Supplement Face-to-Face Time with Digital - but Don't Replace It

At the end of the day, the goal is to free up more time for the most deserving, but rethink how you apply that, too. Perhaps you are in a pattern where you take your best clients out for lunch? Not a bad idea. But it's been proven that breakfast meetings are just as productive, less time consuming (because everyone has to get on with their day), less expensive (generally because there is no alcohol involved) and less likely to be canceled (because the day hasn't stacked up yet but the sense of urgency remains).

A call rotation for the most deserving, where you schedule two or three proactive calls a day to check in with your top 20%, and your protégé reaches out to the 80%, is a proven way to reduce interruptions, rejuvenate relationships and get out in front of developing opportunities so that you can capture more of them. We'll cover service deliverables like that and others in the ONgoing chapter.

**Give It Time** – be patient with your adjustments if they are fundamentally sound. We'll outline how to introduce and position your refinements to clients in the reframing chapter, but once you've started scheduling your time relentlessly and consistently, stick with it.

**Time is on your side** – when you give yourself and your clients the gift of time through a more deliberate approach, you are putting yourself on a pedestal, meaning that if you deviate in the future you run the risk of self-sabotage. You might convince yourself that you can get away with it occasionally but those chickens will come home to roost.

**All in good time** – your respect for the Law of Cause and Effect ensures that you focus more on solid activity and the benefit (productivity) will take care of itself. It also gives more meaning to your success because you savor the wins more deeply, and appreciate what you are building. The Persian poet Saadi wrote that everyone notices the beautiful plumage of the peacock, but all the peacock notices are his ugly feet. Sometimes we are so target-focused that we get down on ourselves and become our own personal dimmer switch, slowly dialing back the light. Then something jars us awake and we wonder, what happened? How did I end up here? Where did the time go?

Paradoxically, those who are the most "unreasonable" about how they allocate time also tend to possess higher levels of gratitude and humility. They are confident without being arrogant. They believe in themselves but they never believe they are superior to anyone else. They are hard on themselves but respectful of others. There was a powerful meme floating around that shows a quote "There is no God" by Stephen Hawking. After Hawking passed away, the picture shifted to the Universe and it read, "There is no Stephen Hawking" by God. Our time here is short and our pursuit of knowledge and enlightenment is never complete. This approach also ensures we focus more on what we can control and less on what (and who) we cannot. Our expectations and perspectives about others and their actions change for the better. Good parents will suggest to their kids that they try hard not to offend anyone – and try even harder to not allow themselves to be offended by anyone.

People want to belong to this type of well-oiled community. As practice management guru Kevin Bishopp likes to say, you project strength and calm when you aren't ruled by the tyranny of the urgent. People pick up on that energy. They are more compelled to share your value with others because it is so much more impressive than that of the common pack. People feel a sense of accomplishment when they join your community because it's not something they were talked into, it was something they aspired to.

## Assessment

The last quadrant is dedicated to assessing your growth on a meaningful and measurable basis. Personal and professional progress is relative and subjective. Your qualitative value has to be measured and appreciated as much as your quantitative is, so be sure that your Key Performance Indicators are in harmony. If we want to get in better physical shape, we have to pay close attention to reducing our intake while increasing our output. Some people get very granular on measuring both, others ultimately gauge it by how their clothes look and feel on the new and improved physique. Actor George Hamilton said that his goal was to always be able to stand up from a chair without pushing off with his hands. Focusing on the core can make that happen. Some people make it a continual goal to be able to put their socks on while standing up. Others want to be able to look left and right by only turning their head, not by having to turn their whole body as age starts to slowly tighten and seize things up.

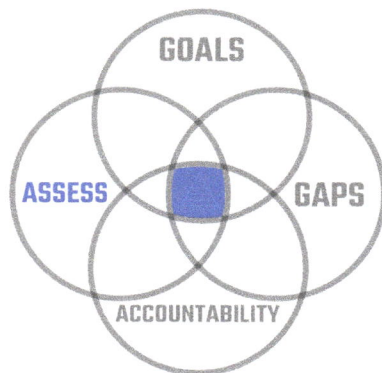

This is where the feedback loop connects to the goals you've set. Ultimately it comes down to "as compared to what?" Are you where you used to be? Where are you, relative to peers and competitors? Where are you, relative to your potential?

On a professional level, a mission critical KPI is to continually assess your capacity. Little's Law is a fascinating premise that must be respected when it comes managing growth and capacity. Every growing enterprise has to be constantly aware of its capacity threshold and as far ahead of this as possible. Keep that front and center as you strive to reduce growth dependency on people and put more emphasis on practice and process.

If you look at a commercial jet closely, you will notice redundancy. There are generally two of everything, just in case. By creating an org chart of roles and responsibilities and a playbook of documented best practices, you are driving your enterprise value beyond recurring revenue and profitability because you are on your way to an IP F4S enterprise – with intellectual properties that someone would rather buy than build themselves. It's a business that is not reliant on one person but rather can rely on any person who can execute a process. Your process and IP provide redundancy.

An IP mindset not only means that the business doesn't reside in someone's head, it also bridges you from a mindset of client service to one of client experience. At the risk of belaboring the point, client experience is thought out in advance. It anticipates needs and issues before they are presented, and is both scalable and proprietary.

## Know Your Ratios

Among radio operators there is a term - "5-by-5" - which speaks to the volume and signal clarity of a perfectly transmitted message. A message has to not only be loud enough to hear, it has to be clear enough to comprehend. In business, it is important to track the improvement of the quality of referrals along with the quantity. It is important to look for patterns around the sources of introductions and frequency of individual advocacy, and the trends around the increase in client empowerment.

## Deploy a Crowd-sourced Process

In your team meetings, engage everyone in being passionate about meaningful and measurable progress. Tie their compensation to three drivers:

- Base Salary – for execution, fulfillment and maintenance of core competency outlined in the org chart – do your job and have it completely documented.

- Bonus – for testimonials and rave reviews, deployment of a new process (such as min/max for greeting card inventory (a maximum of 50 on hand, reorder when down to 10).

- Bell Ringing Tip Jar – when the team moves the needle, everyone wins and participates in the lift through monetary rewards and celebratory events.

It's not just your clients who crave consistency, so does your team, and as a result your enterprise will thrive. People only like pleasant surprises. Surround yourself with people who get that. Count the rewards of great results, and count the costs of missteps and misfires. If someone doesn't get it, doesn't add to the energy on the team and make the environment better, it's not a good fit. Some people see the glass as half empty, others see it as half full, others are just happy to have a glass and see it as growing, because they keep adding to it without limiting beliefs. Respectfully disassociate from the destroyers of a dream - you're doing yourself, your team and the individual a disservice if you don't. As we all come to learn, the least impressive people can be brash and noisy. To use the old cowboy expression, the emptier the wagon, the more noise it makes. Do you have time to spend on things that rattle around? There is a positive takeaway, though. As Carl Jung said, everything that irritates us about others can lead us to an understanding of ourselves. Guard your time, invest it well and always look at the silver linings when reflecting on your efforts.

# Chapter 5:

*Then, Develop a Branding Strategy*

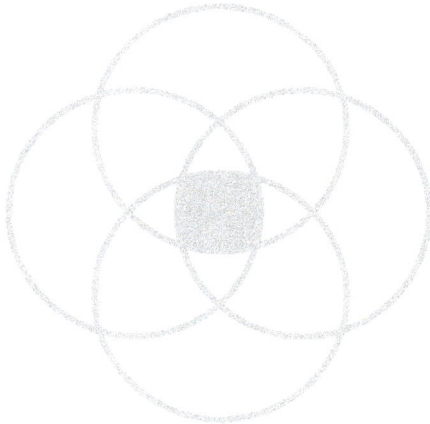

Let's begin this chapter by answering a very important question: What is branding?

Simply put, it's someone's interpretation for value being offered that aligns with a want or need that they have – even if occasionally that want or need is subconscious. Branding activates an awareness for and trust in something that often triggers an instant appreciation for how your value can benefit their life. It's different from marketing. Branding is the client's view of a value proposition, where marketing is the vendor's pitch trying to land and resonate. Marketing is a claim. It's advertising in an attempt to create awareness for your value. It is essentially a promise statement. "You should try this. You'll like it!" As you know, marketing can often prompt a skeptical reaction or complete apathy.

If we were to say, "We are good coaches," that is marketing – again, it's a claim. If you were to tell us, "You are good coaches," that's branding. If a stranger called us and said, "A friend of mine insisted that I call you. He told me that you are good coaches," that would be branding in action moving the needle. Marketing is what you say - branding is what they hear and then relay on to someone else.

Branding is an outward expression of your value that is interpreted based on the prospective client's frame of reference, their current provider and other vendors they are vetting. It activates an awareness for an unmet need which they have that you could fulfill. It is the first impression for a prospective client, not unlike the curb-appeal of a house that's for sale, or the aesthetics of anything that gets someone's attention early in a relationship. When you see a piece of art for the first time or listen to a song or try on a new shirt or taste food that instantly and automatically impacts you – there is an invisible connection, and there is nothing stopping it. You want it. You rationalize it. You convince yourself that you need it. It's like trying to hold a beach ball under water. Nothing stops this. The desire does not fade and unravel the way the impact of a sales pitch can.

Branding is not just a first impression, though. It's a lasting impression. Professional contrast is not a one-off event. It is something that must occur on an ongoing basis for as long as the relationship exists. In the spirit of advocacy, branding impacts how you are perceived and how you are described. In part, it's fueled by how you articulate, communicate and demonstrate your value to stand out from the pack. It's a sequential flow of value, communicated so that somebody can understand and appreciate everything your value does in an ascending way, and then it's your consistent execution that backs it all up after the person opts in.

Branding not only impacts prospective clients and existing clients, it impacts other influencers like strategic partners. Branding is the lifeblood of advocacy. It is reputational and can be relayed. Marketing can create transactions, but does not go anywhere near as far as branding when it comes to referrals. Introductions from advocates are a recurring revenue stream for your business and build the very fabric of your business. Transacting is like sewing without a knot at the end of the thread. Lastly, and it bears repeating, branding helps achieve stewardship, meaning your value is bought, not sold.

Allow us to give you an example. Undoubtedly you know about Sharpie pens. You're probably also aware that there are other knock-off indelible markers for purchase. Branding creates reputational equity, which ultimately activates trust. Put yourself into this scenario: You walk into a store. You're looking for markers and you see a package of four Sharpies for $5. Right beside it you see a knockoff brand, a package containing five markers for $4. Which one do you choose? Most people come to their own conclusions very quickly and they reach for the Sharpies. It's automatic, knee-jerk trust that required no convincing on the spot. The trust was earned in advance and at the stage of readiness the decision is made. If in that store there was a pop-up booth with a person standing there, representing the knock-off brand of markers, they could possibly convince you through marketing and sales-craft that their markers are a better value, but here's the rub: Most people don't like to be sold to. A lot of people like to buy, but that's very different. A lot of people get a charge of energy through buying, especially when there's a deal to be had. Perhaps you know someone who insists on buying everything on sale, even if it's something they don't need? Their savings are undermined by their volume but that doesn't deter them. Even though they can't really afford to keep "saving" so much money, they keep on buying. That's how they're wired. The psychology of buying is a fascinating study. When you're sold, however, there is a likelihood of anticlimax and buyer's remorse. When you buy, the likelihood is lower – not zero, but lower - that you will be disappointed with your decision.

You might be wondering why branding appears as such an early chapter in this book. It's because branding is one of the easiest adjustments to make that gets dramatic results. Consider again the art and science of being a F4S professional. The science being your technical ability and core competency - the art being how you achieve professional contrast. The art, not the science, is often what separates the best from the rest. In client acquisition, once a prospective client becomes aware of your existence, you are trying to hold their attention and have them tune in to your signal. You want them to say to themselves, "I like that. This is what I want." A professional branding strategy is a constant work in progress, not a one-and-done. You establish your brand and you keep tinkering and reinforcing it to ensure that you don't fall into inertia confidence.

To that end, we're going to provide you with a checklist of branding items that you can consider tackling with your team. We'll also provide a deeper dive behind the checklist and then drill down further on many of the items in subsequent chapters. Compare and contrast our list to your current inventory of branding strategies. Hopefully you identify some gaps that are quick and easy to address.

The reason we say that branding is a continual effort is because the law of optimization reminds us that we have to continually refine and optimize to rejuvenate, in order to keep up with natural decline. Think of exercise. Have you noticed that disciplines take far longer to compound than neglect requires to erode them? Don't misinterpret this. We are glass-half-full optimists, but we're always mindful of competitive forces, commoditization and the law of familiarity. You might have heard the joke about the parkour enthusiast jumping from building to building and feeling energized, and on one jump missing the landing and falling. According to the story, someone on the fifth floor heard him yell, "So far so good!" If we allow ourselves to take things for granted, we can engineer our own collision course with obsolescence.

The invisible enemy of branding is commoditization in the sector and loyalty fatigue among your clients, which can sweep the entire marketplace. No sector or enterprise is spared. We've seen Blockbuster Video, newspapers, CDs, Kodak film and traveler's checks – to name just a few - get hit by an asteroid. That is a bit dramatic, of course, but we're trying to gently nudge you to a mindset of constant innovation.

## So, Where do You Start?

Here's an interesting exercise. When we talk to F4S professionals and ask them how their clients would describe them, most say things like, "Well, my clients would say they trust my ability, my integrity and my professionalism." They rattle off qualities and skills and intentions, all of which are important, and there was a time when that was enough. Today, your qualities and skills and intentions are in fact a minimum requirement. What we're asking you to do is to build on that and turn it into something that's proprietary - an intellectual property. Commoditization and competitive factors disrupt clients. When professionals take their eye off the ball, clients start to fixate on the smaller details around decisions which are affected by products, pricing, immediate performance and gratification. We don't want your clients to drift into having a shallow impression of your value. We want them to have a panoramic appreciation for your people, your practice and your process.

We want your clients to focus on what you're worth, not what you cost. We want them to value your worth to the point where they never say, "Hey, can you sharpen your pencil? Is that the best you can do?" or "I've spoken with a competitor and they agreed to lower their fees to get my business." If that happens, we want you to have the unshakable conviction that allows you to say, "We don't compete on price. We don't negotiate our value to try to win someone's business. That's what brokers do. We're not transacting, we're building relationships. We're consultants." With that positioning, you're not just de-commoditizing - they understand what it means to be your client. The relationship isn't promissory on short-term performance, it's promissory of an ongoing experience. You're demystifying your value and they understand and appreciate your value through contrast and respect.

Branding is an essential component for any thriving business, whether it's Apple, Budweiser or Nike, or any of the colossal power houses, all the way down to the bakery on the corner. Likewise, it is absolutely essential for the F4S professional. Why? Because your value can be abstract. How do you shift someone from a mindset of transacting and buying something, to engaging and buying into something while viewing you as being beyond fee-worthy? Looking down the road at a long-term relationship, how do you differentiate and create professional contrast so that your value is bought, not sold, without having to use jargon or pressure?

If you read *The Experience Economy* by Joseph Pine and James Gilmore, they delve into the importance of judgment and skill as it applies to a service provider, but we mention it because it's so tempting to brag about "your experience." We often hear a F4S professional say, "I've been in the business for 21 years." We're not making light of that, but if a prospective client just previously met somebody who's been in the business for 28 years, and that's what you're placing ultimate value on, well, then, the other person must be better? Let your mileage and your experience be the last thing you talk about, because it will come out. It's not the driver of your branding strategy. It will be self-evident. Don't lead with experience as your major defining point, because, as you know, there are people who have one year of experience 21 times. There are people who plateaued and now they're phoning it in. Again, we'll never trivialize your core competency or experience, just always be aware it is a minimum requirement.

How does your value currently stand out? How does it make someone feel initially, and then after the passage of time? You probably know the names Marion Morrison and Norma Jean. Marion Morrison was better known as John Wayne. It's not to say that he couldn't have been as popular had his stage name been Marion Morrison - Shakespeare talked about a rose smelling just as sweet. Norma Jean could have been just as popular as Marilyn Monroe, but there's a reason they (or their studios) decided to re-brand their names. In their world, they were trying to create followers. Some might misidentify this as ego, or having a hero complex, but at a basic level it is providing an aspirational example for the entertainment consumer. A lot of people in the world want to be lifted up, or to escape – to feel like they would have a shot, too. That feeling is an unmet need which entertainment can address. Smart positioning and messaging (or a name-change) can facilitate that. Something moved Robert Zimmerman to adopt the name Bob Dylan and his brand has survived for many decades.

(Fun fact, Hugh Dillon – his actual name – is the lead singer of The Headstones. He is also a notable actor with roles such as Sheriff Donnie Haskell in Yellowstone. If that's not impressive enough, he also played pond hockey with NHL Hall of Famer Doug Gilmour as kids. Hugh is a living legend. Watch the Headstones music video for Smile and Wave – a great mantra to live by – to see him in action in the 90's.)

There is a subtle power to branding. There are quantitative benefits, not just qualitative. In 1954, Peter Drucker wrote *The Practice of Management* in which he noted there is only one valid definition of a business's purpose: To create a customer. In this era, we might modify that a bit and say "to create and keep a customer."

The modern volume of noise and the velocity of information is intense, but your branding strategy is your beacon and a means to an end. All roads lead to attracting and keeping great clients and converting them to advocates. Branding is not just about who you are, what you do and how long you have been doing it. For a majority of your competitors, that's how they think about branding and therefore they are in a competition to tread water because of commoditization. They strive to impress with technical knowledge. They use generic word salads and jargon. They're proficient but couldn't be less interesting. It's like listening to someone explaining their tattoo or describing last night's dream. Interesting to them, but not so much for the listener. They will say things like, "We do things differently here. We take a holistic approach." You might respond (with pardonable cynicism), "Oh, good, you're the one. Finally, I found someone who uses a holistic approach," because, again, technical ability is now a minimum requirement.

Everyone says and aspires to being unique and professional. Branding should not just be bright lights and a coat of paint. It's not just staging a house to try to sell it for maximum value. It's bigger than that. It permeates everything, because it has to be backed up. Potential clients are going to look at the bones. They're going to look behind the curtain. They want to know that there is no over-promise/under-deliver. That you've got the goods - fully and completely.

You might be aware that in motocross racing there's a saying, "jump for show, corner for dough." If you've ever been to a motocross race you know that the jumps are dramatic but that's not where the winners win. An interesting (and vital) element of branding is in subtlety, attention to detail and authenticity – not the razzle-dazzle. A solid, useful brand is an expression of your values, your beliefs and what you stand for. It is as much about your philosophy as it is about your knowledge and ability.

Think about the word "sincere". In ancient Greece, artists were often commissioned to sculpt a statue out of marble. On occasion, there would be sculptors with a questionable moral compass, who, if they made a mistake, would conceal their error with wax. They would drop off the statue, collect their fee, leave, and then, in the hot sun, that wax would melt. "Sin cere" means "no wax". Your branding must be sincere.

Knowledge is what you know and what you think. Philosophy is how you think. This is where sincerity applies. "Do no harm" isn't only for physicians. You'll never succeed in anything at the expense of others, but you will through the service of others. At the same time, don't do harm to yourself by being your own best kept secret. A branding strategy connects what a client wants with how you get them there. Creating an aspiration, creating belonging and creating professional contrast is what your branding strategy will achieve.

## A Solid Example – Your Professional Contrast Statement

As a starting point, it is essential that you master the art of articulating your value. You are undoubtedly a good messenger, but how is your message? When asked what you do, do you tell people you are a professional and that you "help your clients achieve their goals?" Or does your value proposition tell people that you have a process that helps your clients achieve their goals? Make your value a thing, not a skill. We want the world to think of your process as a Swiss Army Knife of value. It's an all-encompassing thing that can do so much and is supported by good people and best practices.

What about when a prospective client asks you, "What makes you different?" How professionalized and standardized – not to mention accurate - is your messaging? It's unfortunately common for a F4S professional to data dump with a stream-of-consciousness, listing off specifics around their technical ability and core competencies.

A better approach combines two fundamentally sound strategies. First, in the spirit of *The Law of Resonance* – which simply says that the value of what you communicate is that portion of your messaging that lingers and resonates with the person long after the conversation - there is an old communication format that achieves that end. You tell someone what you're going to tell them. Then you tell them. Then you tell them what you told them. Reinforce and drive home your messaging in a memorable way. Secondly, frame it with specificity so that you highlight your professional contrast. As they listen to you, they are contrasting your value to that of their current provider and any others they are considering. For example, if a prospective client asks you what makes you different, you could say, *"That's a great question and, as you can imagine, I have been asked that many times. I don't want to oversimplify it, but I think it would come down to our people, our practice and our process. Our people possess all the credentials you would expect and they are passionate about what we do for our clients and we're very good at it, but it doesn't stop there. All of us have adopted a mindset for best practices and standard operating procedures to create a consistent client experience, and we take a lot of pride in that. Lastly, there's our process. We have developed and refined a process that puts every piece of the puzzle together and engages every service provider as our clients' lives unfold and their needs evolve, ensuring they always have the complete picture. Our clients continually tell us how much they appreciate that. So again, it would come down to our people, our practice and our process that really sets us apart."*

The key with this approach is a) brevity - get to the point, b) specificity - don't wander, data dump or drift into a stream of consciousness, c) use a message that resonates – that doesn't fade and activates contrast and d) it is proprietary. It's yours. I can only get this from you. The entire message is not promissory on performance. It's promissory on a long-term client experience.

Believe it or not, the real art form to this is the brevity. It's not easy to consolidate so much impact in so few words. French Mathematician Blaise Pascal hit the mark beautifully when he said, "I would have written you a shorter letter, but I did not have time." It requires effort to be efficient with your attempts at being impactful. In the tech world of e-commerce, there is an expression "too many clicks" which reminds everyone working on a project to let a customer get to the check-out Promised Land as quickly as possible, rather than kill their intent with hoops and complexity.

## The Anatomy of Trust

Ultimately, what a comprehensive branding strategy does is create trust with a prospective client and then maintain it over the long haul once they become a client. Sharpie has accomplished that very well. For a prospective client, your branding strategy activates their critical thinking and ignites their emotions. They see that you could address an unmet need that has developed - or it creates contrast relative to an existing service provider they have grown tired of, and any others they are meeting with to kick their tires. For existing clients, you are locking out any and all competitors and keeping the client "close to the fire" because their appreciation for your value doesn't drift or fade over time. Your message resonates up front and continues to resonate over the lifetime of the relationship.

Communication of every kind can be abstract. It can be hard to put your finger on and really 'see' how it's working. It's part of the X-factor for a F4S professional. There is an invigorating energy that occurs with good communication. You can look to deeper examples of how powerful this energy can be. Albert Einstein was asked what it was like to be the smartest man in the world. His response was that you would have to ask Nicolai Tesla. Perhaps part of that was inspired by Tesla's statement, "If you want to find the secrets of the universe, think in terms of energy, frequency and vibration." If you want to stretch and possibly even bruise your brain, read about what Tesla said about why 369 was the key to the universe. It's taxing to get one's head around all of this, but it is so compelling.

Tesla was a genius, yet one of the less-appreciated aspects of his study was in this field. His beliefs in this area were both spiritual and scientific. If you want to go deeper, read about the premise known as the 11th harmonic. When you learn how one tuning fork will sympathetically resonate off of another tuning fork and how the perfect frequency can shatter glass, you start to understand the power of the invisible. When you look deeply into The Shuman Resonance and how it appears that there is a global pulse of frequency, you start to realize that Tesla was clearly on to something. You can't see the power emitted by a battery. You can't touch a Wi-Fi signal. When you see a comedian who made you laugh, a week later you don't remember everything she said, you just remember that she was funny.

Communication – which is basically what branding is – can be impactful or it can be empty noise, and therefore its value can either flicker out or it can be retained long after it's consumed. In the study of Gaia, a question is presented, "Where does the flame go?" In business, ask yourself, "Where does my messaging go?"

Your branding strategy is a clarion call to the world – "this is how we are different, this what we stand for, this is what we are good at, this is what you can expect from us."

## The Space Between

We have mentioned that each of the individual deliverables you provide, in terms of products and services tied to your technical ability and core competencies, are, in essence, bricks. If you've ever seen an impressively crafted retaining wall, you know that the bricks or rocks used are themselves not very valuable, but the craftsmanship and the mortar that holds everything in place creates the beautiful form and durable function. Your client experience and process are the mortar that fills in the space between each of the bricks of your technical ability and holds everything together. The difference between client service and a client experience is important to fully understand. Client service means that you care, you are professional and that you have high ethical standards to put out fires and to come through when needed. Ultimately, it is reactive and not proprietary – it is an intention fueled by your qualities and skills. Still great, better than most, but not complete. Client experience is a process-driven approach that is thought out in advance and is designed to anticipate issues and provide consistency. It is proprietary. It is an intellectual property of your enterprise, and your branding strategy has to capture and represent that to the world.

## Your Solution Stack

How do you take the abstract nature of your value and make it conceptual? Make it proprietary? The first step is to re-imagine your value so that clients aren't buying individual things from you, but rather they are buying into your entire process - even if there are some parts of your process that aren't relevant to them, yet. You may have some customers who opt in and buy one thing from you initially. You want, at that signing ceremony, to activate their awareness for the complete picture. In the same way some movies start at the end, and then spend the rest of their run-time back-filling the story so that it all connects, you want to future-pace your relationships so that there is an appreciation for your entire range of capabilities, not just the individual need you are addressing at the moment. This is your all-encompassing solution stack - your complete bundle of services that are thoughtfully process-driven to address client needs as they evolve and present themselves. The key of course, in the spirit of stewardship, is to position your process rather than pitch it.

## Do Your Inventory

To help us get there, the first question we ask in a coaching conversation on this topic is, "How many things could you do for a client if they empowered you fully over the lifetime of the relationship?" Many people pause before answering and then respond with, "Well that's immeasurable. We do everything," and then they start verbally listing things off as they occur to them. To which we interrupt them and say, "You don't know, and if you don't know, your clients don't know." So let's remove that mystery for everyone by sitting down with your team and creating a solution stack – a master list of every service and solution you could provide for a client. Not as a menu to choose from but as a mosaic to be aware of going forward. Some clients have needs that are very simple while others are more complex. It doesn't matter, get it all out of your heads and know your number!

It's not uncommon for them to call us back and say with an astonished tone, "We could do 85 things for a client over the lifetime of the relationship." That's powerful. Some do more, some do less. It's not the point. Just knowing your number is the tip of the spear to creating meaningful intellectual property and amping up your fee-worthiness.

Keep in mind that your client will never remember 85 things, and none of those individual things are proprietary to you, either. They're commoditized. I can get them somewhere else, but here's how this works.

## 85 Things – 7 Pillars – 1 Process

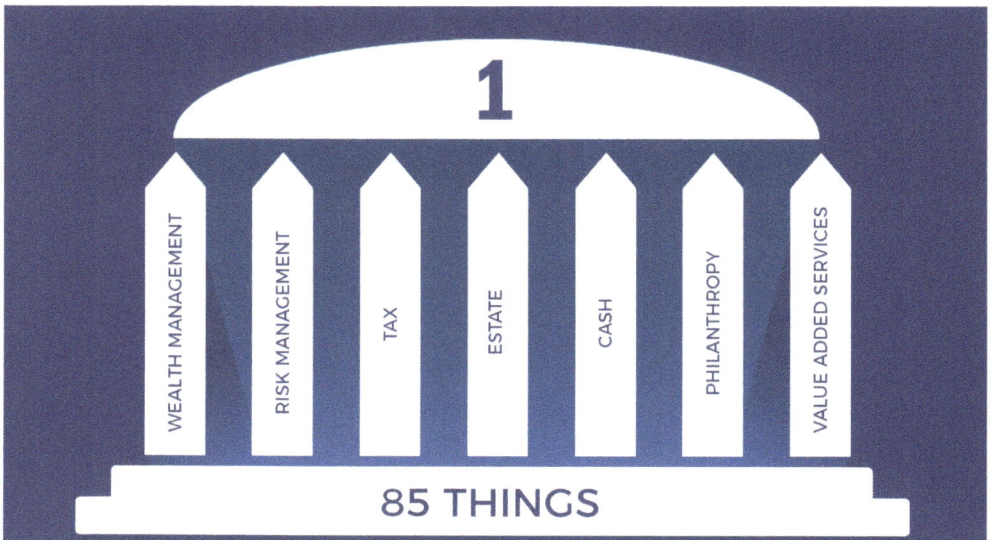

**1**

WEALTH MANAGEMENT

RISK MANAGEMENT

TAX

ESTATE

CASH

PHILANTHROPY

VALUE ADDED SERVICES

**85 THINGS**

This can be applied to virtually any field of endeavor with a bit of customization, but let's say you are a financial professional and you could do 85 things for a client over the life of the relationship. Those 85 things can be sorted into the seven pillars that serve as placeholders for order and clarity.

The first is **Asset Management,** but you're not exclusively an asset manager in the classic sense. Asset management on its own is commoditized. In your world, asset management is an essential part of your process. You don't want to compete exclusively with asset management products, especially the digital platforms that fixate on pricing and short-term performance. There are deliverables out there that will manage assets for 30 basis points or less – much less, in fact.

The second Pillar is **Risk Management:** You don't sell insurance products as a broker, but the many risk management solutions you can provide are an integral part of your process.

The third Pillar is related to **Tax**: You are undoubtedly tax-savvy in all of your decisions, but we don't want you refer a client out to an accountant where necessary, we want you to engage a client's CPA into your process so the client has a complete and integrated picture. This is a big distinction - with all outside service providers, you don't refer a client out, instead, you engage a service provider in.

The fourth Pillar is **Estate**: Continuity and succession, family investment legacy and all of the dynastic intergenerational issues are a big part of your process, and when needed you will engage estate planning attorneys, trust and other fiduciary consultants into your process. This a massive keystone that we'll expand on.

The fifth Pillar is **Cash and Debt**: It's not that you are a mortgage broker or someone that gains wallet share by selling credit cards, lines of credit and other facilities to clients, but when needed you will engage those service providers and make those solutions available as part of your process.

The sixth Pillar is **Philanthropy**: When a client becomes financially independent and the burden shifts from "will I have enough" to "what becomes of my legacy," you begin to focus on benevolent actions such as charitable giving and foundations. When a client starts thinking about what money does - not just what it is – that's all part of your process too.

Finally, the seventh Pillar – **Your Value-Added Services**: This is perhaps the most important pillar of them all and speaks to your X-factor. It's possible that you could provide as many as 10 to 15 distinct additional services to your clients, but they're only value-added if your client finds them to actually be of value. You don't offer goals-based planning, panoramic advice, concierge level service, life coaching and the like just because you're a good person. You provide them because of your well-thought-out process. You don't pitch the idea of a referral as a favor you're asking of a client, you position being a sounding board to a friend or family member as a value-added service you're providing to a client.

## Future Pacing – A Solution in Search of a Problem

Whatever sector and profession you perform in, you can consolidate all of the individual commoditized solutions you provide into a composite process that is proprietary. You might have Seven Pillars, Five Pillars or Nine Pillars. You might use puzzle pieces, building blocks or stepping stones as your analogy to make your process more conceptual.

Whatever the case, creating a solution stack using this positioning enables you to plant seeds and allows someone to look down the road at the trajectory of their relationship with you. Every meeting with the client can include an item on the agenda that speaks to unmet and developing needs. You're building understanding in the client that, as their life unfolds and needs evolve, they have one call to make to address the changes that occur. They are predisposed with anticipation and confidence, and their engagement with your people, practice and process strengthens as their life becomes more complex. They can't outgrow you - they grow into your process. You are their CFO, and in our world that means Complete Family Office. Future pacing mastery is like an exceptional flight attendant or waiter who fills your drink in advance, never has to be asked and anticipates needs like a fortune teller.

We want to make sure your clients shift from transactions to buying into a fluid and dynamic process. This is what competitor-proofs them. This is what captures money in motion. When they describe you to others - explaining how much they trust you, how much they enjoy your client experience and how much they appreciate your process - introductions, loyalty and empowerment go through the roof!

## The Difference Between <u>A</u> Goal and <u>The</u> Goal

An excellent example of future pacing is how a F4S financial provider can enable a client to expand their thinking by looking far down the road and re-imagining how the trajectory of the relationship will impact them. Take a typical first generation, self-made affluent client who sets a goal to become financially independent. They follow the advice of their financial professional, stay disciplined and let compounding incrementally propel them to the goal of ensuring that one day their money will make more money than they do. They are the consummate 25-year overnight success story.

Then there's the professional who, while sitting down with the client, uses the analogy of a Sherpa that guides a climber through his or her journey. Tenzing Norgay led Sir Edmund Hillary to the top of Mount Everest. As you can imagine, planning for and then embarking on a journey like that would be intense. The journey itself is unrivaled in terms of testing the limits of what a person can accomplish, but here is what's fascinating: Reaching the summit isn't the goal. It's a goal. The typical climber spends less than 15 minutes on the summit savoring their accomplishment. This is where the Sherpa becomes invaluable – in getting back down the mountain.

Climbers will tell you that most people get in trouble on the descent. Because of the exhaustion, and often with the anticlimax of the accomplishment, many climbers are vulnerable physically, mentally and emotionally, even with gravity on their side. The goal becomes getting back down, and that requires support on the back half of the journey.

When a client plants their flag at their personal summit, the burden shifts from, "Will I have enough so that I don't outlive my money?" to "What becomes of my legacy and will I help or hurt the next generation?" They have the rest of their life to live after they sell their business or retire. What will give them purpose? How will the next generation cope with the eventual inheritance?

When it comes to continuity, succession and the many dynastic realities of family investment legacy, the professional knows that managing second generation "found" money is different than managing first generation "earned" money. There are many warnings about how those who became suddenly affluent not only devastating a family legacy but also creating a trail of regret, resentment and other severe consequences. As the saying goes, privilege is being born on third base, entitlement is thinking you hit a triple. The books *Beer Money* and *Entitlemania* paint a pretty vivid picture on this theme and are essential reading for all affluent parents and the F4S professionals who work with them.

Sometimes, reading a book like that, especially if you have grown kids, can prompt you to secretly wish you could have a do-over, but when you consider the forces of nurture/nature - and assuming you instilled a strong moral compass, a sense of personal responsibility, grit and ambition - that foundation will serve them forever. The rest they'll figure out. If nothing else, we get to work on the grandkids. (They say if you spoil your kids, you'll raise your grandkids: If you raise your kids, you'll spoil your grandkids. So many mysteries...)

For many people, legacy becomes a very prominent goal on their wish list. Probably the most impressive high-water mark we've seen is the Keiunkan hotel near Mount Fuji in Japan that remained in the same family for 52 generations. As Tom Deans, a very credible and accomplished speaker and author who wrote Every Family's Business and Willing Wisdom would tell you, most family businesses don't make it through the second generation and virtually none the third. We can confidently recommend that you engage Tom to do a presentation in person or via webinar for your business-owner clients and strategic partners, as he will open up conversations that lead directly back to you and your ability to address their needs.

What's fascinating is that you might have an exceptional client with $5 million of investible assets with you, but that only represents 15% of their net worth, with the rest tied up in their business and other holdings. Once they sell, that money often defects to another F4S professional or dilutes and drifts to heirs that do business with someone else. Future pacing addresses that well in advance.

## A Straight Line to Advocacy

Following is a checklist of the many specific elements that help you achieve professional contrast and enhance how people perceive, appreciate and describe your value. We've had a few dismiss this initially because, as they said, "I've already got my pitch book in place." As you can imagine, we jump on that pretty hard because having a good pitch is rarely conducive to attracting great referrals. We also have clients asking about mission statements and slogans. They're fine and they do no harm, but having a slogan that says "Ours goes to 11" meaning you go the extra mile, or "With you for life" speaking to the journey, or "Lighting the path" suggesting the navigational aspects of your value, can be pretty easy to dismiss.

We want you to go beyond intentions. We want you to consider all the things that can strengthen your value. Branding your process creates a brand-within-a-brand that supplements your practice and people. It's proprietary, meaning I can only get it from your firm. It's pace-setting, meaning it speaks to the fluid and dynamic nature of your value. It's portable, meaning if you move on you can take it with you, and it's packaged, meaning you can put it in the hands of others who can adopt and deploy it, giving you predictable, scalable growth.

## The ABC's of Branding

This checklist will walk you through our suggestions so that you can compare and contrast to your existing branded elements and consider any gaps you may have. It starts at A with your value proposition and cascades down to Z which is your proprietary playbook to capture it all as an invaluable intellectual property.

The value proposition is not an elevator pitch (How many elevators do you get trapped in?). It's a brief, concise statement that defines you and leaves someone wanting more. If they're intrigued, they'll give you permission to elaborate. If they aren't, they ask about your tie.

Just embrace the exercise of not winging it and avoid the long-winded data dump. Some people want to know what time it is, others want you to build them a clock. Some want to enjoy the bratwurst, others want to know how the sausage is made. Be led by them.

If you keep it simple - a back-of-the-napkin kind of statement - that speaks to your ideal client, speaks to what they want to achieve and speaks to how you get them there by virtue of your process, then it's fundamentally sound. No jargon. Nothing long-winded. Just activate professional contrast and professional scarcity so the magnetic attraction can start sifting real prospects from the mass of suspects.

The words matter. In deeper conversations, be sure to punctuate many of your points with the word process. "We've developed and refined a process," "That's the next step in the process," "Let's stick to the process." Be like a little kid with a hammer, in that everything looks like a nail. Keep hammering your process. It's like a handle to grab and hold on to, and to hand to someone else.

Again, you're a F4S professional, you think for a living. As Descartes said, "I think therefore I am." If you've read anything by Isaac Asimov, Taylor Caldwell or Somerset Maugham, you know how elegant they are at taking words and making them conceptual.

If you want to go up-market, Daniel Pink wrote an interesting book called *A Whole New Mind,* and in it he provides a scenario where he notes that you can go to Walmart and buy a toilet brush for $6 or you can go to Restoration Hardware and buy one for $106. At the end of the day, they both do the same thing, so why would somebody spend $106 at Restoration Hardware for a fancy toilet brush? Maybe it's because they can, and maybe it's part of conspicuous consumption, but again it's not just 'what it is' or 'what it does' – it's how it makes them feel. It goes beyond that single transaction event. Explaining things in a way people understand is vital to any messaging, and how things make us feel is always the most important aspect. Fredrich Bessel was frustrated when trying to explain, through mathematics, how big the universe is and how far other stars are from Earth. He realized he was trying to describe something to people who did not think the way he did, so he invented the concept of the light-year. All of a sudden, he noticed people got the concept - or at least they claimed to get it.

Try explaining to a child how much a trillion dollars is. It's not easy, but you can say, "If you stack up a trillion dollar bills, it would reach close to 68,000 miles, about a quarter of the way to the moon. A trillion seconds is 37,000 years. A trillion ants would weigh as much as 450 cars. A trillion gallons of water spills over Niagara Falls every three years or so." Context makes things relatable.

## Branding Synergy

If you ever fly into San Francisco SFO, you know that the runway ends at the water. The next time you take off, count the distance from when the plane actually lifts off to the end of the runway. That distance takes about seven seconds to cover, which is not a lot of wiggle room for the pilot, yet they're confident because they've rehearsed it and they've refined it. You can get to that same level. Think of the Apple logo. Think of the Nike swoosh. Think of Corona and the lime. You'd think Corona would have taken a huge knock through name association, but the 2020 debacle barely put a dent in their business. The brand is resilient. Look at the line in the Amazon logo - the smile that connects from A to Z. Those brands are so intuitive they trigger an instant moment of recognition and awareness for those firms' value. We want you to be able to get people to that point as quickly through differentiation.

Defining your process rather than a service is a basic step. If you use a dry cleaner, you might be aware of Martinizing. Now, we're not sure exactly what Martinizing is, but it sure sounds more impressive than dry cleaning. Again, we don't know if the outcome of Martinizing is any better than dry cleaning, but it's not what it is - it's what someone thinks it is. It's how it makes them feel. It sounds like an established thing that you can't get just anywhere. Help would-be clients come to their own conclusion. You don't help people; you have a process that helps people. Many people you meet, especially if they've been introduced to you, have strong predisposition that needs validating, but not through excruciating detail. They don't need to know everything you know. They just need to know that you know, and that will help them feel that they know enough and that you are a good fit for them. Of course, if you're going to tell the world you have a process, it helps to actually have one. We're sure you have an established process, but you might not refer to it as such, and therefore clients do not fully understand and appreciate your value. You might have gaps in your process, but that's easy to address, so let's start addressing those and let's think in terms of intrinsic value.

F4S professional Chris Garcia, and his team in Dallas, have a substantial branding strategy in place – clients identify and connect well with his people, his practice and his process. It's quite impressive. Even more so is the fact that they don't rest on what they've created. It's a living, breathing entity that keeps growing. For example, many of his team members are women and many of his clients are women, so, not taking anything for granted, the team embraced a very deliberate approach to examine and enhance their relevance to women. It wasn't disruptive, it didn't alienate anyone, but it was immensely appreciated as an enlightened extension of their branding approach.

## The Critical Path to Branding

The following is the progressive checklist you can follow to chip away at your branding strategy. Some items are tagged with the Always ON legend - the OS speaks to ONside, The OB speaks to ONboard, The OG speaks to ONgoing and the OW speaks to ONwards.

A. Your 30-Second Value Proposition

B. Your Purposeful Reaction

C. Your Professional Contrast Statement

D. Your Solution Stack

E. Your Value-Added Service Pillar

F. Your Process Icon and Identity

G. Your Story Board

H. Your Content Suite

I. Your VAST Network

J. Your Digital Footprint

K. Your Tech Suite

L. Your Social Presence

M. Your Ideal Client Profile OS

N. Your Intro Kit OS

O. Your Agenda Bundle OS

P. Your Future Pacing Menu OB

Q. Your Onboarding Kit OB

R. Your Service Model and Matrix OB

S. Your Org Chart OG

T. Your Strategy and Tactical Process OG

U. Your Greeting Card Portfolio OW

V. Your Milestone Recognition Parameters OW

W. Your Event Listing

X. Your Community Engagement

Y. Your Office Zen

Z. Your Proprietary Playbook

## A. Your 30 Second Value Proposition

This isn't meant to be a rigid or contrived statement. Just embrace the exercise of crafting a brief message that tells the world who your ideal client is, why they hire you and how you get them there. An example of that would be:

*"I am part of a financial services team primarily for successful business owners, professionals and executives and we've developed and refined a process that puts every piece of the financial puzzle together and engages every service provider so our clients have the complete picture."* Then stop. Leave them hanging and see if they give you permission to continue by asking, "How does that work?" You can then proceed with a more engaged audience. Everyone on your team needs to know this by heart.

## B. Your Purposeful Reaction

One of the most common questions from a client or strategic partner is, "How are you doing?" It's common to respond with a simple "I'm swamped" or something that conveys that you're busy. This is probably true, but what they hear is that you're probably at capacity, and why bother subjecting someone else to that by way of an introduction? Instead, embrace it positively and share a quick example about someone who was introduced to you:

*"I'm doing great. We're hopping but it's all good. In fact, I just got off the phone with a friend of a client who was way off track, and it was fun just connecting a few dots and hearing them calm down and relax. I love what I do."*

## C. Your Professional Contrast Statement

When you meet with a prospective client or potential strategic partner for the first time, and they ask you to tell them "what it is that makes you different," go to this. You can even open a meeting with someone new and start by saying that you're often asked that question:

*"What makes us different? It's a great question and one I've received often over the years. I'd have to say it would come down to our people, our practice and our process. Our people have all the technical skills you would expect, we love what we do and we're good at it, but we don't stop there. We take a lot of pride in adopting an array of best practices that create a consistent client experience and our clients rave about that. Then there's our process that we've developed and refined over the years, one that puts every piece of the puzzle together and engages other service providers, so that our clients have the complete picture. So, yeah, our people our practice and our process are what make us different."*

## D. Your Solution Stack

Because of your understatement and resistance to sales tactics, you may be the proverbial iceberg in the eyes of your clients and partners. They know what they know, and they know what they see, but there is a whole lot more there. Clients should have a complete understanding for your value, not just an appreciation for what you've done for them so far. Full understanding gets you deeper engagement and more referrals, while the other might get you a Christmas card. So, do your inventory, know your number, get it all listed and embedded into your symbol - whether it's the 7 Pillars, the Puzzle Pieces or the Stepping Stones. Your primary deliverable can be the keystone, with supplemental deliverables positioned around it. Wrap it and package it in an all-encompassing process that gives people the complete picture. There is a resource at thebluesquaremethod.com/implementation-resources that will assist you in creating your own.

## E. Your Value-Added Service Pillar

Whether you charge an hourly fee, a retainer or use a fee-based comp model, your value-added services need a placeholder so that they are fully understood and appreciated.

Being a goals-based planner, providing concierge-level service, providing a network of other service providers, being a sounding board for friends and family members, holding family meetings to discuss essential topics and other "above and beyond" services look far more impressive if they are itemized within a specific placeholder rather than just verbally expressed. Perhaps you have other credentials such as assisting client families with special needs, understanding elder care, considering family dynamics up and down the tree for your clients in the sandwich, and various other life coaching elements? Those are warmly appreciated. Give them all a home within your process. Virtually all of your competitors only verbally scatter-shot this approach. An organized, integrated approach, supported at a minimum by a checklist, provides enhanced differentiation.

## F. Your Process Icon and Identity

Referring to your value as being process-driven is a great start. Consider giving it an identity with a symbol that adds personality to your brand. Perhaps greeting cards with images of bridges to imprint your value as the bridge-builder to your clients' goals? The more you imprint that, the more the symbol becomes a Nike swoosh that triggers instant recognition for what your value does. You can go one step further by giving your process a name – calling it something that has its own brand recognition. We've helped hundreds of clients name their process and turn it into an intellectual property that endures for a long time with scalable distribution potential. When you say that you've developed and refined a process called The Keystone Formula, or The 360 Method, or The Stepping Stone Approach - you create the equivalent of an Intel Inside sticker that can go on agendas, collateral, websites and emails, and create a connection for clients. Trademarking takes it all to another level. You can also learn more about our P3 Branding solutions at thebluesquaremethod.com/implementation-resources.

## G. Your Story Board

Capturing stories of wins and breakthroughs are virtual testimonials that provide compelling social proof. They are engaging and persuasive. Sit down with your team and reflect on episodes where you had incredible impact on a prospective client, an existing client or a family member of an existing client. Set a goal to write out 10 stories.

Assign scenarios to each and write them out in a SNIB (Subject, Need, Idea and Benefit) framework. Watch a few video tutorials on the art of storytelling - especially with humor (self-deprecating, ideally) and emotion. Speaking of which, for inspiration do a quick search to learn about Edi Bocelli, the brave mother of Andrea, the legendary singer. You can then watch *The Story behind the Voice*. It's inspiring. We can't say enough about the rejuvenating impact this will have on you and your team, and the persuasive impact it will have on the people you encounter. Some people have built testimonial binders for their waiting rooms and their websites as an extension of this initiative.

## H. Your Content Suite

Content marketing is a powerful driver in your branding efforts, because it gives prospects something to ask for and gives clients and strategic partners something to use as a bridge to introduce people to you. You could consider executive summaries on books you've read, people you've interviewed, or recordings of presentations you've conducted. We've also seen 'Top 10' lists of pitfalls, mistakes or triumphs that you've seen in your travels. All can bolster your position as a thought leader and act as a great hook that you can offer to your addressable audiences to get them to raise their hands and opt-in to initiate contact. Knowledge-for-profit professionals harness their experiences and wisdom in a way that can be consumed by many and have great shelf-life.

## I. Your VAST Network

Establishing a Value-Added Support Team or VAST network, and positioning it within your $7^{th}$ pillar, can strengthen your brand through deeper client engagement and open up an additional avenue of steady, good quality introductions. It has to be positioned as a benefit to the client, not pitched as maximizing circles of influence. In the ONside chapter where we outline how to sift prospects from suspects, we delve into the VAST initiative. It requires commitment, diligence and patience, but is well worth the effort because it positions you as the power-broker at the helm, overseeing evolving needs in real time.

## J. Your Digital Footprint

An exceptional website is non-optional in this era.

Intuitive functionality, search engine optimization, sound content and calls to action, and integration with your digital service model and social media activities, means that you will be found by predisposed prospective clients rather than having to go out and find them. People do a lot of digital vetting well in advance of making actual contact with you, so make it easy for them. Our best advice is to outsource a turnkey initiative to a provider with a sterling track record in your sector. From there, we encourage you to create some video – both evergreen and VLOG – to let people get to know and stay connected with you all the way through the relationship cycle. There is a spotlight for Idea Decanter, experts in turnkey remote video creation for F4S professionals, in the resource chapter.

## K. Your Tech Suite

The array of tech solutions available to you – especially the client-facing variety – are essential for efficiency and convenience, and are a supplement to your high-touch initiatives. Talk-to-text for client meetings for KYC reinforcement, auto-calendar scheduling, integrated CRM and automated procedures have to be considered. Keep your mindset client-centered. The broker deploys sales automation to make the sales process more efficient, to create a transactional win and a commission check. The F4S entrepreneur deploys a full array of automated processes – framed in Always On – to achieve the professional contrast needed to attract and keep great clients, while adding liberation and order to their own life. The learning curves are quick because most of these tools have become very intuitive. The world has embraced online meetings, not by choice mind you, and the comfort level is high while the appreciation for the gift of time is decent. Have a team member be responsible for innovation and optimization and keep pushing the envelope. Keep making your client the voice you listen to by asking them for ideas on new tech and feedback on existing tech.

## L. Your Social Presence

The automated process and integration of the various social media platforms has become quite impressive. Adoption by consumers has matured, and your ability to create awareness with the first degree contacts of your clients has gotten much easier. The key, again, is to delegate this to a team member for consistent pot-stirring, and defer to respectful stewardship rather than pressing salesmanship. There are some excellent resources and tutorials for mastering LinkedIn available.

Done properly, it can create efficient reach for all of your addressable audiences. You can still display professional scarcity, but you are conspicuous in your absence on social – especially as a sought-after thought leader.

## M. Your Ideal Client Profile

Remove the mystery for the world around who your ideal client is. People who chase speak in terms of who they are looking for, people who attract speak in terms of who they are suited for. Professional scarcity conveys that you are not all things to all people. You are all things to some people. Define this on a sheet of paper that is client-facing. Show it to them as you are telling them that you only accept new clients that are introduced to you, and assuming there is a good fit.

Be panoramic in your description. AAA PLUS is the perfect frame. The first A speaks to the Alignment of the client's assets and actions with your value. This isn't about minimums (or even maximums) – it's not about a number, it's about alignment. Write out the demographic reality in terms of where the client is in their life. Write out their socioeconomic reality in terms of the complexity of their needs, based on being a business owner, professional or executive. Define the fit. Then, the second A – which is just as important - speaks to the Attitudinal compatibility of the person. List out seven qualities that emphasize that chemistry is as important as alignment. The third is A is Advocacy – looking out for the people they care about. The PLUS punctuates the belonging and exclusivity because it means, at the end of the day, our clients are People Like US. We're good, hardworking, family-centered, community-focused people who are all wired the same way. The best clients are enlightened about everything and everyone – including the price of value. They don't dwell on why organic food is so expensive, they wonder why inorganic food is so much cheaper. They have natural curiosity about not overpaying, but they are wired with appreciation, humility and gratitude. They don't take the little things for granted. In the morning when they are up early at home, they appreciate that the garbage can in the kitchen isn't overflowing, that the dishwasher is already empty, and the coffee maker is already fully prepared and ready to go. The simple everyday things are wins. They like to see other people thrive, there is no resentment or jealousy. They have appreciation for the possibility for abundance and appreciation for the things that are scarce. Surround yourself in that deliberately.

Let your advocates naturally sift out real prospects and protect you from the suspects.

## N. Your Intro Kit

When an advocate reaches out to introduce you to someone, and you make contact with the friend and have an initial conversation, should they decide to meet with you for a deeper face-to-face or online meeting, it is essential to send out a tasteful Introductory Kit by two-day courier to prime that meeting. This is not a brochure. It is a folder with introductory information about your people, your practice and your process. Details on parking, a sample agenda and a pleasant hand-written greeting card can be included. Be sure to show your clients the kit and explain your fit process so they can describe it and set expectations in a compelling way.

## O. Your Agenda Bundle

Every meeting you have must include an agenda - a simple, printed agenda that spells out how the meeting will progress, time parameters and next steps bridging to the follow-up sequence of your process. All agenda templates should be archived for quick access. After the meeting, the agendas should also be archived along with KYC and action steps. There should be no deviation from this, with the exception of breakfast, lunch and social engagements. Try not to convince yourself that you can do the meeting in your sleep without an agenda. An agenda makes a statement to the client that you are prepared and that you take their needs seriously.

## P. Your Future Pacing Menu

Your total and complete array of services are listed in a progressive format along with a "date activated" box. When you onboard a client, you tell them there are many pieces of the puzzle you can put together over time as their needs unfold. Many of these items are not relevant to the client yet, but you can both review them when you meet in the future.

## Q. Your Onboarding Kit

After the signing ceremony, when you onboard a client, provide them with a tangible item to not only commemorate the relationship being established, but also to harness important documentation around your proprietary deliverables.

Digital resources are fine for the minutia, but specific elements around your practice and process, your future pacing documents, value-added services, etc., all carefully organized, are like the chocolate on the pillow at a fine hotel. Nothing dramatic or earth shattering, but it is eye-opening and with lasting shelf life, nonetheless. We'll break this down further in the onboarding chapter.

## R. Your Service Model and Matrix

Show people your varying array of clients through your classification, and show them the client experience you provide for each segment. This is an open kitchen on steroids, because it clarifies what they can expect and gives them a lot to talk about when it comes to advocacy. It's aspirational for movable middle caliber clients and it provides a sense of achievement for your most deserving clients. It also ensures that you consistently invest 80% of your time on the 20% of your clients that generate 80% of your business. We'll show you sample templates consisting of various touch points and positioning in the Ongoing chapter.

## S. Your Org Chart

Many F4S professionals list out their team members in a vertical display of bench strength. That's fine, but when you also include a client-facing organizational and structural chart that places each team member with a specific role and responsibility, you connect with people who understand best practices and standard operating procedures. In the process, you become more referable to people of that caliber. This document also serves as a cover page for your procedures manual.

## T. Your Strategy and Tactical Process

In the chapter on reframing relationships, we're going to show you how to ramp up, execute and follow through on a Strategy and Tactical Meeting with clients that will open their eyes and rejuvenate their appreciation and understanding for your value.

## U. Your Greeting Card Portfolio

It's a lost art to send a high-quality tangible greeting card to say thanks for an introduction, solidify a new relationship, pay tribute to achievements and milestones, and commemorate holidays - to name just a few events. Throughout the rest of this book, we will provide examples for how high-touch can supplement your high-tech client experience. Using symbols on the cards you send that imprint your value further – images like keys because you open doors to the future, SWANs because clients sleep well at night because of your value, and bridges because you build the bridge as they cross it - also contributes to your branding strategy. For exceptional greeting card ideas, visit lavishcards. com.

## V. Your Milestone Recognition Parameters

Moments occur in a client's life that can be dramatic and life-altering. Your culture as a team, in terms of how you respond, creates an indelible reminder of how indispensable you are. In the Onwards chapter we will outline examples for you to consider.

## W. Your Event Listing

Virtual and in-person events are efficient one-to-many opportunities to connect with clients, engage strategic partners and meet their clients in turn. Ideal Client Events (ICE) for reframing 10 clients simultaneously, Client Advisory Councils to make an important group a voice you listen to for elevating your bar of client experience, client retirement parties, client education events, shredding days, fundraisers and the like, all have an impact. We'll discuss them further in the Ongoing chapter.

## X. Your Community Engagement

Sponsorships, collaborative fundraisers or initiatives, and any team participation events add impact to your social and digital footprint, energy and karma to your relationships and strength to your brand. Take lots of pictures! Faces of people, kids and puppies have an undeniable magnetism.

## Y. Your Office Zen

Multisensory marketing is a real thing. How does your office smell? Do you have diffusers producing subtle natural aromas? If you've ever walked into a Tommy Bahama store, you know what we're talking about. How about your wall décor? Does it have imagery of symbols that represent your value? Furnishings, knick-knacks and the vibe you create all build a sense of comfort and Feng Shui. A beautiful Swarovski crystal SWAN on your desk (that reminds you constantly that your role is to help a client Sleep Well at Night) can be an energizing addition. Do you have parking stalls specifically assigned to clients with sliding placards for their names? Is your kitchen well-stocked? Don't phone it in or just go through the motions. Create an experience that is impactful and memorable. For virtual meetings, sending a client a box of cookies and tea or lunch is a powerful touch and extends your brand via your virtual office. Consider having a stylist, designer, or even a Feng Shui master come into your office and give you their opinions on the flow and what unspoken message your layout and surroundings are conveying.

## Z. Your Proprietary Playbook

The culmination of your efforts cascades into, and is captured and invested by, your digital and physical proprietary playbook. This invaluable intellectual property is impressive to team members, strategic partners and clients as a tangible "This is Our Way" trophy of your commitment to best practices and procedures. Your growth opportunities soar along with your enterprise value as does your sense of fulfillment for what you're building.

Throughout the rest of this book, we will refer to many of these different elements in detail and in an actionable context. This is your straight line to advocacy. This is your checklist, your critical path, and what this creates in your brand-ambassador Advocates is a group who can articulate your value meaningfully and specifically. They can address not just the detail of your value, but the action to take to get the wheels in motion - so that it's not an endorsement that gets lost in no-man's land and undermined by diminishing intent. Remember: Advocates feel they're doing their friend or family member a disservice if they don't introduce them to you. What is the incentive for an advocate to introduce someone to you? They know it's going to reflect positively on them, and they know their friend is in good hands. They will get validation from the friend because they will come back and say how much they appreciated the experience.

Your clients and strategic partners want to talk about you, but if they don't know how, they will describe you with superlatives, generalities and platitudes. Which means you're being endorsed - but not introduced. Advocates take action through an introduction and that's what branding will do for you and your business.

### A Brand Attributes Exercise

When you have your checklist, and you and your team start immersing yourselves in the assembly process of branding, a great supplement is to make a list of your values, beliefs, points of difference and sense of purpose.

Branding is about what your clients want and how you get them there. It's what your value does, not just who you are, what you do, or how long you've been doing it.

What do your prospective clients want? What everyone wants – calm, clarity, liberation and anticipation. It's not promissory on technical performance. It's how they feel. It's self-evident and, when positioned this way, they come to their own conclusions. When they are exposed to branding like this, they say to themselves, "I get it, I want it."

If you'd like some direction and accountability on your approach to branding, visit www.thebluesquaremethod.com and learn more about our P3 consultation deliverable.

# Chapter 6:

## *And Then Reframe Your Existing Relationships*

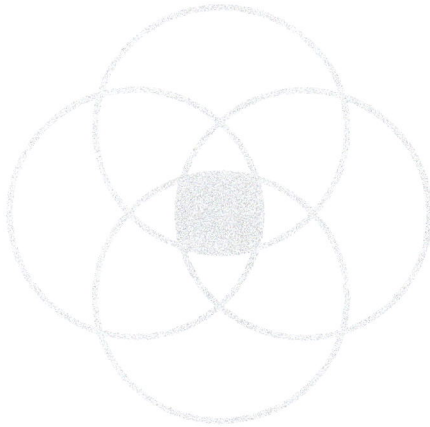

This is where your adjustments start to become client-facing - where you start to introduce your refined and optimized approach to the world. In the spirit of reaching people who count, rather than counting the people you reach, we strongly urge you to have a laser focus on your primary addressable audience – people who are already convinced. Your existing relationships have a degree of familiarity and trust for you – that train is rolling – so let's add to that momentum before you expend the effort to get new ones moving.

Essentially, reframing is reintroducing - and in some cases actually re-onboarding - existing clients to your elevated client experience. It's not that you did anything wrong in the past, but perhaps the old way was a touch underwhelming? You delivered on your technical fulfillment, but the bedside manner that creates conversion might have been lacking. The bar is low in terms of what people expect, because most of your competitors don't go the extra mile, so you've got that going for you. It's not that anyone was disappointed or let down by your old way, but it was no great honor, either. It's possible that you have some clients who are sleepwalking in their appreciation for you. It's also very possible that some of them have developed a bit of amnesia when it comes to remembering how important you are to them.

Let's assume there is a vein of gold within your existing business - this is almost always the case with our consulting clients even at the highest level - but let's make sure we are digging in the right direction. By that we mean "the who" and "the how."

Most start with the 20%. Some even focus on their top 10 relationships, primarily based on their quantitative productivity and qualitative likability. As an analogy, specialists in the oil and gas sector developed new technology to go back to old, abandoned oil fields, zeroing in on the best producing wells of the past and applying their new tech to go deeper to access the oil that was previously out of reach. There are thousands of other old wells that can be re-purposed for geothermal and hydrogen opportunities.

For these companies, it's more efficient than starting from scratch and running the risk of drilling a new 1000-foot post hole. Reinvigorating something that is already in place makes sense – there is more there to work with. Even if it doesn't equate to new business right away, it might equate to new energy in the form of potential advocacy. Once you are efficiently and predictably rolling along, you can proceed to unveil your new way to everyone across your relationship community.

How you unveil is key. There has to be a client-centered reason, positioned in stewardship, which prompts the initiative, so you can point to it without springing it on people out of the blue. To contrast, perhaps you have a friend, a real estate agent or broker of some kind, who is constantly probing you opportunistically, and trying to get a read if there might be a chance at selling something to or for you. It's generally poorly camouflaged, often one-sided, and they are like a coiled spring ready to pounce at any stage of readiness. Their philosophy is, "I'll plant some seeds so that when you develop a need, I'll follow your lead." It's downright needy and smells desperate. There is little to no value-add, nothing is scheduled and they are entirely reactive. They're nice people, but constantly on the prowl and not very good at concealing it. These are the same people who are hurt and offended if you don't happen to call them when a need arises and you take action elsewhere. They feel entitled because, in their mind, they have been nurturing a relationship and they expect to be rewarded. It's the curse of the limited-view salesperson; not building anything and not very referable.

## Step 1. Always Check the Pulse First

In the world of Emergency Medical Services the protocol that's advised if you ever happen to come across an emergency situation is Check-Call-Care. Check for a pulse, call 911 and do your best to care for the person until help arrives. We want you to check-call-care as well. Check the pulse of your clients to see where you stand today. Call them to initiate the elevated approach. Take good care of them once the dust settles.

## CHECK Call Care

How are you currently perceived and described by your clients? Your instincts could get you close to an accurate read. You can tell if your clients trust you if they return your calls, respond to your emails, arrive for meetings on time, and take action on your solutions when needed.

This is not out of obligation to you, and is in their own self-interest, but there is respect, appreciation and trust. While you can trust your "Spidey senses" exclusively, we ask that you consider going one step further.

Make your clients and strategic partners the voice you listen to when it comes to elevating. You can take one of two approaches here. Ease in with a simple, gradual 1:1 approach or go all-in with a concentrated 1:many campaign. On thebluesquaremethod.com/implementation-resources there is a bumper-to-bumper approach called *The Next 90 Days*, and countless clients of ours have deployed it with stellar reviews and impact. If you prefer a more casual approach, then try these simple 1:1 one-offs:

Whenever you get an introduction from a client or strategic partner, call the rainmaker and thank them for introducing their friend or client to you. Tell them how the conversation went and what the outcome was. Then ask, *"If you don't mind me asking, when I met your friend, I was so impressed by them and how predisposed they were. I just have to ask, what did you say? How did you describe me?"* Listen, as they mirror their own version of your value back to you. The persuasive impact of the messenger was probably more impressive than the message, but that's OK. Just know where you stand, and over time you'll see patterns emerge. The bottom line is that you'll be able to go to school on the tweaks you'll need to make, and be able to reframe relationships along the way

When a client praises you or a team member with a heartfelt "thanks for coming through," accept and embrace the praise and then ask, *"You know, as a team we are really trying to step things up and raise the bar. Is there anything you feel we could add to the client experience?"* It's a revealing question. They might tell you they like things just as they are. They might suggest that you add something that you're already doing, but they are not aware of. They might even give you a great idea. In any case, this will add fuel to the reframing initiative as you will see in a few moments.

When a client leaves you, for whatever reason. This one is a tougher pill. It's never fun, but you want it to serve you, not hurt you. Call them and tell them you respect their decision and wish them well. You're also calling because, as a team, you want to build off of this and find a positive so that you can elevate going forward. Ask them, *"If you don't mind me asking, why did you leave?"* Most will tell it was nothing personal, just time for a change. Then ask, "Can I ask what it was specifically that your new provider offered that prompted you to move?"

At this point they might say, "Well I sold my business (something you didn't know about until after it happened) and I just felt that my needs had become more complex. Plus, you've got 300 clients, my new team has 75 – I just felt I needed a deeper level of service." Then thank them! Thank them for the wakeup call – tell them that this is precisely the nudge you needed.

You've been contemplating making some changes, but you've been too "busy" to make it a priority – until now. At this point, ask them if you can keep the door open so that you can stay in touch and possibly show them some of the enhancements you make. Losing a client is often like losing your keys; they may not be gone forever. Once they settle in at their new provider, and perhaps once the over-promise under-deliver kicks in, they may have a longing to return back to your greener grass. Familiarity and loyalty fatigue can be countered before and after a defection – provided you have the right mindset. We've seen it all. Either way, their feedback can serve your reframing initiatives very well, and imagine how powerfully impactful and disarming this story will be down the road, if you do close the loop and win them back.

## Change the Things You Cannot Accept

In business and in life, it's not about wins and losses but about how you play - and if and when you'll stop learning and growing. Getting set in our ways is understandable, especially later in life. Coasting is easier, so it's impressive seeing someone on the back-nine of life still committed to health and wellness, attending yoga sessions and gym classes. It's impressive to see a retired person register for, and crush it, in a blockchain and cryptocurrency Masterclass. It's equally sad to see someone counting the days until they can get away from the ball and chain called "work" because it's never been their calling or passion.

You've earned the right to rejuvenate and liberate yourself. You've arrived at a point in your life where you can operate on your terms. If someone tries to challenge you on your fees (challenge being the operative word because to some, grinding on price is a blood sport), you are at a place where you don't need to justify or defend how you're compensated. Holding your ground and going on the offensive respectfully is very different. How it affects you when you say, "We don't compete on price – we leave that to the brokers out there. We don't negotiate our value – part of our fit process is aligning with clients who are like-minded," is more important than how it affects the client or how they respond.

The final takeaway is to approach reframing with your clients methodically and gradually. As an analogy, perhaps there is a band that you like. You know their songs word for word, and you've seen them perform live. At one concert you notice some music and lyrics that you don't recognize embedded within a favorite song or between two of them. What they're doing is introducing you to the new music they're working on, to rehearse it and refine it in real time. They get to see the reaction of the crowd, they get to reflect on and discuss it later. Ideally, they release the new album when they're ready, not in a hurry.

## Going All In

If you choose to turn up the temperature and pace, and you decide to prime the pump for reframing beyond a slow-and-steady Checking of the Pulse basis 1-to-1, or for 10 or so of your favorite clients, you can shift to a 1-to-many campaign. You can install and deploy a Survey Monkey type of process for all new clients you onboard going forward. This is a simple, automated process, and as you are winding down your onboarding meeting, you can tell the new client, *"Part of our process is that, in a week or so, you'll be receiving an email asking you how we did. We take a lot of pride in providing a quality client experience, but we're always looking for feedback and new ideas."* You can use four simple questions:

- Did we meet or exceed your expectations?

- Did we clearly convey our full array of services and process?

- Is there anything we missed or that you suggest we add to our experience?

- Based on what you know now, how would you describe us to others?

Show them you take this seriously. Tell them that anything less than 5 stars is "a miss" and "we always want to strive to exceed expectations."

Beyond that, many F4S professionals have attempted wide spectrum client surveys and satisfaction campaigns with their existing clients in an email or snail-mail format, but received a lukewarm and underwhelming response. Not that it was negative, there was just not great engagement, primarily because there is so much noise out there.

One notable exception is for the campaign primers where the F4S professional wants to introduce a Goals Based Planning Approach. Jumping ahead a little bit here, but the premise is, that as a team you've decided to adopt an even deeper goals-based planning approach with your clients. You've noticed that all of your clients have unique and very distinct goals and aspirations, but there is a commonality – virtually all of them fit into FORM – Family, Occupation, Recreation and Money. So, as a best practice your team is going to add a process to the client experience that ensures you fully understand what matters to your clients panoramically. For the primer, send a basic FORM questionnaire that prompts the client to get those goals out of their head and onto paper. Then instruct the client to send it back or bring it to your next meeting. If they get into it, you can supplement with W5. When you tell a client that you are raising the bar, and then you start mirroring their aspirations back on them, it becomes a beautiful echo that strengthens their view for your value. As you'll see, it can also become a springboard for the deeper reframe.

## The Next 90 Days

As we mentioned, you can find this initiative on the supplemental website, outlining how you can customize and deploy an incremental approach to know where you stand with your clients, and then feed off of that for rejuvenating relationships.

There are two more "Seal-Team" Special Forces-level 1:many supplemental campaigns you can consider for Checking the Pulse of your clients, both of which can also be found in depth on thebluesquaremethod.com/implementation-resources.

## The Client Advisory Council

Inviting, assembling, probing, and then thanking ten or so of your favorite clients in a professional setting, where you position your goal for elevating your client experience through a pseudo "board of directors" meeting, is as timeless as it is impactful. How to get them there, and setting the proper expectations, how to conduct yourself at the session and how to thank the golden geese that will lay golden eggs for you, is a turnkey and essential approach. It reflects well on you to the people you invite, and for the other people you tell in terms of why you did it, what was revealed, and the steps you are taking as a result. Check the Client Advisory Council idea out and decide if there is merit in it for you.

## Ideal Client Events (ICE)

Steve Phillips, a consultant on The Pareto Coaches Network, took the Client Advisory Council and shaped it in a way that was incredibly effective and efficient. He started to conduct Ideal Client Events on behalf of his own clients, to initiate reframing and elevating their clients. In a dinner setting for 12 of his clients' clients, Steve would talk about his F4S client and marvel at how he or she saw the merit in hiring a coach on best practices, and how seriously they viewed the concept of professionalism and consistency. He would then talk about how important it was, in the spirit of not getting complacent, to keep an open line of communication with clients to find ways to improve. Then the reframing would begin, prefaced by the premise that perhaps the F4S professional had become a bit of their own best kept secret. "Did you know? Were you aware? Many of his best ideas for elevating came from clients, for example..." and on it would go. Lights out, walk-off home-run with absolutely incredible impact. We have made that campaign available in a DIY format that you can deploy in a paint-by-number approach, and we're convinced it will reflect well on you if you take action.

At this point, you might be one of the few we've encountered who either wants to skip these priming steps, or you just don't see the merit. Fair enough. We've met a few who want to "jump past the small talk" or who felt "this seems unnecessary" and we get it, but our logic is simple. Before you listen to or take the advice of a consultant when it comes to improving client loyalty, engagement and conversion, listen to your clients. Make them the voice you listen to. There have been a few of our F4S clients over the years to whom we've had to playfully say, "Lose our number! If you're not prepared to seek and take your clients' advice, you probably won't take ours seriously, either." It's tough love. If you played team sports in school, you probably did not want to be the player isolated by the coach for being complacent or being half-hearted in practice. The thought of being responsible for the entire team having to do laps or extra push-ups might even cause you to shudder to this day. When you saw it happen, it corrected the situation pretty quickly, right? One way or the other? The point being, you're not one to ride a contentment wave today, either. Embrace these steps and build on them. The chances are that your competitors won't, but those who do unlock so many doors.

## Check CALL Care

You now have a better sense for how you're perceived and described, and you've planted a few seeds for what's coming your clients' way in the form of elevated consistency and clarity. Now, it's time to shift gears. The Check is essentially the ramp-up phase of the reframe. The Call is the actual execution phase. The Care is how you demonstrate that you're backing all of this up with real actions that benefit your clients.

The time and place for The Call is ideally when you schedule and confirm your next client meeting, whether in person or online. After you've taken care of scheduling, do your best Columbo impersonation and say, "Hey, before I let you go, one more thing. I want to let you know that..." and proceed to plant the seed.

## Context Matters

There are many scenarios you can frame this within, depending on your own unique situation. If, for example, you are:

**Keeping it Simple** – meaning this is motivated simply by the desire to improve, say *"As a team, we had a bit of a Eureka moment, and we recently found that a few of our clients were not aware of everything we did. We've become a bit of our own best kept secret. (Insert iceberg analogy here) So at the end of our upcoming meeting, I'll be pointing to an item on our agenda where I'll take just a couple of minutes to remind you of our process, so that you have the complete picture."*

**Transitioning Clients** – If you have made the decision to restructure your client experience, tied to their individual classification in order to liberate yourself to go deeper with the 20%, you have to automate, allocate and even respectfully disassociate from some of the 80%. The key is honorable positioning. Automation might mean that you put some of these clients into a managed model or platform for efficiency (and possibly also to improve their outcomes?). Allocation might mean that you assign them to a different person on your team. This isn't a hand-off or downgrade, it's an upgrade in that the client goes to a dedicated person with more capacity and time who is using the same practice and process as you. Remember, your C client could be someone else's A client. Perhaps you're doing the client a disservice by not allocating them?

As for disassociation, if there is dread when you see their number on your call display or on your appointment calendar, if they have demonstrated a pattern of low respect or high hassle factor, it might be time for an "It's not me, it's you" conversation – respectfully, of course. In any case, the priming statement is, *"As a team, we are assessing our capacity, our client experience and our growth patterns. As we continue to attract new clients, we need to get out in front of that by adding staff and expanding roles and responsibilities, so that we can still work with new friends and family members as they are introduced to us, without diluting our standards of service. So, when we get together, I'll add an item to the agenda and that we can spend a couple of minutes addressing that at the end of our meeting."*

**Switching Firms or Exiting** – if you feel you and your clients would be better off in a new environment, or if you are selling your business, subtly ramp that up heading into your meeting. Say, *"Just to let you know, as a lifelong planner, and in an effort to elevate the client experience, we've undertaken an exhaustive due-diligence effort to look for ways to raise the bar for our clients and our team. When we meet, I'll spend a few minutes at the end of our meeting outlining some of our observations."* The key here is that nothing negative ever gets said about a soon-to-be former firm.

For a time, it suited everyone's needs, but looking down the road, looking at the complexity of the evolving needs of your clients, there are some environments that place a bigger emphasis on that larger picture. It's not about being right or wrong in the traditional sense – you weren't wrong to choose the soon-to-be-former firm. Things evolved. It's about what's right for you and your clients going forward. If you are retiring soon and there won't be an internal transition for your "ride into the sunset" - meaning someone from the outside is buying your business - your preparation is of paramount importance. Of course this may arise organically since you have long-term clients who have their own continuity and succession issues, and they are probably starting to wonder what happens to them if you are no longer in the picture. Gradual is better than sudden, here. There is a time and a place to rip off the bandage, but in this case, strive for the methodical approach. Incidentally, be sure that you become a client of the acquiring firm and stay on as a consultant – the optics and credibility are enormous.

**After a Disruption** – if the economy was especially volatile, or your business went through some short-term chaos, or if you experienced a once-in-a-lifetime force majeure (2020? Hello!) you can launch a "Welcome Back to the Future" campaign. Acknowledge that the disruption was difficult, but as a team you always looked for the silver lining. Behind the scenes you weren't playing defense, but instead you were working hard on refinement and optimization. Through it all, you realized that there were some value-added services you could launch and make available, and you can't wait to briefly show them off in your next meeting.

**Growing Down** – as we touched on, and will cover more deeply in Chapter 12, if you've made the decision to dramatically reduce your client count so that you can shift from a breadth to a depth model, call your best and favorite clients and inform them that, as a team, you are excited because you've made the decision to grow your business from 300 clients down to 75! (The client's immediate thought will be, "Whoa, did I make the cut?") Tell them that the upside to downsizing is the opportunity to go deeper into the needs and client experience of the clients you are best suited for, especially as so many of those clients are approaching liquidity events, and with more money comes more complexity. Going forward, you will only bring on AAA PLUS clients. You will be offering a deeper Multi Family Office (MFO) experience, and you will unveil this in more detail in your next meeting. Don't be surprised if a few of your clients says, "Whew, I thought you were breaking up with me. You can never fire me or ever get rid of me. This is great." All of which is code for, "I'll protect you and only refer AAA PLUS people to you in the future."

## Ready to Launch

All this brings us to the moment of truth - the meeting with your client to start executing on the reframe. First things first. We hope you are long past calling your client get-togethers Review Meetings, because ...

## The Review Meeting is Obsolete

The idea of getting together with a client to rehash something that has already happened is just one reason why some of your clients might brush it off and tell you, "Hey it's all cool. I'm busy, I trust you. Whatever you think." You might convince yourself that it's great that your client feels that way. It's not great. It's great that they trust you, but not great that they don't see the merit in getting together. That's where loyalty fatigue and drifting are born. The noise-canceling headphones are now officially off and competitor messages are going to be heard.

We suggest that you refer to your client appointments as Strategy and Tactical Meetings, where you will connect to invest the past into the future, make mid-course corrections and ensure that everything is current, and that everyone is aligned and in sync. It's positioned as an essential part of the process. If a client ever tells you they can't make it, and fails to reschedule, tell them the meeting is happening on their behalf. Your team will meet, discuss adjustments and future pacing elements and send an output of the meeting to the client. (Translation: We'll work around your schedule, but these meetings are essential. They are the center point of our process)

Before we get into the weeds, make a note that there is a video, sample agenda and an outline of the Strategy and Tactical Meeting process at thebluesquaremethod.com/implementation-resources.

A key component of the deployment is the agenda. It follows the flow of a regular meeting – connecting, updating and adjusting – but as it starts to crescendo, the meeting shifts to removing the mystery of your panoramic value and activates future pacing.

An example of positioning in the latter part of the meeting is the agenda item bullet "An Overview of our Process." Note how it allows you to segue to The 7 Pillars and position introductions as a value-added service you provide:

*"You might remember, when we spoke on the phone, I mentioned that our team has been tethered more closely as we refine and optimize our client experience so that we can raise the bar. During this exercise we've come to the realization that, while we have some great relationships, and our clients really appreciate our people, many aren't fully aware of the benefits of our practice and process. We're kind of our own best-kept secret and we want to remove the mystery so that you have the complete picture - not just in terms of what we do and what our value is - but what it does for you and your family over the lifetime of our relationship."*

At this point, turn the agenda over and walk through your version of 7 Pillars 1 Process. Pausing for clarity and to answer questions, when you get to the 7th pillar, emphasize this:

*"One of my favorite value-added services is making myself available to be a sounding board for friends and family members of my clients. As you can imagine, when there is so much turbulence and uncertainty in the world, people look for answers, often reaching out to people they trust beyond their current provider. So, we've been busy with that, but it's incredibly fulfilling and reminds me of why I got into this business to begin with."*

See where that lands. If they embrace it, go deeper (We outline the introduction process in detail in the onboarding chapter.) If they simply say, "That's good to know," then leave it there. You've planted a seed.

When executed properly, the reframe is essentially a control-alt-delete for the relationship – a reboot that rejuvenates and prompts deeper conversations going forward. Regardless of what you are going to address in the back half of the Strategy and Tactical Meeting - whether it's growing down, transitioning, or elevating to goals-based planning - this will be the kick-starter and is certain to be interpreted and received as a lift in the client's appreciation and understanding for your value.

## Everything Old is New Again

In the ONboarding chapter we will go into the importance of adding something tangible to your process. Something that your clients can hold in their hands. You can send a client – a potential advocate – home from a meeting with an organized folder containing items addressed in the most recent meeting. Where does that folder go? Does it float around, then sit temporarily on their desk before being filed away and forgotten? Your interactions should be cumulative and have ascending momentum, even if the deliverables are sometimes mundane. It's still part of the overall experience.

What we're describing is not designed to replace anything digital within your process, but it is designed to be something supplemental they can hold and feel. What is it? It's the Personal Financial Organizer (PFO) – the 'Life in a Book' or 'Resource Journal' - a binder that houses some of the most important documents, not to mention various services and solutions within your process. We're referencing it here because, if you deem that you have a very deserving existing client that embraces your reframe exercise enthusiastically, it might warrant essentially re-onboarding them. Not only because they deserve it, but also so that they can experience it in the spirit of advocacy. Consider that concept when you go through that chapter. We have to say that it drives us a little crazy when a business offers a discount or incentive "for new clients only." It conveys the impression of a revolving door of customer transactions with minimal loyalty or repeat business. It makes more sense that all incentives should be directed at existing customers – people who took the plunge already and might nudge others to do the same – as a reward and recognition for their trust. It's common sense.

## Check Call CARE

There is one more step in the process. CARE. This is where you set an expectation for elevation and follow through on it, immediately. The best way to do this is to send a thank-you card (with your symbol) and a summary of what you discussed – keeping it primarily about the client. The best way to do that is to mirror back their goals, framed in FORM. Technical details and adjustments can be included, too, as well as action steps to be implemented and carried forward. Reference any calendar events, and point to three specific things they can look forward to: Reinforcement of team members new and existing, a reminder of a value-added service, and a reference to any new technology you are adding, for example.

For future Strategy and Tactical Meetings, be sure to send the agenda in advance, following the ramp up, execute, and follow-through approach. Include a phone reminder to supplement automated scheduling, use the agenda in the meeting, and provide a summary of what you discussed – every time.

## Positioned for a Breakout

We receive a lot of excellent feedback from F4S professionals as they go deep into our process. One, not long ago, mentioned that she isn't sure how her business would have fared through the disruption set off by the episode in 2020.

Her view was, in a gracious hat-tip to us, that her preparation and elevation enabled her to capitalize on improved referability while maintaining a calm and consistent vibe in her office and throughout her team, especially when they were forced to work remotely.

## A Tale of Two Clients

Another client of ours - who was admittedly just going through the motions initially with our process – got jarred one day. In the space of an hour, he received an amazing degree of praise and an incredible referral from a raving client, and then got fired by a raging client. It was enough to tip him over to a sense of resolve, because he said, "That's it. I only want those great clients. Not the others." He knew the one relationship was hanging by a thread (primarily because of the client's attitudinal issues), but our F4S client realized that every expenditure of effort he applied to the at-risk relationship was coming at the expense of his favorite clients.

That distinction between expenditure and investment is profound. You have to count the costs and the returns.

The primary thing here, as a client of ours likes to say, is to always "make the main thing the main thing." Focus on your favorite relationships, focus on continual refinement, and focus on driving complacency into a distant corner.

There is a spectrum of outcomes, from worst-case to out-of-the-park awesome. The worst-case is you have validation in your relationships, if nothing else. It's like wrapping them in bullet-proof Kevlar. They can't be taken away. Not a terrible worst-case. At a higher level of engagement, you can see rejuvenation leading to additional empowerment and engagement. Then to the top level – you activate a steady quantity and higher quality of introductions. Again, like staging a home before you put it up for sale, these minor tweaks feel like, to lift from the Snow Patrol song, "Cracking the Shutters Open Wide". Watch. You will have some clients who jump all over this - especially business owners, professionals and executives who "get it." These are the people who understand business development, merit, best practices and professionalism. They will say to you, "Wow, this is impressive" or "I had no idea you could do all of this," and even, "You know what, it's time for you to meet my business partner. I've mentioned you to him but now I'm going to insist that he meet with you."

### Check Call CARE+

For those clients that get excited, and in whom you can see a wellspring of potential advocacy building, ask them: *"Do you have a couple of minutes so that I could quickly show you my onside fit and onboarding process?"*

Show them your introductory kit and the steps in your fit process. Show them your onboarding kit (tell them you will prepare one for them as well). Show them your service model and service matrix. Show them your ideal client profile. It will only take a few minutes but what you're saying is "This is what it looks like to meet with me, to establish an alignment and fit, and to transition over to us. This is what it means to be our client." From that, your client, on the verge of advocacy, can start to internalize and then socialize your process, articulate your value, and together – with their own persuasive impact as a messenger – you now have a message that is unrivaled in its conviction - without bravado and without overstating it. This is how advocates operate.

# Chapter 7:

## *ONside - Our Process for Sifting Prospects from Suspects*

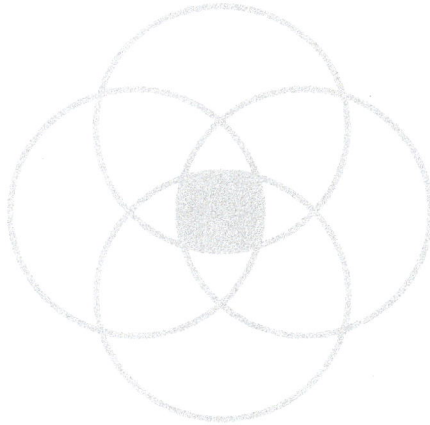

When it comes to consistently attracting a steady stream of prospective clients, and then sifting those that align with your ideal client profile from the masses, you have to be clear on the who, the where and the how. Who exactly is your ideal client? Where are you going to source them from, and how are you going to attract them with professional stewardship instead of pursuing them with salesmanship?

It starts with understanding that the essence of attracting new, high-caliber prospective clients is launched at the intersection of professional scarcity and professional contrast. People are especially drawn to a desirable value proposition that isn't abundant in its availability. As for contrast, people have had their expectations throttled back and suppressed, especially in the last few years. Think of commercial flying, and how the hope now is just for "same-day service." Approaching a restaurant, the hope is for a server that isn't rude and might even try a little bit. When buying a cell phone, one is dazzled not only by competence but especially by the offer to help switch your data over for you while you wait. Effort is a refreshing departure from the bare minimum experiences that have become the norm. Sometimes it feels akin to trying to find the cleanest shirt in the laundry hamper.

Sun Tzu, in his *Art of War*, insisted that every battle is won before it is fought. In history there have been many battles won without firing a single shot, but in your world, you aren't fighting for a new client, you are competing with yourself to avoid the battle of the bland. Putting yourself out there, pushing yourself to be better and putting distance between your value and every competitor that is punching, to varying degrees, beyond their weight class.

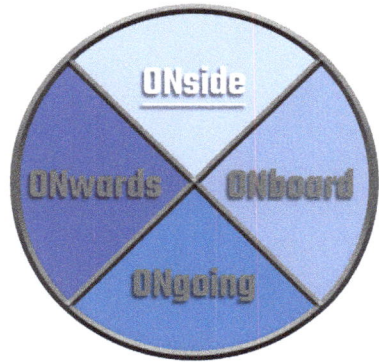

## WHO is Your Ideal Client?

If you haven't already done so, start by crystallizing, precisely and panoramically, who you are suited for. Use AAA PLUS as the frame. Go into detail describing the Alignment of their needs to your value, both now and in the future. List the seven Attitudinal qualities that create long term chemistry and compatibility, and describe the essence of Advocacy – the spirit of being proactively on the lookout to make connections and introductions for the important people in one's life. To drive it home, convey a sense of community, belonging and scarcity, with the Tiffany Blue Ribbon on the box – "We have chosen to only align with People Like US."

Once you've created this self-fulfilling and magnetic document, don't be shy. Show it off. Tell the world and remove the mystery to help them with auto-sifting. Be ready to convey it in three phases:

**The Tip of the Spear** – this is where you simply say, *"when it comes to our clients, we made a decision a while back to not focus on how big we can get, but rather on how small we can stay, which is why we created our AAA PLUS ideal client profile."* Then follow their lead. If they ask you to elaborate, go for it. If not, leave it there.

**The Deeper Dive** – if someone is intrigued and asks for more color, write out the letter "A" three times vertically, and back-fill it with Alignment, Attitude and Advocacy, before their eyes, along with some commentary. Then, punctuate it with PLUS to drive home the point of your small, exclusive community.

**The Full Monty** – OK, so you're not going there exactly, but if someone gets animated in their reaction, reach for your playbook and turn to the page "Who are We Suited For?" Take them on the tour. Walk them through it. Tell stories about the socioeconomic and demographic realities of your clients. Talk about the exceptions you've made with HENRY's (high earners not rich yet), the clients who are great people, tracking in the direction of being AAA, but they are 100% PLUS and a joy to interact with in the meantime.

## WHERE Will You Source Your New Clients From?

The client acquisition source-code is as simple as 1-2-3.

**Your Existing Clients** - It's axiomatic and self-evident that, once activated, clients that convert to advocates will keep you more than busy. They'll go out of their way, carefully sifting and steering people your direction and expecting nothing in return.

In the ONboard and ONgoing chapters, we outline exactly how you can fast-track clients to advocate status with a proven, professional approach.

**Your Strategic Partners** – The clients of other F4S professional service providers you collaborate with can be high-quality, predisposed prospective clients of yours, but with a mindset of stewardship, you can't consider any initiative like this as a referral network. Who is the winner there? A VAST Network – a Value-Added-Support-Team – of accretive, collaborative professionals with a unified goal – addressing every need a co-client has thoroughly and efficiently, well, that's a different story. While there is a force-multiplier of reciprocal advocacy, it's earned by undeniable value being delivered without expectation. Merit is appreciated and rewarded, so long as it is pure. There is a deeper dive for deploying The VAST Network outlined on thebluesquaremethod.com/implementation-resources but, as you keep reading, you'll find some highlights in the next few pages.

**Prospecting in the Second Degree** – Please avoid any form of marketing unless and until you have fully engaged with clients and strategic partners. If you find yourself with additional bandwidth and you feel compelled to go beyond those two sources, the next step, if you are active on LinkedIn, is to start creating awareness for your value with first-degree contacts of your clients and strategic partners. They are the third most predisposed prospective client available to you. They are your second-degree prospective clients. There is a high-road approach you can take to respectfully cultivate awareness for yourself within that community, and we're going to combine some insights on that in the following, but not before we provide some proven strategies for unlocking the VAST Network potential.

## Awaken a Sleeping Giant

For many F4S professionals in your inner circle of strategic partners, and for those connected to your clients that you haven't met yet, understand their wiring. It doesn't always occur to them to proactively make introductions. Their head is down, grinding out their technical deliverables. They might think in terms of 101-level networking, but not all of them are very savvy beyond that. It isn't an innate skill for everyone, and it certainly wasn't taught to them in school. In the absence of the entrepreneurial pedigree – they're running a practice not a business – there is a higher degree of skepticism when it comes to this type of initiative. They might think of it as risk-aversion, but in reality, we would respectfully say they aren't enlightened just yet. It is a learned skill if approached properly.

Couple that with the fact that they may already have a relationship with someone in your space, or maybe they did in the past and it was not great, just realize you've got to take the long view and apply the stewardship dynamic here as well. Consider approaching it with this format:

**Step 1.** With every new client you onboard, mention in that meeting that *"Part of our approach is engaging your other relevant service providers into the process, so that nothing is missed, everything is in sync, and you always have the complete picture. If you see the merit, I will reach out to them to say hello, outline our process, and together we will look for efficiencies and synergies."*

Follow their lead. Some may be reluctant initially and tell you they'll give that some thought and get back to you. Others will jump at the concept and provide you with contact information and may actually even make email introductions immediately. It's all good.

**Step 2.** As you organize and consolidate your thoughts, and logistically order the moving parts of this approach, start introducing this to existing clients at Strategy and Tactical Meetings. Add an item on the agenda, "Raising the Bar" or "A New Value Added Service" and outline the premise. You can say that you addressed this to a degree in the past, but as your clients' needs intensified, you deemed it necessary to professionalize it further and formally add it into your process. It's tough to build a puzzle without the picture. It's also much easier with another set of eyes working in concert.

**Step 3.** Reaching out – It's pretty straightforward when reaching out to a potential strategic partner, especially in, but not limited to, occasions when a client makes the introduction. It's still a very warm call. Even if just a voice mail, let them know you have a mutual client. Let them know that part of your process is to make contact with other service providers to see if they'd like to have an initial conversation about synergies that can elevate the client experience. They might reply suggesting you follow up at later date (after they've wrapped their head around the concept) or they might be intrigued enough to jump on a call.

## Soft launch

A call can work, but an online visit is better. Do a quick search beforehand to learn something about the potential strategic partner. Ideally, find something qualitative in terms of their interests, community and charitable endeavors or history. When you connect, simply say, *"I hope you don't mind that I did a quick search to understand your business and I couldn't help but notice..."* and then ask them how that came about in their life and see if there is some reciprocal rapport.

From there, mention how you appreciate that they're busy and that you respect their time, and quickly explain your value proposition. Then, reference your process and vision for the concept of collaboration in the best interests of the client.

## You'll come to a Fork in the Road

You'll quickly determine if this is going to be a ho-hum encounter or if there is some promise. If the energy is lacking, simply tick the box and keep the door open for occasional check-ins down the road for updates and adjustments. If nothing else, a no-nonsense and all-business seed has been planted.

There will be some who embrace this approach from the get-go. Chemistry is present and enthusiasm is palpable. At that point, an in-person meeting should be scheduled. Tell them that you will send your Introductory Kit by two-day courier in advance of that meeting.

Arrive with an agenda, connect with rapport and then explain at a high level what you are doing with the client and pivot to a conversation about synergies. Be highly interested in them and their approach, and keep referencing your appreciation for best-practices, consistency and an elevated client experience.

When you get to the agenda item "an overview of our process," walk them through it, reinforcing the highly transparent focus on the client. Focus solely on the client's needs, with no hidden agenda about referrals. If you like how they are engaging, then use your discernment, with the 7th pillar as the springboard, to decide if you want to explain your VAST Network concept, in case other opportunities arise where you could introduce people and engage even further. You're sifting and then activating – but organically. You can't force the issue.

If they embrace the VAST concept, ask these three questions:

- Who is your ideal client – who are you best suited for?

- How would you suggest that I describe you if the opportunity presents itself?

- How would you like me to formally introduce people to you?

Based on the Law of Reciprocity, after being asked those questions most, but not all, will then ask you one or more of the same questions.

At that point, explain what makes you different. Explain your 'why' (being a sounding board), your 'who' (your ideal client) and your 'how' (the process you ask people to use when making introductions) - all outlined in the ONboarding chapter. Then, reverse engineer. Show them your onboarding kit, show them your service model and service matrix and point again to your introductory kit. Punctuate it all by reminding them that if they ever introduce someone to you, they can rest assured that this person does not need to become a client to take advantage of your introductory sounding board service. You'll make yourself available and follow that person's lead. If you get some initial traction, even if it's just in the form of intent, plug this F4S service provider into your service matrix under the category VAST, and service them as you would a client, with regularly scheduled touches. Give them a taste of what their clients would experience. All this is outlined in the Ongoing chapter.

You'll soon get a good sense for whether they are truly interested in collaboration, or just humoring you and hoping to get referrals from you in a one-way street dynamic. Your professionalism, your process and your discernment will reveal what's there. A two-way street of respect is essential, as you know. You might recall what many thought was an urban legend back in the day. Van Halen, the rock band that achieved superstardom, demanded, among other things, that a bowl of M & M's be in their dressing room – but the brown ones had to be removed. Pretty obscure. But, in fact, it was the band's indication as to whether the promoter actually read the contract. That attention to detail meant that they took everything else seriously. Your VAST Network initiative is designed to attract and engage other like-minded professionals, and your process will reveal them.

### HOW Are You Going to Attract Them Your Way?

Let's get back to the premise of mining second degree prospective clients to supplement introductions, but note the key word – supplement. This is not the primary driver. To that end, understand that a lot of what we're going to outline here applies to nurturing clients and strategic partner relationships, as well – another form of convergence.

The key is to avoid traditional marketing and advertising. The unspoken reaction when someone sees a F4S professional advertising on a billboard or any other form of "here I am" announcement is, "How good can they be if they are still chasing new business?"

You can rationalize the value of name recognition, and yes, sponsorship banners at Golf Tournaments hosted by your allies are fine, but you want to stay clear of intrusive, interruption-style advertising and marketing. It conveys a need that you have more than it does a value you provide.

## Content Marketing = Thought Leadership

A best practice that can take more time to produce, but strongly reflects and supports your branding strategy, is content marketing. When you create and promote your content, and make it the call to action, you ask the world to ask for your thought leadership IP, rather than asking for appointments or new business. You are attracting with permission marketing, rather than chasing with sales techniques.

When you create content, it is evergreen and always on; always available for consumption. When you turn off the radio, the signal is still there. When you start circulating content, it doesn't collapse like an advertisement, it floats around waiting for the precise stage of readiness. The moment it lands and connects with someone they raise their hand, opting in to learn more.

The sweet spot you are trying to land on with your content and professional services is an abundance of available content from you virtually, and scarcity for the available time with you, personally. That means that you will share your observations and insights with everyone, and make yourself available to meet in person with a select few. It's not a tactic. It's good karma to put information out there with no expectation that it will land, and it is attractive self-interest to allocate your time carefully. It combines service to the community, along with (but not at the expense of) service to self.

So, get to work! Write a white paper on your core beliefs, convictions and observations. Pay an editor to format it properly. It might stop there, or it might evolve to a manifesto in time, and maybe into an actual book at some point. Write it for yourself, initially. Temper your expectations. It's not about how many will read it. It's in case someone happens to read it. It might only be you and your editor, who knows? Be at peace with it, no matter what. Does the world need another white paper, manifesto or book? Probably not. Will you do it anyway and put your heart and soul into it to make it interesting? Hopefully so.

For every book you read, create a summary of your favorite points. *Atomic Habits* and *Traction* are sure to be well received by your ideal clients – both existing and prospective.

Create Top 10 Lists of Family continuity and dynastic tips, Occupational best practices and ideas, Recreational bucket list destinations. Feel free to cover ideas regarding your Message to round out FORM, and invite other subject matter experts to contribute content for your community, and remember, you can revisit this content with updates and re-purpose it in the future.

Record your educational events and make them available. Consider podcasts and video. Most people attempt the podcast route, but quit by the seventh episode because it's slow to move the needle and an effort to implement. You might consider outsourcing that to Proud Mouth. In the resource section you will see their spotlight page for consideration in your pursuit of a heightened thought-leadership reputation.

## Video Skills Will Carry You Far

Musically, can you tell what inspired the above statement? We are in an era where you have to consider video. At a minimum, build out evergreen video that is concise and which someone can view on your website when they visit for the first time. Themes like "what makes us different?" that require no more than 90 to 120 seconds to view are ideal. Cascading and sequential video blogs are great too, but you have to follow the brevity-specificity-proprietary framework. People move on like hummingbirds. They check the hook – the subject matter - and then they check the time duration commitment before deciding to press the play button.

## The Relationship between Quality and Popularity

Again, you have to temper your expectations about visits, clicks and views. There are videos of *Despacito* featuring Justin Bieber that have been viewed hundreds of millions of times (requiring enough hosting power to heat and light several buildings for years). Then you see a Peter Gabriel Video like *Solsbury Hill* or *Don't Give Up* with Kate Bush and note that it's been viewed just a fraction of that. A head scratcher.

At your level, you're trying to put the odds in your favor by automating the attraction and sifting process and staying top-of-mind with the relationships that matter. Go for quality above all, and be at peace with the lag time. Creating content requires patience. It can be as endearing at times as when your dad would follow you around at home turning off the lights you left on. Annoying then, but you get it later.

Creating content can be tedious and sending it out can be anticlimactic, but then something magical happens. It finds its way to the right person at the right time and it makes your phone ring. *Voila*, and like a perfect golf shot, if it can happen once, it can happen repeatedly.

## Through the Funnel and Into the Pipe

If you are still with us at this point, we can assure you that every prospective client that gets introduced to you or reaches out to you of their own volition because of these efforts is predisposed and self-motivated. Your job now is to amplify that further.

That initial contact by phone is a big part of your "curb appeal". Your relaxed decorum emphasizes that you're more interested in solving problems than in closing a piece of business. When you agree to meet and you tell them that "you don't have to bring anything except your questions," it emphasizes that you are more interested in a gradual relationship than an immediate win. It's very disarming. When you tell them that you'll forward your Introductory Kit in advance of that meeting so they can understand your philosophy and get to know your people, practice and process, you are creating anticipation and professional contrast.

## Formulate Your First Meeting Process - Strive for Synchronization

If you've ever been to a large sporting event and a spontaneous chant or wave erupted and took hold throughout a stadium filled with thousands of people, it's essentially a social form of phase transition where the energy in the building evolved into an organic harmonic pattern. After a concert or theatrical show, the crowd bursts into an applause where the clapping is in sync and transitions to a standing ovation – nobody told them to do it. It's said that two metronomes will sync up within 30 minutes. It's said that the hearts of two people in close proximity and with affection for each other will start beating together.

Your goal when meeting with a prospective client is to find a professional version of that. Let your advocates and initial onside steps build predisposition for the prospective client, and then steer and shape the synchronization in the actual meeting without pressure, without attempting to overcome objections and without trying to close them.

Our consulting clients no longer (or never did) use pitch books or presentation decks. They use a beautifully crafted fit process. When they meet a prospective client for the first time, they pump hands and exchange pleasantries and then they say, *"I hope you don't mind but I looked you up and visited your website out of curiosity after our initial call. What really caught my eye was* (something very personal but perhaps obscure that many might not notice or ask about)." The first goal is always to be interested. Being interesting is always a distant second because you learn nothing about someone by dominating the conversation.

Our clients liberate themselves to be spontaneous in the moment by being exceedingly prepared. They don't wing it, ever. They pace the meeting in a measured way, always. They've studied the Socratic Method to master the art of diagnostics and assessment. Many of them frame key points in PAS – they talk about Problems others have had, talk about how the problem was Agitating and then talk about Solutions. Others guide their talking points with SNIB. Every Subject leads to a specific Need someone had, that led to actionable Ideas and meaningful Benefits. This makes things relatable and compelling. Virtually all of our clients use authentic stories and social proof (from other AAA PLUS Clients) to drive those benefits home. Still one of the best examples of getting to the point and activating someone's desire for something is Steve Jobs' now legendary presentation where he introduced the iPod for the first time by saying "With this device, you can put a thousand songs in your pocket." This was long before the concept of a "mic drop" but he could have left the stage right then and the world would have beaten a path to Apple's door.

## Keep Your Goals Clearly in Mind

Speaking of great videos worthy of re-watching, look for Monty Roberts, a.k.a. The Horse Whisperer, describing how he connects with a horse. For some, the approach is to "break" the horse with yelling, whips and a show of strength. Roberts prefers a patient, kinder approach that admittedly takes longer. His view is that the goal is not to break the horse – that's not the win. The goal is win-win – a mutual understanding. It is a thing of beauty to watch.

As a F4S professional, your goal is professional contrast and professional scarcity, meaning you take the "close" off the table.

When you shift from the pleasantries and rapport aspect of the first few minutes and pivot to the professional part of the conversation, the ideal positioning statement is, *"To be clear, nobody has to make any decisions here today. Let's get to know each other, talk a little about your situation and what you're trying to accomplish and take it from there. Is that fair?"*

Then make it about them. As an example, what is the difference between walking into a produce store and seeing a sign in the window that says, "Thanks for your support" versus another saying "You won't have to dig for the good stuff here – it's all good stuff"? One makes it about their benefits, the other makes it about your benefits. It's subtle but still impactful.

Have your assortment of thoughtful and important questions ready to go, prompted by the bullet on the agenda that reads "what's important to you?" (Remember, the agenda bundle is at thebluesquaremethod.com/implementation-resources) then ask:

- What's on your mind?
- What is your most pressing concern?
- What prompted you to make time for this meeting?
- What are you trying to accomplish?

## The Third Chair

Always have an extra chair in the room (some even have an artistic picture of an empty chair on the wall) to symbolize the prospective client's current provider being in the room with you. The idea here is to think in terms of professional contrast, with an emphasis on self-evident professionalism. It's a mindset technique to ensure you are sitting up straight and bringing your A-game to the meeting – not by chasing or competing – by being the most attractive option the prospective client will ever have.

You are striving for alignment, not a close. The "win" is in arriving at a mutually agreed upon conclusion that is natural and feels right. Yes, you will gradually expose the flaws of the current provider and others in the vetting process, but it will be achieved honorably and comfortably for the potential client and for your industry.

## Ascending Momentum

As rapport, interaction and trust gathers steam, you can feel the enthusiasm. One of the best things to do at this point is to not deviate. Keep feeding the self-motivation. Help them come to their own conclusions. One of the masters of this is Randy Schwantz, an exceptional presenter and consultant and the author of The Wedge. Randy's epic statement, "For you to get hired, someone else has to get fired" is as good as it gets when it comes to attracting a client that closes you, instead of chasing a prospect trying to close them.

You'll feel the meeting gather steam as unmet needs and issues needing to be resolved are put on the table. Have some additional thought-provoking questions ready that amplify the doubts they have in their current provider:

- *"If you don't mind me asking, in your most recent gap and risk analysis, did you identify any action items based on how your needs have evolved?"*

- *"When you conducted your last Strategy and Tactical Meeting, what items did you address on the agenda?"*

Randy Schwantz also outlines the importance of being exceedingly diplomatic when the topic lands on the prospective client, hinting at areas where they are disillusioned with their incumbent provider. If you pile-on and hammer at any perceived mistakes, you unintentionally create a guilt by association – in effect, "how could you have been so dumb to hire that person in the first place?"

He then advises you to pick your spots and, at an appropriate time, pose this interesting challenge: *"Complete this sentence for me, 'Gee it would be nice if my current provider did* (fill in the blank.)' "

Then, let the prospective client tell you precisely what they're looking for. "Well, it would be nice if I heard from him on a more regular basis – and not just when he's trying to get me to do something." You can actually defend the incumbent by saying *"Well I'm sure he is very busy and doing the best he can,"* and listen as the prospective client reveals anything else that is bothering them.

Tyson Ray, a F4S professional in Wisconsin, is one of the most truly authentic and accomplished we've ever had the pleasure of working with. He approaches every meeting with a prospective client as a pro-bono session with no expectation, but strives to send that person on their way with a sense of clarity and anticipation. There is zero attempt to convince anyone to come on board with him.

He is incredibly gracious, one-hundred percent present and focused and grateful for every interaction he has, and as a result, people insist that he accept them as a client. Advocates insist that he speak to their friends. Other F4S professionals insist that he show them his way.

A classic example of how he conducts himself is evident in an exchange with a prospective client who was introduced to him. She explained her newly evolved situation and the plan her current provider presented as a course of action – a plan she found to be lacking.

Tyson applauded the plan but pointed out a couple of enhancements he'd make. The stunned prospective client said something like, "that makes so much sense. Why wouldn't my current provider have suggested that?" To which Tyson replied, "Because no one gets paid to give you that specific piece of advice." As you can imagine, she is Tyson's client today, and it was an encounter where Tyson did not have to do any convincing.

## Watch Your Language

Be certain to take any jargon and sales lingo out of your lexicon. Nothing about accounts, households, minimums, production or asset gathering. Never say, "Thanks for the business" to a new client or "Thanks for the referral" to an advocate. Always point to the relationship and the process that ensures you are directionally focused (where it's going), rather than decision focused (you made a sale).

## Look For Clues

Often when you meet people, they tell you who they are – unintentionally - because of their choice of words, the types of questions they ask and the way they treat others when they think nobody is watching. How someone treats service and support staff is very revealing. Self-importance and superiority is definitely not People Like US and not a good fit. Slagging former providers or others in their lives, hinting at personal pettiness, micromanagement and passive aggressive threats of probation are non-starters too. Then, of course, we come back to when someone questions your fees. A solid book is *Never Split the Difference* by Chris Voss – an expansive and even tense read on the world of negotiation. It's such an important study and skill to refine, but here's the key for an F4S professional: As we've said, an essential best practice is to never negotiate your value in order to win business.

You are starting a long-term, sometimes multi-generational relationship that should not be started by lowering your fees. Sure, it's fun to grind on a new car or the price of a hotel room, but these are transactions. The enlightened never try to win a negotiation when it comes to a relationship-centered, long-term engagement.

## A Few Words on Events

Client appreciation, education and other FORM-themed events can be incredibly efficient ways to get together with clients and their friends, strategic partners and their clients, as well as solid and worthy prospective clients. They do require work, so you and your team will probably have to drive them and do the heavy lifting on behalf of your partners, but if you are process-driven with the logistics, clear on expectations in terms of rules of engagement with strategic partners, focused more on the quality of the attendees than the quantity, and committed to recurring impressive events instead of sporadically scheduled and poorly executed ones, they can serve you very well. The best at it take a long view and build an environment of positive energy and appreciation.

## A View from the Cheap Seats

Attracting and sifting requires more effort than expense. Before you start any of this, get a very high up, nose-bleed view to assess your overall plan and temperament. It's one thing to have the idea, but do you have the stomach to execute it? It can be frustrating and disappointing, initially. In your strategic planning, jump to the end in terms of what it would look like if you stopped because you were unhappy with the results, or if it took off and caused unintended bursting at the seams. It's inevitable that it will work, but how long will it take and how much time will it consume? Consider:

**Outsourcing** – be sure that your due diligence is applied with any vendors, confirms specific knowledge for your field and examines measurable success KPIs achieved by others – do not risk being an early adopter.

**Delegation** – assign a team member to act as a logistics coordinator for any of the business development drivers, and to provide concierge service for relationship execution and accountability.

**Automation** – always strive to create automated processes for a set-it-and forget-it mode, especially for LinkedIn, website SEO, service matrix for partners and prospective clients.

Be sure to ask yourself if you even need to do these forms of marketing and promotional events. We've seen it all. Events that led to a break-out, a fake-out and even a few freak-outs. They can be effective, but that doesn't mean they're necessary, and certainly, they should never be at the expense of 1-to-1 advocacy building strategies.

As with events, you want to avoid one-off exchanges of effort and instead focus on what you can build and sustain. There is a confluence with a lot of these initiatives that includes competitor-proofing existing relationships and deeper engagement and conversion to advocacy, but your strategy has to include delayed gratification. When you stir the pot well, and conduct yourself professionally with prospective clients who are steered your way by others, at a minimum they will in turn validate to the rainmaker that it was a positive experience – even if it wasn't a good fit – all of which fortifies the likelihood that they will make it rain again.

## From Intent to Consent

This brings us to the go/no-go after your initial meeting with a prospective client. You told them no one had to make any decisions at the first meeting, you had an agenda-driven diagnostic conversation to see if there was an alignment and good fit, and at the end of the meeting you said, *"OK, thanks for your time. Let me meet with my team to discuss your situation. You take some time to absorb everything, and I'll contact you in 48 hours to discuss things further."* This is done without deviation. It's an example of consistency and a big part of your brand.

If it's not a good fit, respectfully point to your ideal client profile and tell them why, and then make the offer for other options and suggestions. Be sure to call the rainmaker to explain that outcome. If it is a good fit, and they agree, schedule the next meeting, tell them what to bring and prepare for the onboard.

# Chapter 8:

## *ONboard - Our Process for Fast-Tracking New Clients*

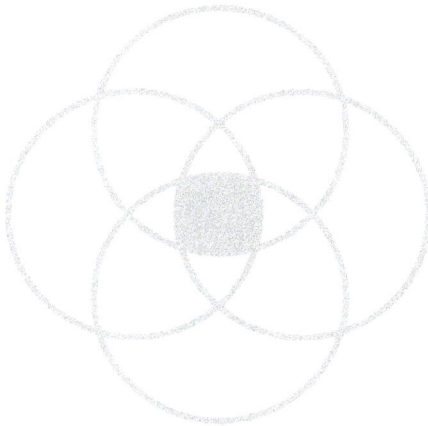

As we shift from the ONside fit process to the ONboarding process, let us remind you of the ultimate key performance indicators that confirm you are executing well. When a prospective client interrupts you part-way through the initial meeting and says, "I've heard enough, I just want to get started," in their view, the stars have already aligned. Thank them, but stay the course. Sometimes, as the initial meeting is winding down, the prospective client – not yet even an actual client – starts telling you about the people they want to introduce to you. Thank them, but park it and come back to it at the appropriate time. Or, soon after the initial meeting, you receive a thoughtfully written email or a beautiful thank-you card sent to you by a very appreciative person who aspires to become your client. These events have probably happened to you in the past, the point is to highlight how rare and powerful it is in business in general, and to impress upon you that you can increase the frequency of such events happening because of process and professional contrast.

## A Second First Impression

The energy shifts from the first to the second meeting. Leading up to your first meeting, the prospective client might have felt some apprehension – but that was squelched quickly – and then moved to a state of anticipation for the potential of the relationship. As you onboard the soon-to-be client, the mood shifts to validation. This is where your actions continually confirm their decision and appreciation that this might even be better than they expected. All of that energy culminates into activation – the concept of conversion to advocacy is taking root. When it catches and the loop closes, they put others into your process to experience it all for themselves.

Think for a moment of the last time you, as a client, were dazzled. Perhaps you bought a new car and when you returned to take delivery, it was parked front and center with your name on it and wrapped with a giant red ribbon. You looked inside and there was a beautiful picnic basket – yours to keep – stocked with goodies.

You snapped a selfie and posted it immediately with you standing beside the car alongside the salesperson (unconscious but immediate advocacy). You breezed through the final paperwork and went your way, and you still remember it vividly to this day. Or, perhaps you checked into a hotel with your family after a brutally delayed journey? When you checked in, the manager could see fatigue and frustration in your eyes and decided to upgrade you. Re-energized, you approached the room with added excitement, opened the door and boom – an ocean view; and then, boom, a separate bedroom; and boom, a kitchenette. MORE than you could have expected. Then boom again, there's a knock on the door by someone with a cheese and fruit plate. Cue the wide-smile selfies.

The thing to keep in mind is the word MORE. People have an expectation for what's going to happen at the signing ceremony. Give them MORE than they expected. If nothing else, you are starting the relationship off on the right foot and you are giving them something additional to talk about. The reasons to sing your praises don't have to be colossal, just unexpected.

It's another lost art that the client experience should be impactful and memorable - and therefore transferable. Speaking of lost arts, there was an era in advertising not long ago when jingles were all the rage. We're not sure if Juicy Fruit moves you, but that jingle played repeatedly, millions internalized it and sales went through the roof. There are multiple jingles from 80s that many from that decade could recite at a moment's notice. Jingles reinforced something – what people wanted. What do people want? They want to be happy, energized, safe, optimistic, and uplifted with a sense of belonging. They don't just want to be satisfied by having boxes checked – that's the bare minimum – they want to feel something.

Good sports coaches know this. Counter-intuitively, they will find something to praise after a loss and find something to fault after a win. They might occasionally get animated with theatrics after a blowout, but they know their temperament has to be measured and consistent. They don't attack the person, they zero in on the action. They will isolate one player after a game, toss them the hard hat and praise specific contributions they made.

They'll go over some technical ideas, but personal development and improvement, along with belief in the team's ability, are the key goals. Coaches often "lose the room" if they deviate from the x-factor, make it personal or hammer only the technical - eventually the team gets numb to the nonsense.

The takeaway here is consistency combined with an impactful, memorable experience. Clients want their expectations met and then exceeded. This helps you de-commoditize, because while the marketplace determines and defines a range of fees in your sector, you determine where you belong on that range based on how far you go beyond the pack – and again, not just because of your technical abilities.

## One Hit Wonder-ful

From a monetization perspective, you have to constantly remind yourself of the two economic drivers that are impacted by this mindset. You create Landing Revenue when you successfully onboard a new client. You then create Recurring Revenue as the engagement goes deeper and they start referring people to you. Many businesses focus on the cost of client acquisition. All of them know that the least expensive is word of mouth because those prospective buyers are the most predisposed. That form of Recurring Revenue is like a royalty. In 1979, Patrick Hernandez released the song Born to be Alive. It was a big hit in the waning days of disco. Now, you might simultaneously be familiar with that song but be hard pressed to think of another song Hernandez created. Over forty years later, he still earns about $1200 dollars every day through royalties for that song. Every day. Fun fact, one of the dancers in his original music video was none other than Madonna Ciccone, which is interesting if you are intrigued by where people get their start in life.

## Get a Sense for Your Framework

As a companion to the agenda and your notepad for putting together a critical path for the discovery session in the onside fit meeting, it's a good idea to clearly understand the framework of a typical onboarding meeting and the tools you'll deploy for maximum effect:

A fully built-out meeting can be categorized into 3 sections:

- Technical Execution
- Future Pacing
- The Tour

It's a good idea to assign windows of time for these three progressive deliverables. Sixty percent of the meeting time is dedicated to transitioning your client over and getting clear on tasks that fall within your TACC. It's not uncommon, in the case of very complex deliverables, that the onboarding is divided into two separate meetings (and scheduled follow-up calls and emails) to avoid overwhelming the client. In this example we'll keep it to one meeting, but you can adapt accordingly.

Twenty percent of the onboarding meeting is dedicated to Future Pacing. This is where you show your client where the relationship can go, and how your process can address the client's evolving needs.

Twenty percent of the onboarding meeting is dedicated to The Tour, where you walk them through specific resources you provide virtually, tangible parts of your process and client experience that they will receive physically, and then introductions to individual team members.

We can't overstate the importance of the high-touch components that supplement your high-tech deliverables. As you will see, there are many pieces that appeal to the kinetic nature of a relationship that are multisensory, impossible to discard and tough to dismiss or file away.

## Assemble Your Resources

You have an onboarding process that you developed long before you picked up this book. The goal is to compare and contrast that process to ours and find the gaps that you feel will have an impact. The next step is to organize your various array of proprietary resources to be deployed in the meeting - agendas, checklists, templates and takeaways - which your client will come to understand and appreciate. We will highlight those as we walk through the three phases.

**Your Technical Execution Phase** – you undoubtedly have a checklist, format and protocol to transition a client to your firm. Some of it is client-facing, while some of it is internal. Be sure that none of it resides in anyone's heads and that no one is ever winging it.

This is essential IP and has to be meticulously structured and implemented. Most of your clients want you to just take care of it and make it go away. They want it to be streamlined and painless. Again, like the data transfer when you buy a new cellphone, they just want it done. That said, keep reinforcing "our process" as you work through things that are client-facing. It is a form of soothing imprinting and comforting music to their ears.

## Putting More Sand in Your Hourglass

A quick word about seeking out options for outsourcing some of the commoditized aspects of your TACC over to bona fide models and platforms that are proven to add efficiency to your overall deliverables. As an example, a financial professional in his 50s was hitting his stride and finding renewed enthusiasm for his business by gradually adopting our process. He did have some trouble letting go of some of things he had been doing for years, but which needed to be re-imagined. He also had some issues with delegation, because of a fear of quality control dilution if he handed it off fully. All very self-sabotaging and undermining.

Then, he discovered he was going to become a grandfather. He was over the moon, and then he revealed some vulnerability. He said he wanted to be all-in as a granddad, but he was afraid that when he was at work he'd be thinking about his grandkid, and when he was with his grandkid he'd be thinking about work. Something had to give. We told him, "Get out of the asset management business!" Wait, what? Get out? We reminded him that he currently worked 45 hours a week, plus or minus. Fifteen on his technical ability, managing hundreds of holdings, 15 on the enterprise, managing his business and (often micromanaging) his team, and then 15 managing his clients. We told him to hand the holdings to trusted, proven managers who "think like you" with scaled models and platforms, hand the enterprise and some of the households to your team, and let them deploy a process to create consistency, and you then invest more time with your favorite clients – many of whom have grandkids, too. No one will get a word in edgewise, but it will be a lot of fun bragging. In the worst case scenario, he could work 30 hours a week and focus on what is proprietary and also meaningful in his life. Best case, he can still work 45, but on his terms, liberated, elevated and invigorated. Getting out of some things that are commoditized can allow you to go deeper into the things that will stand out and make you more attractive to elite clients. It's worth looking into that to find balance, so that you aren't majoring in minor tasks while overlooking the tasks that have a major impact.

**Your Future Pacing Phase** – once you've demonstrated a command of the nuts and bolts of the transition, and set expectations for what the client will need to do - and what your team will be doing after the meeting to get everything in place - you are on your way to MEETING expectations. We advise that you then shift to EXCEEDING them. Start by getting the client to focus on where this relationship can go, and what they can expect from you in the future. A picture may be worth a thousand words, but actions still speak louder than either.

Show things to your client revolving around your client experience, and then execute. The first is your listing of services tied to a revisit of the 7 Pillars, or whatever wrapper/symbol you use. This serves as a brief three-minute overview/refresher to open up the long view. You can then focus on the individual 7th Pillar to emphasize your Value-Added Services. You can plug in your VAST Network initiative here and plant the seed for the concept of advocacy with your sounding board service.

*"Of all the value-added services we provide, still the most fulfilling to me is being a sounding board for friends and family members. Keep in mind that if you ever feel compelled to introduce someone to me, they do not need to become a client to take advantage of this service. If they are important to you, they are important to me, and I will gladly make the time to speak with them."* (In the Ongoing chapter, we'll show you how to reinforce this and go deeper with the positioning over time.)

If you haven't already done so, you can introduce the concept and merit of being a goals-based professional. You've probably, at a minimum, already mentioned FORM - just write down the acronym vertically, and mention that in future calls and meetings, you'll be revisiting their evolving goals as you make adjustments and enhancements to their overall plan and planning approach.

## A Cautionary Tale

A quick tribute to Peter Parker's Uncle Ben, here. You probably weren't expecting another Spider-Man reference, but to paraphrase, with great knowledge comes great power and great responsibility. The lesson is simple, gather FORM knowledge and engage ALL meaningful stakeholders into the process as the relationship unfolds. As an example, an F4S professional had a substantial client pass away, leaving virtually everything to his wife – a lady that attended occasional meetings but wasn't very involved or fully included. The F4S professional scheduled a meeting with her after some time had passed and assumed it would be a simple paperwork session.

She walked in and curtly said, "I'm a school teacher and I don't see the merit in paying you the equivalent of my yearly salary to manage and oversee something that's already in place. I've found an alternative. A lady I trust and who is dramatically less expensive." He was floored. He felt he let her down, he felt he let her husband down and of course he felt he let himself down. It wasn't his intention to ignore her all these years, but the husband was a strong personality and drove the relationship. Knowledge is power and you have a responsibility to capture it and use it, while engaging everyone essential in the relationship, to ensure longevity through any and all external forces and events.

## An 80/20 Reminder

Roughly 20% of your clients generate about 80% of your business. Chances are that 20% of your advocates generate 80% of the referrals. We hope you track referral genealogy and that you track how you allocate your time. Throw the kitchen sink at the 20%. If something or someone is going to slip through the cracks or be put on the back burner as you tighten things up, be certain that it is not anyone in the 20% and especially not those who are AAA PLUS. Raising the bar can be an exhaustive, and at times elusive, undertaking – just don't lose sight of the main thing.

**Back to the Future Pacing Phase**. At this point in the onboarding, as the meeting hits its apex and is starting to wind down – and especially if the client is a AAA PLUS client - we suggest that you present their onboarding kit. A handsome, well-organized binder with a sequence of tabs that keeps everything in order. You might call this a Personal Financial Organizer (PFO), a Life in a Book, or a Resource Hub – it's entirely up to you. Whatever you do, please do not convince yourself that digital resources are enough. The more technology impacts our life, the more the human touch matters. The digital tools you use create efficiency, but can also paint you into the robo corner, because everything that robo offers is digital and virtual. There is a sample checklist of what goes into the binder at thebluesquaremethod.com/implementation-resources This doesn't replace your technology suite, and the binder is not for any minutia. It is for things that are proprietary to your firm and brought to life by your client experience. There is a tab for the client's FORM goals. A tab for your services checklist. A tab for assets held outside the process (that could see a liquidity event and then come into the process). A tab for archiving past meeting agendas. All essential cornerstone documents.

You can include a password wallet. It's not earth-shattering but it is dramatic, unexpected and appreciated, and it will reinforce your value at the client's home as it's placed proudly on a bookshelf. It will be updated as the relationship progresses.

**Your Tour Phase**. In the final phase of the onboarding meeting, show the client your service model to set expectations for proactive and reactive service. You provide a virtual walk-through of the client experience to let them see, touch and feel the aspects of your process physically, and then an introduction to team members, personally.

An extension on your listing of services and solutions wrapped in the 7 Pillars can connect to your forward-looking service model. This projects, over a 12-month window of time, what a client will be receiving from you. That is then tied to your service matrix, which segments the depth of service to the classification of the client. Many F4S professionals have three tiers which can be categorized by A Clients, AA Clients and AAA PLUS Clients. For example, an A client might get a 12/4/2 experience that includes 12 touches through the year through a variety of communication mediums, four scheduled phone calls and two virtual meetings. AA clients receive a 17/4/2 experience, 17 touches, four scheduled calls and two meetings – one in person and one online. AAA PLUS clients receive a 34/4/4 – 34 touches, four calls and four meetings - three virtual and one in person. This is the proactive service component that is above and beyond any reactive service needs that come up throughout the year.

## As Compared to What?

The primary goal is to be able to say "This is what you can expect from us" as you point to the service model and matrix (samples found on thebluesquaremethod. com/implementation-resources) "This is what it looks like to be our client," and "These are your days – scheduled, and of course on top of that we will react and respond to situations as they come up." This is back to validation and activation. You are reinforcing their exceptional judgment in joining your firm. You are also activating conversion because you are making it very clear why they should make an introduction – because their friends and family would also be in good hands.

Contrast is a key aspect of this approach. When you go to an outlet store, they will often put two prices on the tag – what the item is worth and what you will actually pay for it. Through contrast you feel like you've accomplished something. When you compare and contrast a client experience for a AAA PLUS client as compared to a less complex client, you are activating a sense of achievement – "this is who I am - I've arrived – I'm worthy" and an aversion to backsliding to a lower tier. They want to maintain their position. It also gives you an out. They will better understand that, if they happen to introduce, for example, an AF client – a "kid of a client" or a Family member of an AAA PLUS client – whose needs are less complex, they shouldn't expect the same level of service (and maybe not even be accepted onboard at all unless with an associate?).

From there, you can also point specifically to how you arrived at your AAA PLUS Ideal Client Profile framework and remind them about your Sounding Board value-added service. "And this is why we only accept new clients who are introduced to us, provided it's a good fit."

## The Cascading Effect

All of this culminates in your org chart and playbook. Tell them, "We take a team approach to bringing all of this to life," and show them your org chart. Show them your associates – other people with the same commitment to practice and process – who work with A and AA clients. Show them your bench strength of roles and responsibilities that make you worthy of advocacy. Then say, *"Before I walk you around to meet some of the team, the last thing I want to show you is our procedures manual. We're kind of operational nerds around here. We take a lot of pride in refining what we do, and we get many of our best ideas from our clients. So, if you think of something down the road – a tweak or enhancement – please let us know and we'll run with it and make sure it gets added."* Pow! The inside voice of the new client is in overdrive. "Seriously? I've never seen anything like this. Who are these people?" Some may even tell you that they want to adopt some of your practices into their own business. Some may ask you how you came to develop this mindset and approach. Virtually all of them will say to themselves, "Finally, this is what I've been looking for."

Walk them around, let them put faces and voices to names to depersonalize their solo connection to you, and amplify their connection to your people, practice and process. As you're heading to the door, let them know that, over the next 45 days, they will receive steady correspondence, some of it technical and time sensitive, and other items related to service and communication. Then send them on their way.

## And They're Gone

But certainly not forgotten. At this point, the key is to keep it going so that there is no "fade and forget" normally associated with the possible anticlimax of becoming a new client. Here are four simple steps:

- That day – send out the nicest thank-you card demonstrating appreciation for their time, make a FORM reference and point to how much you are looking forward to the future together. All chemistry, nothing sales-y.

- A week later – send a letter formally welcoming the client along with a listing of your bench strength roles and responsibilities and contact information.

- 2 weeks later – send their assembled onboarding kit and ask them to bring it to future meetings.

- No more than 45 days after the signing ceremony – make a first statement review call now that the dust has settled, just to check the pulse regarding clarity, comfort and confidence in their decisions.

A quick note on cards. There is a section at thebluesquaremethod.com/ implementation-resources on this topic with ideas and solutions for taking action. Just know this: No matter how sophisticated or complex your client is, no one dismisses the value of a tasteful card with a thoughtful comment or tribute written inside. When it comes to ROI on time and money, few things can rival this touch and few things are more tangibly effective at triggering an introduction.

# Chapter 9:

## ONgoing - Our Process for Total Client Engagement

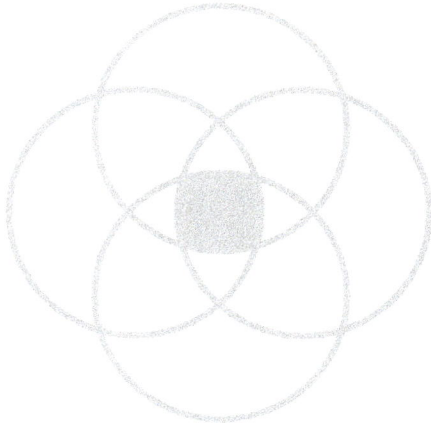

As you can gather by now, the recurring theme throughout this book is "have a process." It can seem tedious at times, but the multitude of benefits on the other side of development and deployment are worth the effort. As we've also pointed out, there are many resources waiting for you at thebluesquaremethod. com/implementation-resources so you don't have to find inspiration as you stare at blank sheets of paper trying to come up with this from scratch.

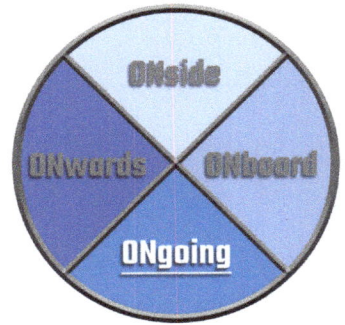

As things come together for you – identifying and addressing gaps – things fall into place like a perfect game of Tetris. You are building something different, better and proprietary. The congruency you display, by backing up your statements of "having a process" by actually having one, puts additional distance between you and the pack. Still, in the pursuit of balance, don't let yourself tip too far over into the science of building a business – remember the art. It is one thing to not "go through the motions" when it comes to best practices and standard operating procedures, you also need to combine it with your calling as a professional with a purpose. Your process gets enhanced by your standard of care. You have standards – meaning you standardize - but also you set the bar high because you care. You care, so you take good care. It's not a play on words. You care about your clients, you care about your team, and you care about the reputation, legacy and personal fulfillment that comes from a balanced life well-lived. Respectfully, you aren't heading down a path where you will die at your desk because your sole obsession was with making money. That's not what will define you. Instead, you are tracking in a direction that Tom Peters would refer to as *In Search of Excellence* – personally and professionally.

This chapter is all about Total Client Engagement which, in a nutshell, means:

- You competitor-proof your clients by insulating them from external forces.

- You gain their full empowerment as their life unfolds and needs evolve.

- You consistently convert clients into referral-generating advocates.

All of which contributes to your fulfillment, productivity and enterprise value.

Look at how all of those benefits cascade down to what you are building. Every investment of effort adds momentum towards your primary motivation – a balanced and well-rounded life.

The question you have to keep asking yourself and your team members is, "do we deserve all of that?" Based on the way we conduct ourselves, do we deserve their loyalty? Do we deserve their continual empowerment, and do we deserve their introductions? We encourage you to put a simple "respectful nag" on your desk or the wall in your boardroom. A subtle, gentle nudge on the desks of your team members or a prominent declaration on a wall that your team, clients, prospective clients and strategic partners can see, saying only this:

**de/serve**

You'll recall that the word 'deserve' stems from the Latin words "to serve." That will keep the concept of merit squarely in your mind and heart on a daily basis and can create an intriguing conversation started by your guests. They are sure to look on your wall and ask, "What's with that?" giving you the permission to explain your core code of conduct.

Again, service is brought to life in reactive forms based on your standards of care – your philosophy – and they are brought to life in proactive forms by your standard operating procedures – your process.

## Let Us Get this Straight

Part of our core mantra is that service is branding. Service is marketing. If that sounds like a generic statement to toss in for the sake of it, allow us to clarify. A while back we had a consultation with a pretty substantial F4S professional who reached out to us because on the surface his business was thriving, but deep down he was underwhelmed by the quality and quantity of referrals he was receiving. In our gap analysis, it was revealed that he had a fairly significant advertising budget. He sponsored a few worthy causes and had a promotional campaign at the chamber of commerce, both of which he was very attached to, and we weren't about to tell him to stop. It was the other 'pure' advertising "here I am" tactics that we weren't fans of - ads in local magazines and the like. Later on, he pushed back hard on things like the Intro Kit and Onboard Kit as well as some other service elements. To which we said, "Let us get this straight, you write checks for advertising to strangers without batting an eye, but you don't see the merit in these branding strategies that cost about the same amount of money. It's not even a wash. The ROI of this will be profoundly better in time." He wasn't getting it. We asked, "It obviously isn't money that's the issue, is it the work and hassle factor that is required to get these deployed that is bothering you?" To which he replied, "Look, my clients see the ads, they tell me they see them so they're obviously working."

This prompted us to have a very respectful fire-side chat about the difference between name recognition and the quantitative impact from branding. The fact that they saw the ads isn't the point. How did the ad make them feel and what action did the ad prompt them to take? Do the ads drive referrals, or do they make people wonder why you still have to do advertising? Do the ads increase the awareness of professional scarcity and contrast, or do they undermine them?

## Stealth Marketing

Service is subtle, underground business development that motivates people to appreciate you more, to engage with you more and to share you with more people. Nothing is more persuasive than the nudge from a friend who clearly has conviction about something or someone. Marketing doesn't do that. Branding and service does.

## Reactive Service

Clients of a business generally call with a service need, and with an expectation of just having that need met. Simply addressing that need in and of itself – validation through execution – is often the totality of the experience. Nothing extraordinary happens, they just get it taken care of and they go back to live their life. This is not an indelibly memorable experience and nothing much to talk about with someone they know.

Many service professionals have a "just in time" mindset when it comes to their client interactions. When you visit a doctor, you're sitting in the exam room and the door opens. The doctor reaches for the chart on the back of the door, and you realize it's at that moment that he or she starts thinking about you and your situation in real time – just in time – without any preparation. They stop thinking about you at the end of the meeting when the chart goes back up on the door, and they head to the next room. It's a transaction, and, fair enough, you had a need. It was addressed in some form and off everyone goes, but how memorable is it when you get a surprise phone call the next day following up to see if everything is OK and in order? It's not a big ask, but it stands out. Maybe they don't see the need, and maybe you don't expect it, so no harm, no foul - but how did we get here – to the point where basic is now the high-water mark?

Imagine you walk into a dentist's office for your appointment, work through their experience for a cleaning with the hygienist and a routine checkup and then, toward the end, the dentist walks in and makes an appearance. They get briefed by the team, do a quick look around, perhaps address an issue, but seems a bit rushed and a bit distant, because you know they are already thinking about the next patient in the next chair. Yes, dentists have a well-oiled, process-driven machine, but how much more powerful is it when the dentist walks in and makes a reference to something you discussed in your last visit – unrelated to your teeth? What if the office sent you a nice card – not one with their logo on it but a beautiful handwritten art card - saying it was nice to see you after your visit? All of that supplements the exceptional technical ability you received.

Contrast that to a meeting with a lawyer, accountant or consultant who seems to be over-explaining something, and it occurs to you that maybe they are dragging things out a bit because they are clock-watching to drive their billable hours. Imagine, instead, that you're meeting with a professional who seems incredibly prepared and process-driven, working through their agenda with a high tempo, and they round it all out with authentic interest in your other FORM related issues. Imagine they send an email follow-up, with a summary of the technical aspects, as well as a reference to non-business-related interests, along with, say, a link to a pickle ball tutorial site (Had to work it in somewhere).

The point being this: You care enough to go above and beyond your technical delivery and core competency when you respond to a service need and provide an experience that is memorable and worthy of telling others about.

## Proactive Service

This is where you elevate how you are perceived and described, while adding undeniable worthiness to your goal of deserving Total Client Engagement. It's how you serve a client in a way that's unexpected by the client, and better than anyone else trying to lure them away - and we all know many are attempting that every day.

An important distinction with proactive service is that it has to be of value. We've all been on the receiving end of proactive service that was either generic or, worse, pandering. In the early 2020s you might have said to yourself, "Do I really need to receive another email on how to wash my hands properly?" (Or perhaps we've been doing it wrong all these years?) There is a lot of trite and therefore disposable messaging floating around that's cloaked in an intention of service and value, but which is just going through the motions – and ultimately is just noise.

Discernment, common sense and effort are required, otherwise you run the risk of actually turning someone off with what they perceive to be a dumbed-down message.

## Thematic Communication

A big part of your client experience and service model will be proactive communication, which can be categorized in three primary points:

- Where your industry is going in terms of ideas and innovation.

- Where your market is going in terms of trends and patterns.

- Where your clients are going in terms of their interests and ambitions.

Ask yourself, will this be of interest to my addressable audiences, or do they hire me to make this go away? When you think of an investment, you consider Return ON Investment, meaning the upside opportunity, and you think of Return OF Investment, meaning the downside risk.

When you invest your time in service through communication and content, there is an incremental force that builds. Recipients either look forward to it because they got value from your previous installments, or they start to dread it because they received no value from your earlier efforts. Dread leads to dismissing and opting out. Anticipating leads to a gradual build of appreciation that can create a reaction: Loyalty, empowerment and conversion.

## A Case in Point

One of the best examples you will see of a steady stream of thematic communication service - that also brings value to strategic partners and even prospective clients on the fence - is Brian Wesbury's *Monday Morning Outlook* blog. Once a week, he and his team – a deep bench of professionals – send a concise one-pager providing "an antidote to conventional wisdom." Savvy thought leaders know that ongoing research, observations and ideas should not reside solely in their heads as knowledge. They should be converted to content that can be shared, which results in recipient feedback that can be assessed. You don't have to be as frequent as weekly, initially. The barometer of effectiveness is not tied to frequency – it's tied to anticipation and appreciation. Part of that is tied to the quality of the information, part of it is tied to the brevity and consistency of the message. Weekly, monthly, quarterly – set your rotation and stick with it.

When it comes to subject matter for your clients, think beyond your technical prowess. Be panoramic. Get into the weeds when necessary, but give it context too. Reference how it can be of impact and relevance. Consider a story related to how someone has acted, or can act, on it. Add elements of FORM. Family health and wellness insights, Occupational wins and story lines, Recreational hobbies and interests. All rounded out by insights and observations around your core Message that are timely and actionable.

## Getting Granular

Let's shift from high level intention to deep implementation. Let's work backwards by looking at a service model that is shaped for your very best clients – your 25 or so AAA PLUS clients and then go from there. (Who knows, in time this might serve you so well that you alter your business to only have 25 clients – but hold that thought – more on that later.)

As a sample, your most deserving AAA PLUS clients could receive as many as 34 proactive touchpoints throughout the year:

- 26 scheduled distributed communications

- 4 scheduled call rotation phone communications

- 4 scheduled meetings – 3 virtual and I in person

Now you might be thinking that seems intense and maybe even excessive. With an automated process it's easy, and you can't over-serve if the communication is of value.

The most common activities are:

- Monthly email blog with insights, observations, commentary and spotlights.

- Greeting cards for birthday, Thanksgiving and special occasions.

- Invitations to events, webinars and non-business-related themed gatherings.

- Articles of Interest tied to FORM on paper and digital third-party content and links.

That could be as many as 20 touches from those four bullets as a starting point. Updates on your people, practice and process can be added, and the rest is rounded out by your proactive communications regarding appointment scheduling and for technical issues, renewals, changes and required actions. They all count and they all matter, and it ensures that your favorite clients don't go very long without hearing from you in a diverse manner. Diversity is the operative word. Adding variety to your communication keeps things fresh. Kevin Bishopp and Jackie Wilke, the creators of the *Insights and Innovation Blog*, use a great analogy to describe multichannel communication. When you listen to music on an AM radio station and then listen to it on an FM or satellite stereo system, the difference is dramatic. It's even more so when you listen to surround sound. It envelopes you and prompts you to anticipate and pay attention to where the sounds are going to come from. You're more engaged and attentive to the signal.

## Look Both Ways

You don't need 34 touches out of the gate, by the way. You may reach that in time, but head in that direction initially. At the same time, you have to populate your AA, A (and beyond) models and matrices to build it out. It's a great exercise and you will feel accomplished when it's all in place.

## You Can't Dis-Card a Beautiful Card

You already know to keep the digital cards to a minimum, or you've eliminated them entirely. You probably also know that we are big fans of Lavish Cards – a company that not only offers a concierge level of service, advice and fulfillment of cards, but also has a portfolio of cards that have incredible impact and shelf-life. From symbols to support your personal brand, to personalization ideas like sending a holiday card targeted to lesser-known occasions that are meaningful to the client, Lavish Cards is next-level in terms of their track record and client feedback. We provide some details in the resource chapter.

## Scheduled Calls

Still the most impactful proactive service driver, and one that has endured after all these years, is the call rotation. A scheduled reach-out – where you may just leave a voice mail – that is recurring through a rotation cycle of your choosing. Generally, every 90 days is ideal. These calls are nothing earth shattering, there's no agenda to provide a profound insight or to push a product or action – you are just touching base. "Hey, just thinking about you. Wanted to say hello. How are the golf lessons going?" Whether they pick up or you leave a message, just be upbeat, optimistic and make a reference to something FORM-related going in their life. If you've ever been on the receiving end of this approach, you've personally felt the rejuvenation of the relationship immediately.

It takes time. Time needs to be carved out and allocated to your schedule, and it takes time to have any impact. It's easy to do, and of course it's easier not to do, but nothing you do from a value-added service perspective could ever supersede it. Some F4S professionals push back on us, saying that their clients "are so beyond that," all of which is squashed when we ask them to test it for just 90 days. "Say no more. The process is in place. I get it," is often the response we get after three months.

Additionally, this sets you in the mode of being perpetually scheduled and process-driven. The primary reason why an affluent client fires a F4S professional is because the experience was random and unscheduled - the relationship dynamics rarely went beyond technical deliverables, and in the absence of FORM, the chemistry and relationship was shallow.

## Never Eat Alone

Many F4S professionals go above and beyond in the face-to-face interactions that are more about relationship management than business development. Despite the bedlam of the early 2020s that temporarily derailed this kind of initiative, this is a tremendous habit and ritual to consider. Keith Farazzi's book *Never Eat Alone* makes a strong case for dining with relationships. Some go so far as to adopt 3-2-1 lift-off approach. This equates to three breakfasts, two lunches and one dinner per week with clients, partners, and team members - and even good prospective clients. That's a significant commitment, but as many would say, I've got to eat anyway and it will do no harm. Tricks of that trade include focusing on breakfasts, because they are generally brief, inexpensive and less likely to be canceled. Establish a restaurant that is dependable, and buy a monthly credit in advance, so there is no distracting payment at the end – and tip massively. Arranging a box of muffins or sandwiches for the business owner, client or strategic partner to take back to their team is a nice touch.

## Your VAST Network Matrix

Speaking of strategic partners, an initial matrix to consider adopting for your VAST Network community is 6-2-1. Six scheduled touches, two scheduled calls and one face-to-face dining meeting per year. This is, of course, above and beyond the technical collaborative work you do together to address a client issue. As the relationship flourishes, and they demonstrate a level of buy-in and engagement, you may move them all the way up to a AAA-PLUS level experience for exceptional VAST members.

## An Unintended Consequence

Occasionally, an F4S professional is so inspired by the narrowcasting to a few (rather than broadcasting to the many) mindset that they reduce their client counts dramatically. Sometimes it's to grow up-market, sometimes it's just about simplicity. It's always gradually, respectfully and professionally done, but we've seen F4S professionals go from 300 clients down to 100 clients and then down to 25, without drastically impacting the bottom line along the way, and always propelling the professional towards their own Blue Square. Sometimes we get the call or the email, "Thanks a lot! I reduced my client count to a number I loved, went deep with them and got into a groove and now I'm back up to 50 perfect clients through referrals, and now I have to work hard again!" We know they're (mostly) kidding, but those are the potential perils of professional scarcity and professional contrast. A nice problem to have, to be sure.

## The Content Conundrum

We've made the case that your content must be brief, valuable and incremental. You can make it available to everyone in your sphere, and encourage those people to push it to others who they feel would find it to be of interest. If your content is solid, you generally don't even need to ask for the push. It happens organically. Considering the signal to noise ratio, you have to be realistic. There is a lot of content competing for attention. We had an exchange with one F4S professional who wrote a book that he considered as a credibility Trojan horse that he would offer to the world for free, but it was an out-of-the-blue initiative, with no foundational or promotional build leading up to it. Some of his clients asked for a copy, but even those numbers were lackluster. He then took it to LinkedIn and other platforms and started pounding away on his offer of a free book on connection invites to strangers. He stopped out of frustration because it all landed with a thud of virtually no engagement. "I don't understand it, it's a free book!" He said somewhat incredulously.

We said to him, "What did you expect? How much is a free book worth to someone who doesn't know you? Have you ever seen the discontinued bin at a bookstore overflowing with .99 cent books collecting dust? There is no trust, no one endorsing you or recommending the book with 5-star ratings, and maybe the unspoken objection is that they feel you will spring a sales trap if they do request it. It goes beyond 'what's the catch?' A book requires an investment of time. Busy people rarely make an unknown entity a priority." A bit harsh, but you have to consider the perspective and the interpretations of the people on the other side of your offer.

In the world of wastewater (a strange segue), there is a saying, "The solution to pollution is dilution." Think about that in terms of the absorption of your message. Dilute it by breaking it down and sending it out in a stream over time, to sequentially build a case for your thought leadership. It's tough to burst out of the blocks with a blast. When Mount Etna in Sicily erupted not long ago, it belched more pollution into the atmosphere than all the cars and factories do in the world in an entire year. Now, with the help of trees and other factors, the world seemed to absorb it pretty well, but with you, you have to take the long view, chipping away and building a following of people who choose your content over something else. (By the way, we're not making light of pollution, but the innovations and awareness led by the next generation, including Naomi Seibt and Morgan Vague, are impressive and worthy of our attention. If you want to be jarred about an unmet need out there that has to be addressed, look no further than at a picture of a cross-section of a barrel containing nuclear waste. The people who figure that one out will deserve a Nobel Prize.)

## Events as a Service

We spoke earlier about how client and partner events – both in-person and virtual – can be very engaging and effective touch-points. Having a subject matter expert (whether yourself or a third party) conduct a presentation on a topical issue will resonate with some. Having a sommelier do a virtual wine tasting for a small group of clients (who like wine) can be well received. Even remotely, you can arrange to have four small bottles delivered to a client's home and have the event delivered over a virtual platform. It's not quite the same thing, but it's still not bad, and it's less expensive because you needn't deal with venue, taxi and other costs. When it comes to virtual events, sending food is always an added bonus that provides an ROI.

For physical events, consider being a Conscious Collaborative Company, which means you engage in community-minded events for the SPCA, the Food Bank or other local not-for-profits, along with partners and clients. Take lots of pictures of your team chipping in to help, and circulate the photos. Advertisers will tell you that faces and puppies in content and promotions stop people in their tracks, but keep it real. We are in an era where selfies are part of the culture, but many are growing weary of the posing and staging. It's the pure and authentic that stands out and gains traction. (And what's with the food pictures? Do we need a picture of someone else's Thanksgiving dinner – aren't we all eating the same thing at that time?)

### Family Meetings and PIDA

Many F4S professionals now offer an online family meeting to discuss topics such as family investment legacy, continuity and succession, dynastic insights and examples (good and bad) and emerging trends (think blockchain). A solid agenda with interesting content is a must. Ensure there is an opportunity for others in a family - who you may only know by name - to ask questions. This sort of meeting is a proven winner. There are some excellent videos and books to help you give this some structure.

### Personal Interview with Dad's Advisor

Don't be surprised if a few highly-motivated offspring of your client chime in and show an openness for a deeper dive on a one-to-one basis, albeit online. It's an opportunity to relay some of your favorite chestnuts and ideas. "If your outflow exceeds your income, your upkeep will become your downfall," is a favorite that can only be enhanced with a quality Dad joke about the difference between tax evasion and tax avoidance (it's about seven years). You can draw a comparison between NFTs and Tulip Mania – the most famous market bubble from the mid 1600's – to prompt an interesting conversation about human nature and what "it's different this time" really means. You're not trying to take a position on something, but to make someone think critically.

We'll talk about the mentor-protégé dynamic more in The Torch chapter, but we hope you embrace the notion of being available to support the next generation on some of the fundamental laws of life. The Walter Mischel study from years ago, where he offered kids one treat now or two treats later spoke volumes about the concept of delayed gratification. Paying yourself first, diversified investing, conversations about grit and adversity, stories about the difference between knowledge and wisdom, critical thinking and so much more can be beneficial to both of you.

## A Multitude of Benefits

Going through this exercise to blueprint your service tools and deliverables will benefit your team, impact your ability to differentiate your value for prospective clients and strategic partners, but most of all, will revitalize your existing client relationships.

When you reframe your long-term clients, and you show them your refined and elevated approach – even if it's a work in progress – you'll be amazed at their enthusiasm. When you go from vapor to paper by supplementing your digital tools with tangible things, you'll see them look at your IP deeply and with respect. When you remove the mystery of your complete value (watching out for the iceberg effect), be prepared for a client to say, "Finally! I actually understand what you do!"

## And Finally, Why Don't They Refer?

Everything we've discussed to this point will make you undeniably more refer-able, but there is one more piece that needs to be put into place to convert referability into a steady stream of good quality introductions: Communication. You must always position and articulate the concept of an introduction as a service you are providing, not as a tactic to drive your business.

## The Anatomy of a Referral

On a macro level, you have to get clear on the mechanics and motivations of CONSISTENT referrals. Start by asking yourself two questions:

- Why don't they?

- Why should they?

Most of your clients don't "go there" because they are unclear of how it looks to get involved in someone's life and potentially put their own reputation on the line. They are undermined by a subconscious "no good deed goes unpunished" mindset, so they don't get involved, even when the opportunity is presented. It's not that they're unconvinced or unmotivated, there is just some uncertainty about referring, so they don't. Some may be out there singing your praises and endorsing you because you are dependable, but it sputters out quickly when it lands in the friend's mind. Unless and until a client or partner is crystal clear about how it will reflect on them and the friend, there's a blockage.

There is a nurture/nature dynamic at play. With some people, you don't have to overthink it. They are just wired to be "power brokers." They like to come through for people and they are on the lookout to make connections. You can nurture it with others. It doesn't have to be a fluke.

Look at the word coincidence – stemming from the word coincide – a need a friend has, that aligns and coincides with the confidence a client has for your value – the friend bared his or her soul, the conversation prompted an instant thought of you, and boom – an incredible coincidence of wants and value. Your client wants his or her friend to be taken care of and wants them to be in good hands. Your client also wants you to thrive, but in that order, not the other way around. It's not because of a sense of obligation to you. It's about doing a friend a solid.

## Lead with Purpose

It all has to be built on a rock-solid foundation of service. You have to position the concept of speaking to a friend of a client as a service you are providing to the client - without any expectation that it may lead to business. The client has to then, in turn, view it as doing a friend a disservice by not lighting the path to you – and that is the nexus of advocacy. It feels just as good to come through for someone as it does to be taken care of, and as it does to attract new clients to your business. Win/win/win.

Pure and simple – it's framed in purpose and process:

Step 1 – define the what and why

Step 2 – define the who and how

## What and Why

It's an introduction, not a referral. Take the word referral out of your language and focus more on the activity rather than implied productivity. Then, tell people why you do it. It's rooted in your sense of purpose. Helping people is why you chose this profession, and it's easily the most fulfilling part of it. Punctuate that by saying, "*if you ever happen to introduce someone to me, they do not need to become a client to take advantage of this service. If they are important to you, they are important to me.*"

That form of professional scarcity and stewardship is also your bridge to clarifying who you're suited for.

## Who and How

Be sure to tell the world who they should introduce – you'll talk to anyone who is important to the client – but you only accept new clients who are introduced provided it's a good fit. Describe your ideal client based on AAA PLUS and remind them that you are all things to some people, rather than the other way around.

Communication on who is important for many reasons. By sticking to your defined approach, you've added a circuit breaker that prevents you from going beyond your capacity. However, it needs to be reinforced, because occasionally you might have a client tell you, "I was thinking about introducing my friend, but I don't think he's big enough for you." Which might seem like a sensible interpretation and reaction, until you find out that the friend has a successful business and a variety of needs that would, at least on the surface, suggest an alignment of interests. Professional scarcity can be a double-edged sword. If that ever happens, remind them first of the PLUS component – that the primary factor of fit is that they are People Like US. Secondly, remind clients that an introduction to be a sounding board for a friend is not tied to "how big they are," and then let the process figure the rest out.

Now, we reach the pivot to outlining for a client "how to get things rolling."

*"There is a process in place that my clients use to make an introduction. If you feel compelled to steer someone my way, step one is to give me a call. Tell me about your friend and get the wheels in motion. I'll take it from there. I'll reach out and have an initial chat. There is no expectation it needs to go any further than that. I'm led by them. If they want to meet, I'll schedule some time and send out my introductory kit so that they can learn a little about my people, my practice and my process in advance, and then we can go from there, and you can hold me accountable that this will be a good use of their time."*

Provide specifics in terms of what will happen, and then instructions for the actions they can take. Based on your compliance realities, you can encourage an introductory text or email, or even a direct message on social media. Whatever the method, clarify the process precisely. When they are well coached, they will know to be on the lookout for triggering events, and know how to bridge their friends' dissatisfaction with an easy-to-understand statement – "My guy works with business owners and he knows his way around liquidity events like no other, I can make an introduction."

Remember: Advocates call you directly on behalf of a friend. Clients endorse you and tell their friends to call you, and you know how that generally works out.

## "Where is the Puck Going?"

Walter Gretzky, the ultimate hockey dad, gave his sons that invaluable advice many years ago. Be sure to adopt the same mindset. Pay close attention to where the relationship is going. Steer it and shape it with great service and great stories about the people you have met through introductions, and the problems you've solved. Be patient and keep refining.

We happened to be in an office with a client of ours in Dallas a while back. He was driving his business nicely and in the right direction. As we were chatting, his phone kept buzzing. So he picked it up and then smiled. He told us that it was a client texting him to say that he told a good friend to call him. He was giving his F4S professional a heads up, but also probably looking for a bit of an "atta boy." We said, "hey good stuff, more proof that you're referable." To which he replied, "Oh yeah, watch this," and he started reading his text response to his client as he was writing it.

"Thanks so much for waving our flag. Means the world to us, and in fact puts us on cloud nine, but keep in mind, there is a process in place. Next time, it's best if you call me directly and make the introduction, instead of telling your friend to call me. That way, it's far more likely that we'll connect, and I will be able to get your friend the help he needs." There was a long pause and then another buzz, to which the budding advocate wrote, "Yeah, my bad. I forgot. I'm on it. I'll tell him that I'll get it rolling." That's a perfect example of staying consistent, resetting perceptions by communicating clearly and coaching clients on how to be advocates for their friends and for you.

## Talk to Me

One last point about communication: Train yourself to think and talk out loud so that clients always know where they stand, and where they are in your process. Take nothing for granted. They crave clarity. Don't misinterpret this, we're not referring to information overload, just clarity on where they are in the progression.

Think of it this way; you are at the dentist for a root canal. You know the team is good, and they know they're good. You have massive anxiety for the procedure, but it has to be done. You're well under way, and amidst all of the multi-sensory aspects of noise, smells and sensations, you start to wonder, how much longer is this going to take? You start grabbing the chair firmly, your toes start to curl. You're now bracing yourself for a slip, a mistake or some bad news.

Your mouth is full and you can't talk so you pull out your phone and start texting. You ignore the hygienist's repeated pleas as she tells you that "you can't use your phone in here" and you simply hold it up so they can read your message, "Are we almost done?" To which they all in unison say, "Oh for sure, you're doing great and we're going to wrap up soon." Relieved but still agitated, you say to yourself, why did it have to come to that? Just tell me where I am and how close I am to the finish line.

The moral of the story is, don't wait to be asked. Be proactive. Ask your clients at the end of an encounter if they have suggestions for how their interpretation and understanding for that segment of your process could be enhanced. Avoid activating thoughts of uncertainty and you will activate a more loyal client who will want to share their appreciation for your value with others.

On thebluesquaremethod.com/implementation-resources, there is an entire resource with scripting and positioning to assist you in bringing this to life and customizing it to suit your own style and preferences.

# Chapter 10:

*ONwards - Our Process for
Reacting to Moments of Truth*

The core premise of the ONwards quadrant is to connect the aspect of reactive service – the yin – to the yang of proactive service. You already know that a process-driven approach to proactive service, combined with a philosophy of elevated reactive service, will set you apart. Proactive service speaks to your desire to create consistency and dependability. Clients know they can count on you – for themselves and for the people they introduce to you. It creates an ongoing recognition for your value that is ever-present.

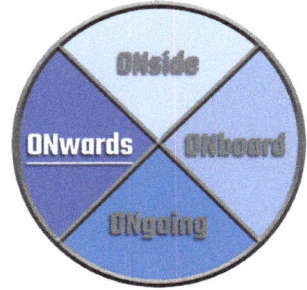

## In Your Sleep – but Wide Awake

From an operations perspective, a process-driven approach to service is repeatable – dependably – by anyone that embraces it. You and your team could do it in your sleep. It's "set it and forget it." Examine the word forget closely. Sometimes there is an unintended consequence to habits, rituals and processes. They can put you in a trance. They are so automatic that we can check out to some degree. If you have ever left the house in the morning and headed to work wondering, "Did I close the garage door? Did I turn off the iron?" and as you pull into the parking lot you thought to yourself, "How did I even get here?" It's a routine that you have gone through hundreds of times with varying degrees of consciousness.

When you connect your process to a philosophy of reactive service, it means that when a situation arises, you move heaven and earth to respond. Even just that sense of urgency and resolve is impactful, and look what it does: You get a call from a friend in a panic, because one of their kids had a wisdom teeth eruption. Your friend asks who you know that is exceptional. Being able to relate because you've been there, you insist – actually insist, that it's a non-option – that they contact your dentist. In fact, you offer to call on their behalf, and not just because of the skill set at that office, but because of how they responded during your own emergency, and the bed-side manner afterward. Your friend's child is in pain and you want to help it go away. It's more about the friend than trying to help the dentist hit her quota for the month, and when the dentist's office figures out that the friend was referred by you, they will make it a priority to find a slot. That is how it's done. The advocacy loop closes because of enhanced merit.

## Community = Productivity

Back to that standard of care for a moment. Business is about far more than just tactics and economics, it is also about how you interact with people. Marketers are notorious for placing too much emphasis on the inanimate and mechanical aspects of business development. Talking about traffic, pipelines, views, click-throughs, followers and other metrics – which do have their place - but it has to include the human component. It's not about how many followers you have on social media, it's about the degree of their engagement. They're not following you, they want to engage with you and your value, to consume it to their benefit and share it when inspired.

So think about the community of your inner circle and the degree to which you've created an environment where you all have each other's backs. The stories where a community of farmers build a new barn for a neighbor who lost his in a fire are very inspiring. The stories of farmers that show up at a foreclosure auction, to ensure that only the original owner had the winning bid after their run-in with the bank, is the stuff of legend.

## Make the World Stop

The bottom line is this: Moments of truth, milestones and critical life events occur in the lives of the people in your inner circle. What is your philosophy and process for responding to them? These can be anticipated events that have built up over time, or they can be lightning strikes out of the blue.

The best practice is that you have a philosophy that says you will act, and you have a process that means you aren't scrambling when you do.

A good football team will have a set of clearly defined plays that they will practice repeatedly, so that when it's go-time, the reflexes are in place. Occasionally, the quarterback will see something on the other side of the ball that concerns him, so he calls an audible and the team shifts to a new play immediately.

Your proactive services are your set plays, and they are as consistent as the waves rolling up on the beach. Your waves of service may be steady over time because of your process, but then there is a random event – an outlier – like a rogue wave that gets your attention.

## Don't Bury the Lead

On a slow day, a newscaster will cover a blend of pre-formulated human-interest stories, along with coverage of cats being rescued from trees. Notwithstanding their tendency to sensationalize things at times (sarcasm intended) when a big story is uncovered, it is breaking news. Voices are louder, the tone is firmer, and intensity is dialed up to match (or occasionally exceed) the severity of the event. You get the point. Some events happen in the lives of your clients that warrant your response. This is how the best in business think and conduct themselves. Remember, Think and Grow Rich speaks to the mindset of the very best. There is an old saying, "Millionaires will occasionally invite a billionaire to speak with them to get inside their head. To know how they think." (There is another saying, "millionaires don't believe in psychics but billionaires do" – not entirely sure what to make of that one yet?)

Not only can a moment of truth, milestone or critical life event impact your client, it can also impact your professional relationship, sometimes even rendering your current plan obsolete. It can have an emotional impact as well as a tactical one.

## Expectation Management

In marketing, the hope is that when you send out a message it will be received. You advertise and hope it drives business. That's how it's supposed to work. When you trigger a service process, you hope you will get a response. We just want you to expand your thinking and outlook a bit, to take this is into consideration; Look for a response, but don't expect one.

The only thing that is different is that you are in a place of Zen. You are at peace with the response to any form of marketing or service. Not everyone agrees with this and that's fine, but the same rules that apply to marketing can hold true to your extraordinary efforts at service. You expect a response, but you don't always get what you were hoping for, and sometimes nothing at all. Sometimes the recipient forgets, or they got distracted or maybe they are just overwhelmed. In the same way you don't donate to a charity for the praise, you don't go above and beyond for the accolades. It's your own standards and decorum that drive it, not the potential feedback.

## Situational Awareness

In high-intensity team sports, we are often advised to keep our head on a swivel. Always alert, ready to adjust, and not to be caught napping. Being a F4S professional is a noble undertaking. You cast a significant shadow on people and their families, navigating them through incredible turbulence and uncertainty, and you keep delivering. There can be an emotional toll, as well. In one week, you can have a client tell you that they just attended their best friend's funeral, another tells you their kid was accepted to an incredible school, and then another tell you their spouse has cancer, and yet another tells you that they got an offer on their business that was way, way over the fences.

Sometimes it's a joyous occasion worth celebrating and responding. Sometimes it's extremely somber and heavy. Sometimes, it's somewhere in between.

The first thing to consider as a response is this, "I'm honored that they would share that with me." Pause and absorb that. Just because it often happens that someone would include you in their celebration or setback, doesn't mean it's not an absolutely big deal, and that you shouldn't take action accordingly. It speaks volumes when you are one of the first calls they make.

The second thing to consider is, "How will I respond?"

There is a bit of a Goldilocks approach to consider with your response, a spectrum of what is "just right" for the situation.

- A call and a card.

- A call and a card and a book.

- A call and a card and a gift.

As a team, sit down and define your philosophy on the concept. Define the process and the budget you will apply. Team and corporate culture is not mandated, it is created and magnified by the buy-in and willingness to implement. Document scenarios, go-to vendors, mini-max your inventory for cards, and reference the importance of applying FORM when responding to moments of truth, then record everything in your playbook.

## When the News is Good

When a client has a positive achievement or milestone, at a minimum, make a call to celebrate with them and send a card with heartfelt congratulations. Use the 24-hour rule on the message. Write it down, circulate it with team members, and on the following day take their input into consideration, as well as your own evolved modifications. Only then do you carefully transfer it to the card – carefully, for the sake of legibility.

In addition to celebrating, this win may mean recalibrating the client's plan with you. You can mention that, as part of the process, you will make yourself available for a dedicated Strategy and Tactical Meeting to address these new issues.

When it comes to books, focus on physical books, not audio or digital books. For impact, defer to FORM to supplement the shelf life that comes from receiving it, holding it in their hands, reading it, and then keeping it on display.

On thebluesquaremethod.com/implementation-resources, there is a Top 10 List of perfect books for the most common occasions, as well as a deeper dive that includes the books we've referenced throughout, as well as a few others. The books on those lists will either strike you as being perfect for responding to a moment of truth, or they will prompt you to come up with your own idea based on what you know about the client.

## Gifts

The idea that has the biggest impact, and is the easiest to fulfill, is a gift basket. It's turnkey, fast and dependable. If you have ever been on the receiving end of a quality basket, you might have said to yourself: "Wow!" and "How?" 'Wow,' meaning it had so much drama and impact. 'How,' meaning how did it get here so fast?

The beauty of gift baskets is they are shared – handed around like a trophy with co-workers at the office or with family members at home – sparking conversations about "Who sent you that?" Incidentally, always ensure there is a "keeper" of some kind in the basket – something they will retain beyond the basket itself. That will add shelf life to the impact. Corkscrews, coasters and wine stoppers are just a few ideas for memorializing an event for the ages.

You don't have to get into the gift giving business, and you don't need to break the bank when it comes to gifting. Just be thoughtful, targeted (think FORM) and timely. Here are some suggestions:

## Family

When a child is accepted to a university, go online and find a unique item (search – name of university - swag.) Perhaps a hat or sweatshirt for the parents, too?

When there is a wedding, a Tiffany frame might not be on the registry, but that blue box and ribbon will always be appreciated.

When there is a new baby, a silver coin in the birth year is timeless – because it's God's money paying tribute to God's ultimate gift.

When someone downsizes, a framed artisan-rendered picture of their family home might cause a tear or two.

When someone buys a second home, perhaps a coffee table book of the area.

## Occupation

When someone retires after hitting their number, perhaps encourage and offer to co-sponsor the retirement party.

When someone sells their business after getting their number, a framed picture of a mountain symbolizing the achievement.

When a client or VAST Partner is heading into their busy season, a gift basket for their team to help offset the chaos is appreciated.

## Recreation

When someone arranges for a family reunion, say "I want pictures." They will send a few as the trip is happening. You can have one printed and framed and maybe even treated by a rendering app to add artistic impact.

## Message

When someone celebrates a milestone anniversary with you, perhaps have lunch or dinner to mark the occasion. Again, it's not about the right or wrong idea, it's about what's right in your view and that you took action.

## When the News is Bad

The highest form of emotional intelligence is how you help someone who just shared news with you that was not so great and caused them grief. You might know someone who is almost angelic in how they cushion and absorb someone else's pain, not by giving advice or an opinion. Avoid things like, "you're only given what you can handle," or "it can only make you stronger," or especially making it about yourself and the time you had your own setback. (Dads and their "back in my day" speeches are a different topic for another book.) No, these people have a special gift for just listening intently, offering kind condolences and gentle offers to help. One of the most authentic forms of unsolicited comfort ever offered in a moment of a severe setback is "We are here for you. No one expects you to get through this on your own."

The "call and a card" for this type of situation are appropriate but, if able, your presence would be a tremendous supplement to sending them anything. After the call or visit, a card with a sunset or butterfly, along with a simple message about what awaits us in the future:

*"You don't have a soul. You are a soul. You have a body."* – CS Lewis

The early 2020s caused so many disruptions and fractures. Often lost in all of that were the many people who were part of the collateral damage. Surgeries missed. Last visits missed. Funerals missed. People forgotten about and slipping through the massive gaps in the social safety net, because so many were prohibited by, or distracted by, the primary story line. It's just a reminder to pop our heads up occasionally, to look around at who gets caught up in the wakes and undertow of life, and determine if there is an action we can take in turn.

By the way, you wouldn't be the first F4S professional to add a funeral director into your VAST Network. When people are in the fog of grief, it's indelicate to say, "I know a guy," but powerful when you say, "Do you have someone who can take care of the arrangements? Because if not, I do."

A passing of someone in the life of your client can be devastating, to say the least. Be mindful of the other less severe, but still painful, gut-punches that are critical life events worthy of your attention. Many people mean well but their intent diminishes - but not yours.

For example, you have a client heading into surgery. They're putting on a brave face but you can tell they're nervous. Perhaps a bundle of magazines (yes, they are still a thing) around themes of interest, or a gift basket to the hospital for their recovery time.

You have a client who has had a personal or professional setback. Not life and death level, but perhaps depressing or demoralizing. If it's not too severe, perhaps a shout-out message from a favorite sports figure or celebrity on Cameo. It generally gets a laugh and jolt of energy. If it's a bit of a darker episode, again a call and a card, and perhaps an offer for lunch, or a hike (or ax-throwing to blow off steam?)

If you ever have someone in your sphere lose a pet, a framed picture is cherished – especially if it's artistically curated through a renderer like *Night Café* or *Paint Your Life*.

Take a moment to envision what it would be like to be on the receiving end of a meaningful tribute or acknowledgment of something occurring in your life. Think of the impact, and think of the shelf life. Yes, a dinner is appreciated and memorable as an experience, but the steak is savored right up to the point that dessert arrives. Something personal and tangible can create a different response. Imagine the wife of your best client saying to her husband, "It's beautiful and very touching, but how did they know?" To which he replies, "It's their job to know."

## Recurring Moments of Truth

Some things straddle ongoing service and moments of truth service. Onboarding a new client and responding to a rainmaker when they make an introduction should be standardized, but celebrated, by the team as profound KPIs. This is a recurring moment of truth. That you get to impact another new family, and that you were recognized with such a compliment and entrusted with such a powerful responsibility, warrants that the world stop, the moment gets savored, and defined actions are taken.

## Your Own Moments of Truth

As we prepare to segue to team dynamics, let us add that you have your own moments of truth that will occur, and how you respond to them reflects powerfully on your leadership qualities.

**When there is a service hiccup** – when your process "jumps the tracks" and client service suffers, it is essential (after discussing with the team) to call the client to: a) thank them for pointing it out, b) apologize and own it, c) embrace how you hate the thought of them being inconvenienced and d) explain what you intend to do to remedy the situation.

No excuses, no rationalizing and nobody under the bus. Just a sincere response that shows how seriously you take this, and how you always strive to do better. It's not about over-reacting or under-reacting, or whether the client is taking out their bad day on you. They had a bad experience and there is a learning opportunity to be taken away from that.

**You lose a client** – we touched on this in an earlier chapter, but it bears repeating. Thank them for the jolt. Ask them why they left. Tell them what you're going to do about it and do everything to leave the door open.

**You're at the end of your rope** – a client unloads on a team member and is way out of line. Notwithstanding the benefit-of-the-doubt considerations and understanding all sides, generally a person who does that has the likability of athlete's foot and should be –respectfully – disassociated from. You've probably tolerated them to a degree, up until now anyway, but in the spirit of team harmony and personal standards, a professional exit is in order.

Calm seas never produced a skilled sailor. Epictetus, in ancient Greece, said, "Circumstances don't make the man, they only reveal him to himself." He also said, "We must ever bear in mind—that apart from the will, there is nothing good or bad, and that we must not try to anticipate or to direct events, but merely to accept them with intelligence." Considering the era he was in when he formulated those views makes them that much more compelling when it comes to addressing life's ups and downs.

# Chapter 11:

## *Bench Strength -*
## *Our Process for Team Development*

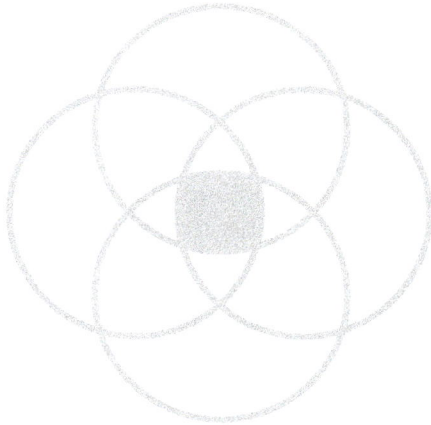

A profound African proverb suggests that if we want to go fast, we should go alone. If we want to go far, we should go together. There is so much to like about that premise, including the use of the word "go." When your business-building momentum kicks in, you can decide how far you want to go with it. If you decide to keep going, your next step is to pop the hood and study the concept of team dynamics. Those who take this seriously view this as the afterburner for going to the next level.

The next two chapters are effectively a book within a book, with an emphasis on adding scale, reach and sustainability to your growth engine. Between those two chapters is an activity template with which you can do a "state of the business" assessment through a thought-provoking strategic planning exercise.

For now, let's focus on your team – as it is now, and what it can look like and accomplish in the future. We have a soft spot for start-up F4S professionals. A new chiropractor will find a location and a receptionist (often a relative), hang out their shingle and grind away. A new dentist will do the same (in this case, literally grinding) while adding a hygienist to the team. An accountant or lawyer will draft in behind an established firm to cut their teeth, before establishing their own shop. A new financial professional will take a "boutique" approach which, in truth, initially means smiling and dialing to friends and family, and then to the outer rings of their degrees of separation, feverishly trying to squeeze every drop out of the sympathy/obligation orange – occasionally getting someone to throw a small bone, and saying "be conservative – don't lose this!" and then eventually cold-calling strangers to find additional new business to get over the viability hump. This sequence of events could be described as Darwinian.

Sometimes they are fortunate enough to become a protégé to an established mentor, and sometimes they roll the dice by acquiring an existing business, and their feet are instantly to the raging fire of complexity and moving parts. It's very revealing about the degree of determination and conviction, to be amongst the fittest who survive all of that.

That might bring up some memories from your own beginnings, but they are all in the rear-view mirror. Now you are running a thriving business, and you are approaching or have already hit your stride, and are coming to a fork in the road: "Where do I go from here?"

These next chapters are designed to help you look down that road and start contemplating options, conducting scenario planning and identifying specific adjustments, many of which include team dynamics.

The end goal of a highly functional team is that they make your life easier while making the business stronger. The team liberates you to do what you are paid to do. As the saying goes, Frank Sinatra never moved a piano. He stayed in his very unique lane of competency. Your job, in turn, is to create an environment where people can thrive, enabling them to embrace and represent your philosophy, and develop, refine and deploy your process. It is a two-way street. It's not about someone doing you a favor. It's an alignment of self-interest that creates a multiplied outcome.

## A Spectrum of Expectations

At a minimum, your team is there to liberate you to ensure that you major in the main things – not minor in the minutia. They have a Pre & Pre Protocol which means they create PREdisposition in people you are about to meet, and PREpare you for the encounter – all following a predetermined format and process. They will do a quick scan of social media on the person you are about to meet and provide you with any insight. They will prepare the tools and templates you need well in advance. They will refresh your memory of previous actions and any history of recent interactions, and they will run with the next steps to fulfill on what occurred in that meeting. All the while, they handle the fluid stream of issues from the mundane to full-on firefighting.

From there, you empower them to ratchet up their protection of your time - acting as gatekeepers and sifters. They hold you accountable and enforce consistency. You embolden them to not deviate and instead put the process above you, the person. You insist that they schedule recurring team meetings, and stick to it with the same importance as given to client meetings. "This team meeting is happening."

- Once a day you have a five minute huddle to discuss wins and hiccups.

- Once a week you have a one-hour meeting to put issues on the table.

- Once a month you have a two-hour meeting to connect the past to the present and future.

- Once a quarter you have a half-day strategy session to assess your progression.

- Once a year you have a full-day, deep-dive, off-site meeting to celebrate and recalibrate.

From there, you shift to a crowd-source/open-source culture in which your team is encouraged to bring ideas above and beyond observations to the team meeting, to keep optimizing everyone and everything – personally, professionally, and exceptionally. It's powerful when a team member tells you something FORM-related concerning a client that you were unaware of. It's powerful when you give the green light to ideas like, "let's have real coffee and tea in here served in beautiful mugs." Or "Let's have a toaster oven pumping out freshly baked cookies prior to meetings." Or, "Let's have a serious accountability conversation with a VAST Network partner who talks a good game, but keeps dropping the ball."

## Let's Get Serious

All of this can escalate to significant buy-in to the next level. It's not that we have to do this, we get to do this because we understand it. It makes perfect sense and everyone will benefit. This is where the culture of your enterprise and the standards of your team find another gear.

## The 90-Day Dash

As you embrace this, look to the consolidation and standardization of your resources, tools and templates. A simple gap analysis in a team meeting, following a checklist and discussion of relevance and merit, is a good next step. Talking about the reasons why you need an org chart, ideal client profile, service model and matrix, introductory kit and process, onboarding kit and process, or other aspects of the Always ON framework, will lead to a lively discussion. As goals for completion, next steps, accountability and a 90-day window of time is more than reasonable.

That is the high-level first step. Once you close that door, it will open the next 90-Day Dash. Everything that you, as a team, pulled together in the first wave is germane to your overall intellectual property and client experience. The Rule of Three, which states that every task your team performs, three or more times, and has three or more steps, cannot reside in anyone's head. It must be documented and organized within your own proprietary playbook, a manual of standard operating procedures and best practices. Your goal is for the team to get these documented in real time - as they perform them - consolidated and organized in your weekly meeting, to allow you to standardize 80% of your procedures within 90 days. A lofty goal, but doable with a sense of urgency and unified resolve. Be sure to tell your clients about this undertaking as a soft primer for eventual reframing.

Once that dust starts settling, tell the team that you want to review the impact of the exercise with a 12-month delta. By then you should see the qualitative and quantitative benefits of the effort.

## Human Capital

These compressed, focused efforts at refinement bring something out in all of you. You get to be reminded that, as an entrepreneur, you are in business for yourself, but not by yourself. Everyone is pulling in the same direction. Your team feels a deeper sense of purpose and belonging, all of which contributes to the pursuit of their own personal Blue Square. Your own role as a leader is emerging as you do this.

Think back on the leaders you've had in your life, whether a parent, relative, coach, or mentor. Think of some of the qualities that became apparent to you as you realized, "I really respect this person." They were fair, consistent, direct, confident, strong and respectful, to name a few attributes. They tended to defend against injustice. Martin Luther King said it so well, "In the end, we will remember not the words of our enemies, but the silence of our friends." Leaders respect a level playing field, especially if there is an unfair advantage or an underdog dynamic. You might have heard of the "Sheepdog Analogy" which states that in the world, there are wolves and there are sheep, and in the middle ground there are sheepdogs bound by duty. There are powerful pictures floating around on the internet of an exhausted, blood-soaked dog with a spiked collar around its neck, fresh from a battle, resting peacefully amongst very appreciative sheep.

Pure leaders lead from behind. No bravado, no fanfare and the last in line to eat at a buffet table. They are also very rational. Peter Drucker outlined how friction and confusion create under-performance. An environment of fear and uncertainty can also create a tentative workplace at best, or one of inaction at worst.

Leaders don't seek power, they strive to empower to create synchronicity and synergy. They create an environment of healthy competition – it's all transparent and accountable. Everyone knows where they stand, but it's not to belittle, it's to lift up. It's a form of "co-opetition" in which the team competes by cooperating. All boats rise. They are the perpetual fountain of optimism, rather than the drain of negativity. They are happy for a skilled team member who leaves to pursue other options and they encourage those that detract from the team to find greener pastures. Some people are just not a good fit.

Incompatibility is often more about chemistry than competency. There are arsonists out there who will complain about the noise of the sirens. You're doing everyone a disservice by not encouraging those that detract to move on.

Leaders are as demanding as they are diplomatic. They do push, often relentlessly, but not for shallow outcomes. This becomes apparent when you see them in a social setting. They are highly respectful to members of a service staff. At a party at their home for their team, if someone spills a drink, the leader will talk about The Angel's Share, from the world of whiskey. If someone drops and breaks a beautiful plate, the leader will throw one down and say "OPA! Now it's a party."

It's just how they roll. Partly innate, partly developed from intensely watching other leaders in action. They create an environment of productivity and high expectations, but they bolster that with fun and balance. Mark Twain said, "People treat you how you train them." In this context, it's not about training or indoctrination, it's a culture of buy-in, adoption and deployment of proven best practices. It's not only Total Client Engagement that you earn and deserve from your clients, Total Company Engagement is something you earn from your team. That mindset is the glue to bringing everyone together.

An exceptional F4S team is led by Mark Stevens, Eric Watson and Philip Lazzari in Maryland. This team takes the concept of "team" to another level in terms of honoring and respecting each other's unique contributions, while being connected through process, all to deliver an unparalleled client experience worthy of a white paper.

## Going Further

If you want to take team dynamics to another level – both in terms of adding structure to your process and enhancing your philosophy toward human capital – consider adopting Tuckman's Model as an approach to understanding individual personalities and strengths.

Whether you are coming together as an existing team to tackle a significant project, responding and regrouping leading up to a staff departure, or adding to your bench of talent, Tuckman's model is a great starting point to frame and structure your approach. Tuckman's model was developed in 1965 and is still the best simple, intuitive and straightforward project management and team development framework we've seen. It has four components:

Forming – your blueprint, roles and responsibilities and fit process.

Storming – getting to work in a systematic and urgent manner.

Norming – professionalizing, standardizing and refining as you go.

Performing – assessing both the meaningful and measurable KPIs.

## Tackling a Project

As big fans of branding, and after encouraging you to name your process as an extension of your practice, we also urge you to name every 90-Day Dash you embark on. You could call it Project De/serve – because you want to be more deserving of loyalty, empowerment and advocacy (and with that, for all to be deserving of a bonus.) Maybe call it Mission: Walk-Off, a project so important and impactful it has the drama of a walk-off grand slam to win the game. Or just Elevate, because you are raising the bar for everyone involved. In branding, when you name something, it gives it an identity. It's something to rally behind and makes the concept more real.

Then, create a cover page or mission statement, framed in SNIB:

Subject – Elevate our client experience – Raising the Bar.

Need – Praise the existing approach but there are gaps to be addressed.

Ideas – Assemble input in a checklist along with roles and responsibilities.

Benefit – It's a 3x win – a win for the client, a win for the business and a win for the team.

## Total Company Engagement creates Total Client Engagement

How do you respond to a departure? It could be a maternity leave, a family move across the country, a retirement, or simply someone moving on. The approach is very similar to the project example above, but there's a specific emphasis on the org chart to ensure agreement that everyone stays in their respective lanes – and that there is crossover to support and offer cover as the regroup and reset are being worked out. An emphasis on silver linings is key to keep things positive and to focus on the future.

## Adding Talent and Strength to Your Bench

When it comes to adding people to your team, there is no hurry, no panic, and no skipping of steps. Stick to the plan, trust the process - especially with an emphasis on Forming – and establish who is a good fit.

At a high level, you can take the AAA PLUS aspect of the ideal client profile, and configure it to the team to mean:

Assets – credentials, references, and what they bring to the technical table.

Attitude – looking at the x-factor around their philosophy and outlook.

Alignment – will they contribute to the harmony of the current team.

Ultimately, do they appear to be People Like US, as far as their standards of care and attention to detail are concerned? Do they seem happy (because that is tough to teach)? This is why HR professionals tend to look at a potential hire's social media activity.

Going deeper, you can frame your Form and Fit to the PSP acronym:

Philosophical – do they see the world the same way you do?

Strategic – will they bring value to your clients and enterprise?

Practical – can you afford them? Can you afford not to have them onside?

A modified version of the *Rule of Three* can be applied here. Three separate meetings in three different settings with three different people on your team. It's not an exact science, but it has been stress-tested to put the odds in your favor.

We're such big fans of Tuckman's Model that we want to pay it tribute with a bit more detail. There are many videos out there putting different spins on it, but it is a fascinatingly simple and effective approach.

Bruce Tuckman posited that every elite team goes through these four stages – often more than once as new members are added or situational changes occur.

## 1) FORMING

We made the point several times that you need a plan, and you need to keep planning to move confidently forward, making adjustments and assessing your progress.

In Tuckman's model, 'forming' covers the team's initial steps – learning about each other, learning about goals, process, opportunities and challenges. At this point, Tuckman points out that individual members have to begin letting go of their individual comfort zones and begin to orient with the team's model. Part of the shift is to de-personalize from maverick talent and place an equal emphasis on people, practice and process.

## 2) STORMING

History is rife with stories of great intentions around "Here's what we need to do...here's what we're going to do...here's what awaits us on the other side of this..." and so on, and a failure to launch or a rapid fizzle-out occurs because the focus was more on the intention than on implementation with a sense of clarity and urgency.

Storming is all about integrating the troops behind an initiative and/or adding your new professional or teammate. This stage will see all members building trust, resolving conflicts and establishing long-term group dynamics within the framework of your playbook and process. This is where the rubber meets the road. Team members will have learned and are internalizing the business messaging, they are now sharing ideas creatively and getting into the groove with your overarching process.

This is a potentially combative step, as team-members are comparing and arguing their understanding of the process and the message (though your control of the process will minimize this) but keep in mind that you will need to ensure tolerance for team members and their differences as they get up to speed.

To quote Tuckman, "without tolerance and patience the team will fail. This phase can become destructive to the team and will lower motivation if allowed to get out of control." As the controller, your job will be to gauge where your team is. More on the potential landmines and unforeseen issues in a moment.

## 3) NORMING

In norming, your process becomes the norm. *The Rule of Three* is respected. Standard operating procedures are being documented and archived in your playbook. Cooperation in your team is now habitual and the entire enterprise begins to move forward more rapidly. At this point, the business should be beginning to run like a Swiss watch even when you are not present.

Camaraderie and cooperation should begin to pervade the team by now. Team-members will be taking responsibility and understanding their roles – they'll be "owning it" and will have moved past inter-team friction and into synergy. If you are onboarding new team members, along with their legacy clients, the ramp-up, execution, and follow-through process – essentially a modified version of ONside and ONboard, is humming along beautifully.

## 4) PERFORMING

To quote Tuckman's original paper, "With group norms and roles established, members focus on achieving common goals, often reaching an unexpectedly high level of success." You'll see many qualitative Key Performance Indicators that are meaningful and quantitative KPIs that are measurable.

What's not to like? Effectively, the performing stage is the payoff – it's the liberation and order of having a valuable and potentially scalable business (franchise-ready?), with an elite team that can onboard new members with minimal friction and deliver top-tier service to clients. Your team, at this point, is alive - and to an extent self-directing - within your overall process.

## A Moment to Discuss Quirks and Cracks

If you're a dog lover, you know the maxim, "Rescue dogs save us, not the other way around." There will be people who come into your life who have been dealt a tough hand, and all they need is a chance to prove themselves, or perhaps even a second chance. Moral compass issues are a different matter and not for this book (can a tiger change its unethical stripes?), but mistakes and errors in judgment don't have to be deal breakers – especially if the rules of engagement are clear, and expectations for code of conduct are defined. Many entrepreneurs can point to people on their teams who didn't have the best resume or best credentials, but did possess skills and qualities that are tough to teach - even if they weren't apparent when they brought that person on. It emerged and flourished, opening up like a flower in the sun, because the conditions were perfect. People who study, think like, and become effective business owners trust their gut, take a few chances and take the long view.

On this topic, if you haven't already been around this block, we encourage you to look closely at the different personality styles that will inevitably gravitate to your enterprise. This will enable you to get a sense of the mistakes that get made, tensions that can develop and how to apply empathy, perspective and patience to your goals and expectations.

## DISC: Understanding your Communication Style

We developed a stand-alone coaching and consulting deliverable called C5 Team Dynamics, which is specifically for rapidly growing teams to take what is often considered to be a soft skill, and an imprecise science, and make it part of their human resources and human capital investment. We built it on the foundation on the DISC System and brought it to life with a Certified DISC Practitioner with great results. You can learn more about C5 at thebluesquaremethod.com/implementation-resources.

A way to raise your team's efficiency, and to most effectively move through the storming and norming stages of team building, is to look at your communication style. How do you communicate most comfortably, most effectively? How can we take the skills that you already have and enhance them for the betterment of communication in your circle?

How effectively does your team communicate? Do you have a thorough understanding for the different styles and compatibility? As far as your clients are concerned, they, too, are different from you in many cases.

For some clients, talking to them is absolutely natural. For others it might be a bit of a struggle. So how do you enhance it so that both you and your clients are more comfortable, so that you can truly enhance that connection?

When we look at understanding your communication, we want to know both what your style is and how it's perceived. Your communication may not be perceived as you are hoping to portray it. Understanding your communication style also gives you a strong appreciation of the differences of other people and their styles, their likely response, and a stronger connection.

It's not unlike the book *The 5 Love Languages* by Gary Chapman. Communication is a skill that can be improved upon in terms of talking, listening and understanding. In business, communication is the universal language of observable human behavior; it's the language of how you do what you do.

Your natural communication style isn't good or bad. It just is. It's how you communicate. It's how you're perceived and it can always be honed, refined, and fine-tuned, to ensure that you're seen and understood as you would like to be seen and understood.

In the DISC view, there are four broad categories: Dominance, Influence, Steadiness and Conscientiousness. We want you to think about the people around you, people in your firm, people on your team, and clients that fall into these categories.

**Dominance:** These people look for results. They often speak fast, focused and almost in bullet-point form. "Hey, let's go do this" or "I want to get this done. Let's get it done right now." Direct, forceful sentences. They may use big gestures. Another way to pick them out of a crowd is that they are looking for the facts. They're not interested in small talk or secondary concerns, they just want to know what the central facts are. Even if you're talking about personal information or small-talk, the conversation could be purely factual. "How was your day?" might be responded to factually. "Got to the office early. Got lots done. Had a great day, had a great lunch. Went home to relax."

Note the type of verbiage and the short, focused factual sentences. That's a high-D.

Another thing that you may notice about a D is that they have a bottom-line focus. On a team, they look to the bottom line as far as value to the team is concerned. They are forward-looking and challenge-oriented. They are going to be innovative. They are going to initiate activity when under stress. They could be more demanding than others, and could, in some situations, overpower people that are not a high-D in turn. That's something to keep in mind when looking at communication within a team or with a client. If you're comfortable in that situation, the chances are you are a D as well. If it makes you uncomfortable, the chances are you're not - but know that this is one of the core behavioral traits that are out there. It's not personal. It's not about you. It's about them. This is how they communicate.

So what can you do to communicate better with somebody that's a strong D?

Make sure that you communicate with confidence. Be direct and to the point. State your case. Have that conversation and be on time. You can have a great relationship and great communication with a high-D person if you approach them in that way.

**Influence:** The influence-based communicator is a fast-paced, people-oriented communicator. They may not be as direct as a D when they're talking, but an "I" will often use large gestures. The odds are that they are smiling, they are talking to people, they are around lots of people and they're talking with their hands.

A high-I, generally, is very confident and convincing. They are enthusiastic and optimistic. It's likely that when you see somebody standing in the middle of a group and they're laughing, talking and holding court, that's a high-I. If you've got a team member like that, what value do they bring? They bring optimism and enthusiasm, obviously, but also creative problem-solving. They motivate others and are committed team players, as well.

Is there a downside? There could be a little too much talking at times. Possibly a bit too much socializing - especially for people that are very direct and people that are very task oriented. That's something that you want to keep in mind. When a client walks in and they are just over the top, chatty and talking and smiling and having a great time, that's a high-I.

If you want to enhance the relationship and communication with someone who is a high-I, you are going to want to jump in there with them. Take part in the enthusiasm and pay attention to things that they are saying, and things that they are enthused about. Be friendly.

If you are not a high-I, you might find it a little bit frustrating if you are focused on the task at hand and a person comes in and just wants to chat. That's where the communication, understanding and appreciation comes in.

Remember that a high-I is a people-oriented person, the D is more task-oriented, but both, despite their differences, can be overpowering if you don't understand that these are their styles.

The high-I could be one that pays a little bit less attention to details and might be a little bit too talkative, too. These are things that you have to be aware of. Keep in mind, some are hunters and some are farmers. Both feed your growth engine, but in different ways.

**Steadiness:** The high-S is looking for stability and security. Sometimes people with this communication style will be typed as friendly, amiable, diplomatic and supportive. They're relaxed and sincere. The pace of communication is often slightly slower than a high-D. The "S" is also looking for facts, but they're more people-oriented and less interested in an immediate bullet-point answer.

Communication-wise, they can be indirect. They'll use some gestures, often not overly large, and generally more controlled. One of the cues for recognizing an "S" from body language, is they'll often have a poker face while conversing. They're not going to show a lot of emotion.

Team-wise, an "S" is a very dependable team player. They'll work for a leader with a cause. They are patient, empathetic and logical. They are service-oriented, steady, controlled and friendly, so when you have somebody like that on your team, you know you have a perfect match for people looking for pace and consistency – clients who themselves are high-S. The way to connect with high-S team members or clients, is to make sure that you're giving them the facts, the assurances, the security, and the process that they're looking for. A client might be looking for more assurance that they made the right decision. That's where your consistent onboarding process comes into play, to reassure these people that they've made the right choice.

**Conscientiousness:** You'll notice the "C" by how they react to procedures and constraints. A high-C is definitely a data person. They're accurate. They're analytical and conscientious. Given that they know data, they might overuse it at times. A high-C person might always back up their discussion with facts and figures, which will be correct even if not necessarily required. They have very high standards. They will define, clarify, and make sure that what you're doing is right, backed up by all the facts in the world. These are very comprehensive problem solvers. Having a high-C on your team is going to ensure that there is a step-by-step process being followed, backed up by facts and data.

As far as clients go, if you've ever had a client request a massive amount of information, and not just ask for it but read it cover-to-cover and ask you about it afterward, you have a high-C. When you're communicating with a high-C, you want to make sure that you are listening to their facts, and make sure that you're giving them the information that they're looking for, and that you follow your procedures. Let them know what the procedures are, and detail any constraints that might be there as well.

As a team impact, just be aware that you could get bogged down with details and could suffer some "analysis paralysis." Be aware of that, and you will enhance your experience and the experience of the rest of the team as well.

When you have an understanding of who you are and what your style is, it can give you the power and the tools to enhance your communication around the team, and with clients as well. Remember: We aren't just one category. No one is wholly one style, though one may be dominant – everyone is a mixture of all four in differing degrees.

Understanding your styles helps not only in knowing how to communicate – it lets you know how NOT to with specific clients or team-members. You might find yourself in a situation where one standard or procedure within your firm is actually perceived as a negative to certain communication styles. This understanding gives you the option to do a full analysis so you can customize your communication with specific clients.

## Enhance Team Communication

Now that we've covered DISC in general, we have a question: Is every member of your team similar in behavioral communication style? Different styles come together to create a powerful experience. If you are a diverse mix, that's great. If you aren't, there may be cues here, and some ideas that you can use. Not just to enhance the team that you already have, but to give you some ideas on who is going to be the best person to add to the team.

Don't just look at who is on your team; evaluate how your team communicates and how they interact with each other, and how you and they interact with clients. If you find deficiencies in communication, you may be able to tweak a few things and see improved rapport.

When you think of your team, there are many skills and areas of focus in play. Some are extroverted, and will take that first step toward starting communication. Some are more introverted and will have a look at what's going on before they jump into an initial interaction. Some people are focused on team dynamics - they want to make sure that everyone is happy and that the team is working together smoothly. Another may be thinking about improving communication with the clients, or discussing the different clients and their individual feelings, needs and wants with the team. A third might be more focused on making sure that there's structure, and that all procedures are followed, and the paperwork is done correctly.

There's huge value in every single one of those people, obviously, and of course everybody is a combination of these styles, but some are more natural at one than at the others.

When you look at your team, are all the roles filled? As mentioned before, sometimes teams end up loaded with people that are similar to themselves. If that's the case, just be conscious that the next person that you add to the team could address gaps in your available communication skills. An examination like this also highlights team members who may be over-extended and taking on too much. Bottom line, embrace the exercise to expand your leadership awareness.

Assessments like this will absolutely increase efficiency in teams. It also clearly identifies gaps such as characteristics that are missing from your team. It's not just about who you are right now, it's also who you could be.

How do you use this on a practical day-to-day basis? You enhance the team experience through regular meetings, a full understanding of roles and responsibilities, a process in place to ensure that all the roles are filled, clarity for everyone on what their role is, and what everyone else's role is. It makes everything more efficient for yourself and for your team and clients. Take ownership and embed the lessons learned in your service matrix. Lastly, be aware that not everyone is motivated by the same thing. Money, recognition, added responsibility, extra free time and other incentives need to be carefully considered when it comes to rewarding your team with a "bonus."

The entire DISC exercise is a perfect example of working on your business, not just in your business. Thinking of your team as a tapestry or a tartan that is interwoven, or a mosaic of small pieces forming a bigger beautiful picture, should always be the focus.

Furthermore, and from a deeper qualitative perspective, putting in this effort makes a statement of how respectful you are, in terms of understanding people and striving for harmony. It's not being intrusive or overbearing. It's respectful to be sincerely interested in what makes another person tick. Ranchers will say, "It's important never to lean on someone else's fence." Be proactive but not pushy. Be curious but not judgmental. These are qualities that ensure you foster a positive environment while not accepting any corrosive, soul-sucking dividers. Because they are out there.

With that, let's shift to the conduit – Strategic Planning – to work through what growth model best suits you.

## STRATEGIC Planning - The Conduit between Organic & Scalable Growth

You've taken in a lot of information up to this point. If you are clear on your path in terms of where you want to go, and what needs to be done, you can skip this sub-chapter and move on through the last chapters of this book. If you have some uncertainty, or some mixed emotions, around the balance between your contentment for what is, and your ambition for what could be, this exercise might help you pull things together.

The primary benefit of this is to solidify your organic growth model to reinforce your understanding of what gaps you'll need to address. You can then determine if that's as far as you'll take it – you'll keep growing your business organically on your terms, as you live your best life and head to your eventual exit and liquidity event – or you'll keep going and invest all of that into the next step in your progression and become franchise-ready. Which, again, simply means your organic model is a template that you can leverage in other ways. We'll also factor in aspects from the four Venn diagrams we outlined in the True North Chapter.

In our approach to strategic planning, we are providing two options: A high level approach that you can zip through quickly following our STAR format, and a deeper dive that turns the word STRATEGIC into a logical and sequential path of checkpoints that force you to think things through and get answers to some outstanding issues on paper. They're both exercises that we've used with our coaching clients with solid outcomes.

On   thebluesquaremethod.com/implementation-resources   there   are resources you can access for both options, if you decide to work through one of them on your own or with your team. In this chapter we will walk through the STRATEGIC framework to get your wheels turning.

This approach is formatted to encapsulate key issues that we've covered up to this point in the book. This is built on the assumption that you aren't reading this book in one sitting, and there are certain elements that ring true long after you were initially exposed to them, and which are worth revisiting. The exercise enables you to take a breath, take a look around, and take the time to determine what path is best suited for you. There is a recap element built in, to pinpoint ideas that are outlined in a way that allows you to revisit and distill key points from these pages so that you can commit to an action plan.

The first years of the 2020s were strange, to say the least. Perhaps your view is that, from a business perspective at least, the last few years have been good or great - or let's close the book on that time frame and move on. We believe there is a renaissance coming just around the corner. Like a slingshot pulled all the way back – almost on the verge of breaking – we feel there will be a release on many levels. There may not be a better time to be a F4S professional, and in fact, there may not be a better time to be alive than the years ahead of us. That being said, optimism is great, but it's action that needs to be taken, so let's plan it out.

In general, many business professionals put off doing their own deliberate strategic planning recently because things were so bizarre. Many of us simply reacted to what was thrown at us. Right was left, up was down. Disruptions swarmed on every level. Looking ahead, though, hopefully this will catch you at good time and supplement your own DIY approach.

The objective and purpose of all of this brings us back to Maslow's hierarchy: Self-actualization - becoming the best version of ourselves. It's worth repeating our paraphrase of Hemingway, the goal is not to be superior to another person. The goal is to be superior to our former self. That is true progress.

To get there, we have to immerse ourselves into the mindset of kaizen, the Japanese concept based on the premise of constant change, constant improvement and constant assessment. It's a big part of plateau avoidance.

To build on that, these are some of the questions we ask our clients – and a refresher on the ikigai Venn diagram. Do you love what you do? Are you developing a process that drives your enterprise value based on intellectual property? Are you growing through the vein of gold by constantly converting clients to referral-generating advocates? Are you monetizing fully, which may include positioning a shift from organic to scalable growth?

That's the professional development element that propels you towards the Blue Square - your bullseye. The degree to which you harmonize that with the personal side - meaning you never lose sight of your sense of gratitude, your sense of purpose, your sense of balance and your sense of personal fulfillment - is essential. Are these part of your guiding beacon and do you place a proper level of importance on all of it?

As a starting point, we begin with a defined view of the future. Yes, there are forces out of our control, but despite that, we are going to chart a course and set the sails. You don't need to crush it with complexity, but we do hope that you will go through the exercise of getting your goals out of your head. Take it seriously, professionalize it, standardize it and frame it. We kick it off with these simple questions:

*Are you today where you said you were going to be five years ago?*

You had goals five years ago, and that time frame came and went very quickly. Where are you? Most people we talk with say they've gotten close or exceeded their expectations. Reflect on and savor that.

*What does Nirvana look like for you in the next five years?*

The likelihood is that the next five years are going to go by even faster than the previous five did. Describe it, define it, and get it out of your head. If you want to go deeper into the goal-setting exercise, go through that simple but revealing approach called W5:

## W5:

What are you grateful for? In the spirit of investing the past into the future, do you have appreciation for what you already have, as you aspire for what you don't yet have? Take a moment and just define on paper all the things you're grateful for.

Where do you see yourself in the future? Get it out of your head. Write out your wish list. Give your wish list a placeholder by framing it in FORM. What are my goals for Family? Education, travel, various aspirations, continuity, succession, legacy, all of that. Occupation: What are my goals? What am I trying to accomplish with my business, myself professionally, my team? Recreation: What's on my bucket list? And of course, Money. You might end up with a list of seven, you might land on 17 – whatever the case, look at them on paper, don't just think about them in your mind. Then add timelines.

When do I hope to accomplish these goals? Just put numbers beside each: One year, two years, three years and so on. This is designed to prompt you to think about cause and effect and the importance of detaching from a full expectation of an outcome. Anxiety and frustration are born in the place between what you expect will happen and what actually happens. Yes, you hope to achieve those goals in a reasonable period of time, but you will focus more on the activity required than the productivity attained.

Why is this so important to me? Jim Rohn, a thought leader from back in the day, said it so well, "When the why is clear, the how pretty much takes care of itself." We'll never downplay the importance of sculpting out a blueprint for the how, but the why is the fuel and the blinders that prevent drifting and self-sabotage. Lastly:

Who do I need to become to make all of this a reality? The clay must stay soft. Who do I need to surround myself with? What do I need to read? What credentials do I need to refine? What habits do I need to embrace? Crystallize and then galvanize your vision on paper. Decide if you want to have this conversation with your team and then decide to the degree that you want to standardize your goals-based planning approach beyond that. Many professionals do, and it's incredibly powerful in terms of engaging clients further.

Let's keep going.

## Always be STRATEGIC

**The S in the STRATEGIC acronym is Strategic Summary**.

"You'll see it when you believe it." The strategic summary is self-fulfilling. It's a personal aspirational statement that builds on the earlier nirvana question. If everything could fall out of the sky and into your lap in the next five years, what does it look like? One of our favorite examples came from a consultation with a team. We asked them, "Are you a billion dollar team currently managing 500 million? Yes or no." There was a long pause. Then the lead said, "I'd like to think so." It prompted an in-depth conversation about the future, their ideal life and it became their beacon. Today they are a billion dollar team. It's powerful to add a comma, but they did it on their terms. So, define your strategic summary in one paragraph. What does a panoramic view of nirvana look like, written down? Brief is better. Keep it short and to the point. Another leader of a team – Anthony Valente with The SVS Group in New Jersey – who is playing at a high level in business, but also living a high octane personal life on race tracks, set his strategic summary simply as 40 & 40.

Literally that simple, and very self-explanatory and motivational to him. In five years he wants his firm to do 40 million in yearly revenue and he wants to be on the race track 40 times per year. (At the rate he is going, 50 & 50 is more realistic.) What's great is that his 'why' is balanced with an unwavering commitment to the 'how.' It's not a dream or a fantasy. His entire mindset revolves around merit and client-centered value – not to mention team-centered value.

**The T is for Top Clients**. Many of the teams we consult with are growing up-market. We're going to ask if you have your ideal client profile completely defined, based on AAA PLUS, on a sheet of paper that you could show anyone? Remove the mystery for yourself and for the world. It's not who you're looking for, but who you're suited for. Remember that you have three types of clients. You have the clients who need you, the clients who deserve you, and the movable middle in between.

The most deserving clients, your existing AAA-PLUS clients, are often the least demanding. So we tend to sometimes take them for granted. We don't want you spending time with people who need you at the expense of people who deserve you. The movable middle are the people who are tracking in the direction of becoming an ideal client, so be mindful of the upside of that tier-two group. This stratification is fueled by the Pareto Principle, the 80/20 rule, and is addressed through a service matrix. If you've got your ideal client profile defined, great. If you've got your service model and matrix defined, great. If you don't, that's a simple gap we're going to ask you to address. Hold yourself accountable to be that "open kitchen," and show the world who you're suited for.

A lot of needs will evolve for your clients over the next five years, as well as those of the people close to them. We want you to get out in front of that because, as you progress based on demography and momentum, your clients will have their own liquidity events, milestones, and moments of truth. The more they feel they belong to something unique, and that their future needs will be addressed by your people, practice and process, the more they're a lock to empower you and introduce you to others with their own needs. When events happen, and people from the outside start chirping and putting ideas in your client's head that 'maybe they've outgrown you,' and it might be time to deal with somebody else, you want to have future-paced the relationship so that they are insulated.

**The R is for Right Sizing.** We're going to ask you to consider the concept of growing down. The colliding forces of *Little's Law* and *McNamara's Fallacy* might be salient issues in your life - now or soon.

Managing smaller numbers of clients, so that you can manage a larger and more complex array of needs, requires careful planning. Part of branding and practice management consulting is designed to help you achieve professional contrast, where it's self-evident that you are superior to the pack. Part of professional contrast is brought to life through professional scarcity, which means there's a sense of achievement in qualifying to work with you. Clients understand that your goal is not to see how big you can get, it's how small you can stay. Growing down is often the springboard to growing up-market.

Of course, growing down can come in different forms. Based on 80/20, maybe you've already done this as a team. The lead professional works with the 20% of the clients who generate 80% of the business, and the protégé associates work with the 80% of the clients who generate 20% of the business. This can never be perceived as a hand-off. Ultimately, it has to be positioned as an upgrade for everyone involved. We say that because your business must be a panoramic business, not a book. You don't have a book. It's not even a book of business. It's a business. In time, this may continue to evolve to a situation where you work with the 20% of the 20%. We have many clients who themselves work with 10 to 25 people directly, and they oversee delivery by their team to everyone else.

The ideal business is framed in people, practice and process. Your clients trust and appreciate the people. They appreciate the client experience brought by the practice. They appreciate the process, not just for what it is, but for what it does for them.

Certain clients need allocating. If you move clients to a different person on your team, that person is still executing within the same practice using the same process. Transitions are positioned to highlight that you would be doing that client a disservice by not allocating them to a different person. For other clients in the need category – children of clients and those with less complex needs - a deeper degree of automating the relationship using technology can be considered.

There are some clients that are far beyond automate or allocate, of course. It needs to be a disassociate approach. It's just not a good fit. Usually these are attitudinal disconnects where the client is constantly questioning and trying to negotiate your value in one direction. They're micro-managing and being disrespectful, and they're clients where there's an element of dread with you and your team when you see their number on the call display. Disassociate respectfully. You're not firing clients. The alignment of interests is just not there. Going forward, liberate yourself by narrow-casting to focus on clients where the alignment is absolutely perfect.

To unlock capacity and bandwidth for the most deserving, you need to remember the distinction between your core competency and your proprietary assets. In the case of a financial professional, you don't just manage money, you manage a business and you manage people; treat all three with the same level of importance. How you manage money is not proprietary - it's commoditized. Your business and your clients are yours. Treat them with a heightened level of importance.

**A is Activities**. As a team, we'd like you to determine, in your scheduled meetings, the six to eight activities/gaps that you need to identify, address, or refine. Look to the Always ON resource as a starting point.

One of our favorite activities that teams have added has been in branding and introducing a process to their clients that is proprietary. It has an identity that has a personality. It's incredibly powerful to ensure your clients understand and appreciate where your relationship is going. In the spirit of planning, you want your clients to fixate directionally, not on transactions individually. Not just where they are today, but where they are going. That's what future pacing is. It makes sure a client understands there are parts of your process that aren't relevant to them yet, but as their life evolves, as things change, you'll be out in front of it all. They want to know where they stand today and where they are headed in the future. They don't outgrow your process. They grow into your process. That's especially important with the dynastic drivers, liquidity events, and other moments of truth that start to involve other family members.

Your clients already like and trust you. They already have a connection with your practice. Let's have them have the same level of appreciation for your branded process as they do for your practice and your people. That's how you competitor-proof. That's how you capture newly developed needs and money in motion, and that's how you create advocacy. Your clients internalize how they feel about your people, your practice and your process, and they socialize that to others.

**Technology is the second T in the STRATEGIC framework**. Here's a question: Have you found your sweet spot between high touch and high tech? There is so much technology available to you, but you have to be careful not to over-innovate. Innovation is about efficiency, not complexity. Feature creep is a thing that has seeped into technology, providing users with features that aren't needed and which contribute to an increased probability of a breakdown. Essentially, a digital form of planned obsolescence. One example of simplicity intersecting with quality craftsmanship is the Solo Stove.

Based on very simple technology originating from WW2, these products aligned simple solutions with simple needs in the marketplace, but ensured they were well made and dependable. It's refreshing to not overthink or over-engineer something, but rather to differentiate with simplicity and quality. The goal is balance.

Have you embraced video as a team? Have you created an evergreen video for your website and any other activities where you tell the world what makes you different? Something to help a prospective client vet you in advance of meeting you? Something to activate professional contrast? Remember that gem from Randy Schwantz, "For you to get hired, someone's got to get fired."

In order to put the wedge in that prospective client's relationship with his or her current provider, they need to come to their own conclusion that you are an upgrade of superior value. You're not trying to convince somebody you are better. Instead, you want it to become self-evident as they compare and contrast while they are kicking your tires. Video can accelerate that professional contrast exercise. Have you embraced podcasting, or any other 1-to-many deliverable that positions you as a thought leader while efficiently communicating with clients, strategic partners and prospective clients? Do you have a digital marketing and branding driver? Are you engaging in social media? You can still achieve scarcity and contrast with these forms of communication. Undoubtedly and by necessity, you've become pretty competent with WebEx and Zoom. You might have even started to do your Strategy and Tactical Meetings over Zoom and your clients love them. They are agenda-driven and it gives everybody the gift of time. For many of our clients, especially at the highest level, they have four meetings with a client in a year. One is in person, three are online.

Those who take it seriously book their meetings for Tuesdays, Wednesdays and Thursdays only. Mondays and Fridays are reserved for professional development, business refinement, and other forms of working on, rather than working in, the business. When you schedule your Tuesday, Wednesday and Thursday client meetings, be sure to position and deliver them as "Strategy and Tactical Meetings," not review meetings.

We hope that you're embracing technology and that it is serving you well. There are many ways that you can outsource minutiae and outsource what's commoditized. When it comes to the concept of outsourcing, we're working with many teams right now who are, in essence, getting out of the core aspects of their business.

They outsource as much as they can. They've shifted their mindset from households and holdings to platforms and models. They outsource it to somebody who's got scale and a sterling track record. They take that saved time and invest it into their businesses and into their client relationships. For some, they've come to the realization that, again, they're doing their clients a disservice by maintaining the status quo, by not embracing a tailored outsourcing approach, at least to some degree.

The more efficiencies you can find, the more process-driven you become, the tidier your books and more predictable your business development is, the more it contributes to the value of your business. Every business is built to be sold in some way and at some point. The beauty of these investments is that you are slamming money in the bank, because every investment of effort you make, contributes, not just to your productivity and profitability, but also to your enterprise value.

There are a lot of people and a lot of entities right now who would rather buy a business than try to build theirs further. What are they buying? Are they just buying the clients? Are they just buying the AUM, or revenue and EBIDTA or are they buying the predictability of sustained growth because of your IP and playbook as well?

The multipliers are going through the roof right now. So again, please understand every investment of effort you make drives maximum value for your business.

**The E is Enterprise Value.** A lot has been said regarding enterprise value up to this point. If you've gotten this far in our book, your perspective might have changed one way or another. Like any solid lifelong planner, the key is to get out in front, no matter how distant the end game is. Ask your network if they know of any business brokers, trust professionals, mergers and acquisition specialists or anyone else in the space of dealing with the sale of a business, the handling of inheritance and any other aspect of money in motion. Interview these people. Get to know a typical day in their life. Understand the problems they solve and the trends that are developing. Gain insights and expertise and determine to what extent you want to build out your Value Added Support Team. You get to further develop your own knowledge and that can be applied to your clients' liquidity events as well as your own.

Take a local business broker out for breakfast to pick their brain. Just to get your head around it, buy an hour of time to speak to an attorney like Ted Motheral, who understands both the buy and sell side of a potential acquisition.

Think like an entrepreneurial CEO and always strive to broaden your horizons, and eventually orchestrate your own desired results on your terms through knowledge, preparation and a position of strength. Remember that you are not a transactional F4S professional. Your efforts are not expenditures, they are investments into your IP and your EV.

**The G is Growth.** We want you to fully build out the concept of organic growth through conversion, driven by the loyalty ladder, primarily around converting clients into referral generating advocates. The beauty of engineering an advocacy environment is that you become more aware that triggering events which prompt people to consider their options work both ways. Yes, you strive to activate advocacy within your own circle but you also strive to insulate against it so that your own clients never defect. Many F4S professionals take organic growth, Total Client Engagement and competitor-proofing very seriously. Barry Porter and Jim Axelson lead a high-caliber F4S team in Southern California that continues to organically grow in all market conditions. When asked if they aspire to pivot to a scalable growth model to fully capitalize on their IP and momentum, their response was a unified and instant "no thank you." What's fascinating is that they had an immense aversion to any form of growth they felt might distract them or disrupt their client-centered approach. They weren't complacent or coasting, they still invested more effort and resources into their business than virtually any other team we worked with, but the ambition was crystal clear – to never plateau personally or professionally, and to always stay out in front of their clients' constantly evolving and very complex needs, and that was more than enough to keep them fulfilled.

To each their own. There are some that aspire to keep climbing. When you reflect back on the "grow up-market" progression we outlined in the True North chapter, you might have started to consider a potential radical shift - your organic business can be so well-built that it is a proof of concept. Because you have so completely rounded out your organic growth model, you can shift to scalable growth. You could go out and acquire a business. Someone who's got no continuity and succession plan, somebody who's plateaued. Maybe they'll sell and stay? Maybe they'll gradually ease out? Perhaps you want to attract others to draft in behind your process and not be left to their own devices? They just want to work on their client relationships, they don't want to get bogged down in the minutiae. There are countless combinations, all of which allow for scalable growth. The intrinsic value of your IP is never more evident than when you put your playbook of procedures in someone else's hands and say, "Go, this is our way."

Scalable growth is the next frontier. When you bridge that interlude between organic and scalable growth, your enterprise value goes up even further through a force-multiplier. You are not only fully building out your legacy around your life's work, but the monetization as well. Those who achieve scalable growth are those who achieve an inflection point on many levels.

A shining example of this is Eric Applewhite and his team at Harbor Group in Boca Raton. They have never taken their eye off the organic deliverables of client service and an intergenerational client experience, but as they continued to grow, they added the scalable component by taking on soon-to-be-retiring F4S professionals and adding associates, all of whom had to follow The Harbor Way. That process proved to delight new clients that transitioned over but also liberated the professionals because they followed a proven process. It's a textbook example of well-executed and well-managed growth.

**The I is Individual.** Part of the benefit of this exercise is to remind you that the best way to take care of your clients, the best way to take care of your team, is to take impeccable care of yourself.

We meet many F4S professionals who lead their teams - but to a degree, everybody else's happiness, fulfillment and success seems to be coming at the lead's expense. They're working themselves weary, compromising on balance and wearing themselves out to a point of anticlimax. It's a form of self-sacrifice. Self-sacrifice breeds contempt. It can be thankless. It's not appreciated to the extent it should be. Self-interest can be far more positive, breeding respect because you've adopted the philosophy that says, "I'll take care of me for you." The enlightened capitalist will never try to succeed at the expense of anybody. They'll always strive to succeed and achieve self-actualization through the service of everybody. They touch the lives of team members, clients and strategic partners for the better, but you've got to power up your magnet and work on yourself. Schedule time to take care of yourself from the standpoint of exercise, diet, yoga, spirituality and whatever elements will add fuel and energy. It's a trite and worn-out cliché, but you're either running the business or it's running you – and either is by choice. Now, an extension of this is the last letter in the acronym, which is:

**The C is Community.** In 1961 JFK was inaugurated. As you know, one of the greatest takeaways from his inauguration speech was "ask not what your country can do for you, but what you can do for your country." Some historians believe that Cicero, in ancient Rome, actually crafted a version of that phrase originally (Read *A Pillar of Iron* – an epic book by Taylor Caldwell telling the story of Cicero – a book that she dedicated to John Kennedy). We would just ask you to replace the word country with community in this context. Ask what you can do for your community, with no expectation of accolades or return of any kind, because it's the right thing to do, and because it activates karma. Partner with your team, partner with your clients, partner with your other service providers.

There's a lot of need out there and the last few years have been very hard on a lot of people. It's easy to like those ground-level grassroots organizations that are directly impacting needs with no layers of bureaucracy in between. There are organizations dedicated to seniors or deeply involved with veterans. It's moving, it's powerful, and it adds so much energy to your sense of purpose, your drive and your personal fulfillment, and also to your legacy, because it's pure.

It's time to take action. Schedule your meetings with your team throughout the year to deliberately frame out your strategic plan (see thebluesquaremethod. com/implementation-resources) and then execute on it. Don't dominate the meeting, engage the team with the Socratic Method. Ask great questions, be curious, empower them and really listen.

When you populate your STRATEGIC framework, it takes on its own life, because it's now a document, not just a collection of ideas floating around. Don't let it remain simply an intention. We want you to increase the probability of self-actualization. You're a lifelong planner. You plan for your clients. It's not just that you create a plan, you also do ongoing planning based on external dependencies and their critical life events. The ask is simple, make the time so that you can apply as much importance to planning for your own business and life, as well.

# Chapter 12:

## *Inflection Point – The Shift from Organic to Scalable Growth*

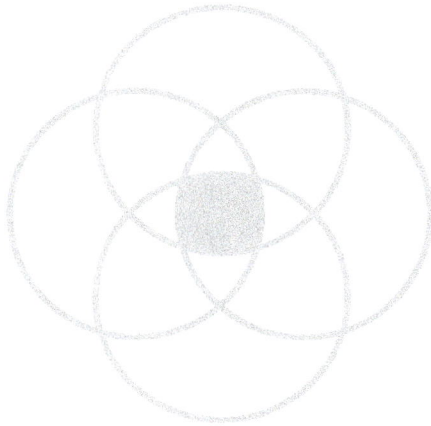

Many F4S professionals are so incredibly refined and polished that when they read through the table of contents for this book, this chapter will jump off the page and they will start here, almost beginning at the end. Covey would be proud. They have the mindset, they have the ambition, and they have the worthiness to make this form of growth a reality right now. The foundation is built, so if we just described you – welcome.

For everyone else, the growth road you are traveling on is approaching a fork – but we'd like you to think of it more as a tuning fork. You have to listen to your instincts to determine what is in your best interests, and what appetite you have as you progress from here. Do you stay the course with your B-to-C model, methodically and organically, growing through Total Client Engagement and then eventually exiting on your terms? This is your life's work, but you can't take it with you, so enjoy the ride until you hand it off to someone else for maximum value. Someone will buy it for a premium because of your IP. You'll be picky and make sure your clients and team are well taken care of, and your legacy will be secured.

Or, you flip the switch and invest your IP and momentum into a B-to-B franchise-ready model. You can start to replicate the value from your organic template. You can create multiple income streams. Perhaps you will monetize by selling your playbook to others in your field? They can buy "your way" and elevate their own business. Perhaps you will say, while my business brings on 50 clients one at a time organically, we can also go out and buy one business with 50 clients. It's not uncommon for a process-driven franchise-ready buyer to acquire an undervalued business from an owner generating $800k in revenue, and, through the transition and onboarding of those clients, transform it into a million-dollar revenue generator quickly, because the service bar was relatively low, previously. The wow factor was so pronounced for those new clients that they reacted as dormant seeds of untapped opportunity that sprang to life in a better environment.

## Keep Re-imagining Growth

Many people in your sector are approaching retirement, but they have no protégé or continuity plan. Their clients have their own dynastic issues and are starting to ask, "What happens to us when you hang it up?" Furthermore, so many people in your sector are feeling the friction and compression, not to mention the AI competition, and are wondering about their viability in the not-so-distant future. Not everyone can adapt. While some are chameleons, many are sitting ducks. Your value proposition could prompt them to draft in behind your process, free themselves from their lack of scale and intense minutiae, and focus on what makes them happy and what makes them money.

The opportunities are virtually unlimited, as is the growth potential, based on the degree that you want to shift even further to a CEO role and oversee an enterprise with exponential growth potential. We've all read the stories of entrepreneurs that toiled and tinkered on their prototype business for years, cracked the replication code and saw the hockey stick outcome. That's the essence of capitalism. If you study the history of humanity, until recently, many generations of the masses were desperately poor. As innovation, scale, and the ability to pursue opportunities kicked in, an entire class of people thought, "I can take a shot at this." Slowly but surely, the middle class emerged and millions were lifted. Merit and good fortune has never been an exact science, but as Winston Churchill said:

> "The inherent vice of capitalism is the unequal sharing of blessings. The inherent virtue of Socialism is the equal sharing of miseries."

Add to that, Thomas Sowell's take:

"Equality of rights does not mean equality of results."

Rounded out by another gem from Churchill:

> "Socialism is the philosophy of failure, the creed of ignorance, and the gospel of envy."

PJ O'Rourke was a fascinating man in that he shared his evolution from being a liberal to a conservative capitalist with his readers as it happened. He once believed that the left was the side that was looking out for the common man. He came to the realization that the most compassionate and generous people were capitalists who strove to create wealth, not redistribute it - all in the spirit of teaching people how to fish. He grew tired of those who cloaked their agendas with talk of fairness and social equity.

His many great lines include "If you think healthcare is expensive now, just wait until it's free."

On a macro level, capitalism truly is the most of the good and the least of the bad. On a micro level you already know that. The question is, how far do you want capitalism to take you?

Larry Harvey is a quintessential F4S entrepreneur in Houston, Texas. He has developed the highest standards of service and care for his organic clients, many of whom have been with him for decades, and he has also empowered his team to build out multiple income streams and complementary lines of business with exceptional synergy. The organic clients give him fulfillment and purpose, the scalable business keeps him charged up and highly motivated with no plateau in sight.

The F4S business environment is a fascinating business model and very conducive to scale. For comparison, look at other sectors that don't just transact, but can create recurring revenue, lift and scale. An auctioneer has no overhead, minimal downside risk, is recession proof – in fact business can actually improve in tough markets - and he can grow based on reputation for results and organic momentum. Then, on the other side of the spectrum, study The Ritchie Brothers model, and you are staggered by what started out as a very humble little business venture and eventually became a global powerhouse.

Look at the storage locker business. It has a low barrier for entry in terms of cost, potential customers have been accumulating stuff that they can't bring themselves to get rid of, and they are happy to pay a monthly fee to hide it out of sight. The owner of the storage lockers will sell your stuff if you stop paying, freeing up space for the next customer, and they sit on this little bamboo tree until it pops (Bamboo trees grow slowly and then suddenly, if you didn't know). Storage businesses wait for the city growth to finally reach their doorsteps, and then someone comes along and buys the dirt. The owner takes their significant check, buys some cheaper dirt on the outskirts of town and plunks down the lockers. Repeat. A little boring engine that could.

Look at Software as a Service (SaaS) tech firms. Develop an IP that solves a problem, then raise money based on lofty projections and attract multiples that defy logic. That one is hard to fathom, sometimes.

Now back to your business. You're taking all aspects of your enterprise value seriously. You've got a fundamentally sound business. The metrics are impressive. Client loyalty, longevity and engagement are measurable. The EBITDA is strong. Your fee-worthiness is undeniable.

You have tidy books, documented procedures, a sticky staff and IP with meaningful intrinsic value. Maybe you should just sit on that, enjoy the ride, and wait for a buyer down the road who meets your criteria, while paying you 6x rather than most of your competitors who get 2x?

Ted Jenkin, a serial entrepreneur in Georgia, actually helps people achieve that. Jenkin is a F4S professional himself, who now also assists others in maximizing their exits – many of whom sell and stay. In many cases, the lead sells all of or a portion of their business on the condition that everything remain intact as they take some money off the table. Liberated on many levels, the lead has never been more motivated or effective. There are entities that will buy "your life's work" as an asset acquisition but don't want to disrupt the mojo.

Or maybe you will be like the team at CFO4Life in Dallas, Texas. The absolute embodiment of a process-driven business that puts the client first on every level as they continue to refine and optimize their business to improve the B-to-C experience. They also created the Plan4Life Process that they not only deploy for their own clients, they insist that other F4S professionals who gravitate to their team deploy it as well. Their self-imposed mandate is that scalable growth can never be pursued at the expense of their core clients.

## What Do They Want?

If you get to the point where you say, "it's go time" on the B-to-B model and you're confident in your B-to-C IP and adoptability, the next things to clarify before you go to market are your hook and your B-to-B process. The hook itself has nothing to do with how great you are. Potential opt-in candidates will figure that out for themselves as they go through your fit process. The hook has to be all about them and what they want. There are far more buyers than sellers, and your mindset has to be relentlessly focused on professional contrast and professional scarcity through your entire cycle. It starts with defining precisely what the ideal candidate wants from you.

Whether they want to sell the entire business to you and bow out, sell and stay (even on a consulting basis for a while), sell you a remnant so they can grow down to 25 clients, draft in behind your process, outsource some of the commoditized to you, or just acquire your IP and apply it to their business, their motivations fit into these 3 categories:

**Liberation** – they want to restore balance, simplify their life and pursue other FORM related interests. It's a version of their own Blue Square.

**Legacy** – they want their clients and worthy team members to be upgraded.

**Liquidity** – they want to monetize fully.

The order of 'wants' matters. If all they're concerned about when you talk to them is money, that's probably a clue that there will be some hair on this deal, and for that reason it would not be a good fit. Yes, getting maximum value is important, but their "why" has to be addressed fully.

Larry Andrews, a F4S professional of the highest order in La Jolla, CA got out in front of his own and his clients' continuity and succession issues by bringing in his son, Larry (L2) as an associate. To his credit, L2 was already bought in to the SOP world of best practices and process.

Methodically, with the team, they defined roles, identified gaps and reframed their relationships in order to raise the bar and activate deep future-pacing and planning – with tremendous impact on and feedback from clients. Unknown to Larry, a soon-to-be retiring colleague in the office observed the entire evolution and approached Larry to "please accept responsibility for my clients. I know they couldn't be in better hands". After meticulously validating the fit and alignment, mapping out and executing the transitional process and documenting it all along the way, the departing colleague was delighted, the new clients are ecstatic and L1 and L2 have a "just add water" process that has been fully proven, ready to deploy again and again.

On the topic of liberation as it relates to a motivator, we were on the other side of the process, brought in by an acquirer to answer questions posed by an anxious seller who just wanted some clarifications about "what this would look like." In speaking with him, he was well prepared but trying to control the conversation. We answered his questions and picked our spots for when we could ask a few back. It was revealed that, in addition to vetting potential acquirers, he was also trying to figure out whether or not he should exit stage left, or stick around for a while after the transition. We asked him directly, "Is this your calling?" To which he replied, "Calling? More like a cauldron. There is so much about this business I don't like anymore. I am the proverbial boiled frog." To which we invited him to elaborate on what caused him pain and to also talk about what he still did like about the business. It was bipolar in that his tone on the phone shifted from dark and ominous for the dread and hassle factor, to upbeat and cheery around the things he loved. So we asked him, "What does it look like for you in a typical week if all you did was talk to your favorite clients, engage in the activities that you are strong at, and enjoy and get back to a few things in life that you've put on the back burner?"

"Well, that would be perfection," he replied.

At that moment he started scenario planning with us the steps he would need to take to get "my act together" – an initial checklist. He literally came to his own conclusions that "this is what I want and I am excited again about my job."

## Will it Work?

To put the odds in your favor that there is an alignment requires a variation of a fit process that has to be thought through well in advance. Remember, you won't be chasing or pursuing anyone, you will be attracting with a compelling value proposition and process. Like every relationship, how you start it, position it and see it through will have a huge impact on how it will unfold over the long haul. Again, the fit process is:

**Philosophical** – You see the world the same way. You're like-minded. He or she is wired to stewardship and is not a hunter-gatherer. They see the merit of becoming a client of your firm themselves. They see the merit of staying on as consultant - for a while at least. They are absolutely ecstatic about the precision of your process.

**Strategic** – He or she is unwaveringly, adamantly, bordering on obsessed about the well-being of clients. It's not a transaction. This is not a sale. It is a professional transition with a singular focus on elevating the client experience. No ego, all Legacy.

**Practical** – The last thing to discuss is the economics. It's important but not the primary motivation or the deciding factor.

To add predictability to your eventual encounters and interactions, we also encourage you to capture and chronicle (Rule of Three!) the details of your approach for your first and second acquisitions. It's a malleable format that you can use to ensure your acquisition and transition are well-defined, well-executed and repeatable. That process is incredibly valuable once it's built out and proven.

There are two more components to be addressed, but before we discuss them, if this overall premise seems like a good idea, but you don't want to reinvent the wheel, visit www.thebluesquaremethod.com/implementation-resources. For those who want hands-on guidance with their deployment, look at our Elevated program to learn what engaging with one our accountability partners would entail.

## Populate Your Pipeline

This is not the type of initiative that gets rolled out with an advertising campaign. It must be an underground effort, especially in the beginning, to ensure discretion and methodical management. Instead, release the hounds – bird-dogs, that is. Vendors and wholesalers are effective at stirring the pot. Start networking and presenting at conferences. Speak to M&A brokers and lenders (especially while the cost of capital is low). Include lawyers, accountants, bankers and any other professional with expertise on your space who can also share your story with those they come in contact with. When you broach the subject, discuss your vision and readiness. Emphasize process, emphasize fit and always strive to emphasize professional contrast and scarcity.

## Transitioning Early Adopters

As much as you want to have your process fully built out to help them to see the merit of opting in, you also have to build out the process to move (all or some of) the team and (all or some of) their clients over to you. Be transparent with your first B-to-B relationship to ensure you have a foundation for them in place so they know you will be working with them – building the bridge as you cross it - and refining as they make the move.

This is a hybrid of the B-to-C ONside and ONboard process, but with a few twists, and is framed in Ramp Up, Execute and Follow-Through phases.

**The Ramp Up Phase** – anyone on the verge of transitioning to you has to prime the pump with their clients, to plant seeds and create awareness for what is coming down the line – and do it gradually. We've been involved in transitions that were immediate (for a variety of reasons) and while it can be done, it's not ideal. Methodically and without urgency is better. The best way to prepare their clients is for them to relay an appropriate version of this:

*"Just to let you know, as a lifelong planner, our team is currently going through an exercise for the purpose of raising the bar when it comes to our client experience. I'm taking the long view, looking down the road to get out in front of our clients' evolving needs. We're very excited about this and will keep you posted on the enhancements that we make."*

Admittedly cryptic, this message is designed to open the conversation. Most will say, "I look forward to hearing about that," while some might want to pick their brain for more details. In that case they can just say, *"It's a little bit early in the process but I'll keep you apprised when there are some specifics."*

**The Execute Phase** – either on the phone, or preferably in person, they can speak to their clients in concrete terms about what is taking place. Work it out within a SNIB to get the positioning in order:

**Subject** – After some extensive due diligence focused on areas that can elevate the client experience, we have made the decision to (describe the transition).

**Need** – Over the years I've seen my client's needs become more complex, and as a lifelong planner, I wanted to make some adjustments that would raise the bar for them now and in the future.

**Ideas** – My due diligence revealed three specific things that reinforced my decision to go in this direction.

**Benefits** – The primary benefits to my clients are (continuity and succession, a deeper emphasis on panoramic planning, streamlined access, etc.)

Then, outline the call to action and lay out the next steps. "We have developed and refined a process to make this transition as seamless as possible." Outline salient points around fit (they will determine if they see the merit through an ONside process) and then ONboard (setting expectations for what it will look like.) The driver here is that they will buy in because they trust you and the transition is in their best interests.

**The Follow-through Phase** - once the transition to the new model/ environment/experience has occurred, expectations were set. "I believe elevation was mentioned," will be swirling around in the minds of the clients that followed. In the onboard, the full suite of deliverables for AAA-PLUS clients should be displayed. As with any motion, opportunities for reframing can be deployed to reveal untapped opportunity. In time, silver linings appear around automating, allocating, or even disassociating further down the client roster. With an ongoing open kitchen approach throughout the early stages of the new and improved relationship, you can anticipate an uptick in conversion.

## Go No/Go?

As with any investment of time and money applied to a new venture, you have to do a risk assessment. Some ventures appear to be destined to provide a risk-free return, and then, after a sizable expenditure, it turns out to be return-free risk. An element of the sunk-cost fallacy often kicks in.

Do you have the appetite for this level of intensity? Are you committed to the thorough due-diligence and preparation required to add the probability of success to the outcomes? Will you execute and follow-through with a process? Do you have the stomach to deal with the heartburn of frustration that will surely occur when dealing with new people and many moving parts? Will you empower your bench with the resources to manage this more complex venture? Many F4S professionals have made this leap, and while it wasn't a straight line or without hurdles, the outcomes have been impressive. Be sure to check out Elevated at thebluesquaremethod.com/implementation-resources to learn more and schedule an exploratory conversation with us.

# Chapter 13:

## *The Torch – Your Legacy and the Mentor-Protégé Dynamic*

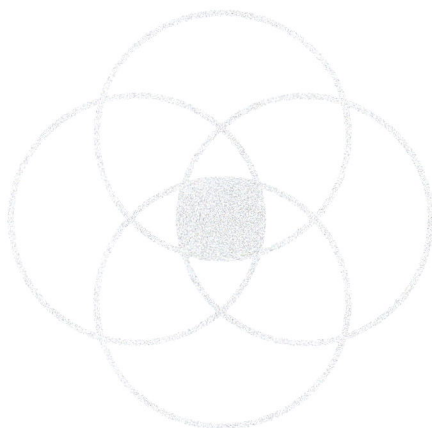

As an extension to the professional advice you provide within your process, there is an opportunity to consider another avenue where you can have an impact. There is an unwritten rule in the world of entrepreneurship that says that, as you progress down your own path, look for people whose path you can shine a light on. In your pursuit of your goals, be mindful of who you could throw into your sidecar and propel forward. As with a successful sports team that finds the perfect blend of veterans and rookies, the coach will let the seasoned subtly offer leadership and direction to those with potential and flashes of brilliance, but who still have much to learn.

Patek Philippe, the last remaining family-owned Genevan watch manufacturer, captured the essence of that in their slogan, "You never actually own a Patek Philippe. You merely look after it for the next generation."

Jim Rohn said that the goal of business isn't to just make a profit, it's to leave a profit, too. The suggestion is to always strive to leave things, people and the world better than you found them. Some people are ambivalent about how they make money. For them, money is the goal. Others are more purposeful and financial success is an outcome of their business achievements.

In ancient Rome, Janus – the god of doors – had two faces. One looked to the past and the other to the future. Legend has it that the key he held in his right hand symbolized his role as the sentinel, the gatekeeper, the protector of doors that opened to new beginnings. It's a pleasant thought to shape that into our own vision. We can open doors and offer protection to the next generation.

This chapter focuses on what often appears to be the lost art of giving and receiving advice. Providing advice is a study, but to the enlightened, the person giving also receives. It's a mirror to evaluate one's style, tone, timing and the impact of our approach. We get to hear it and self-assess for credibility and congruency. Those whose heart is in it never ask for the recipient to be a better listener, they ask of themselves to be a better communicator. The exchange might prompt us to search for more answers, too. As the saying goes, a candle loses nothing in lighting another. In this case, its flame might even strengthen, and with so much negativity in the world, your efforts stir up some karma that will land somewhere. One positive act will surely counter a negative somewhere and at some point.

There is a misconception that the appetite for guidance today is waning. There has to be an awareness for the recipient's stage of readiness, and delivery requires tact, but searching for direction is something that is innately human. Whether it's self-identifying with your spirit animal, being energized by a hero or just trying to not reinvent the wheel, we all crave, in some degree, to be led – especially early in life. Many put on a brave front fueled by a "fake it 'til you make it" approach, but most people, unless they become jaded, are sponges. They will soak it in if they feel it's of interest and will help them.

The historical origins of advice are fascinating. Socrates is considered the founder of western philosophy, with a specific emphasis on ethics, extending back 2,400 hundred years. He also taught Plato, who took the Athenian torch and ran with it, opening an academy of thought. In his timeless work The Republic, Plato posited that society should be led by people who demonstrate wisdom, self-discipline, justice and courage. There was Aristotle, a student of Plato who went on to expand on the study and appreciation for logic, among many other qualities.

There are countless historical figures who laid the ground work for us when it comes to studying and relaying wisdom. Will and Ariel Durant captured a massive amount in their epic project *The Story of Civilization*, an 11-volume series that took a lifetime to create and takes years to consume. It's over 13,000 pages of examples and warnings from the past. It's impressive to look at, let alone read, and you feel smarter for just owning it, but every page teaches something powerful.

Some of the best stories and lessons that teach us what it means to strive for excellence are not only from those who achieved their goals in life, but also those who came close. Mathew Robinson competed in Berlin at the Olympics in 1936 under intense conditions, and still broke an Olympic record - only to finish second to Jesse Owens. Throughout the rest of his life he developed a reputation as someone who gave tirelessly to his community with little fanfare, especially considering he was the older brother of baseball legend Jackie Robinson. While one achieved more fame, they both quietly went about pursuing things bigger than themselves that will stand the test of time.

## Why Leadership Will Always be Needed

There are two invisible forces that have always battled throughout history. On one side you have the forces of darkness. Dividing, stealing, slandering, deceiving, attacking and gas-lighting, while always claiming to have the moral high ground.

To what end? To control, to consolidate, and because of their insatiable appetite - to destroy. The parasite will always strive to destroy the host, even if it's a wolf cloaked in sheep's clothing. This is why the world needs more sheepdogs.

On the other side, you have the force for good. Building, innovating, helping, earning and achieving through merit, honor and value, but they are often playing defense, too. These are the people who know that something that's happened 100 billion times – a human being born - is still a miracle. They have immense wonder and appreciation, as well as intense ambition and aspiration. It's truly a thing of beauty – but they have to be perpetually vigilant. There have been many attempts to subtly awaken people to the dark forces.

There are also great examples in art that outline the conflict. Take *The Wizard of Oz*, with its Scarecrow lacking a brain, Tin Man lacking a heart and Lion lacking courage, yet still helping Dorothy down the yellow brick road. They confront a wicked witch and her terrifying flying monkeys, only to discover she was a paper tiger undone by just a bucket of water. The heroes are then applauded by her minions following her demise - and then the curtain gets pulled back. So many lessons.

Lewis Carroll's *Alice in Wonderland,* and almost anything by CS Lewis, among others, were just trying to make sure we knew where we stood, what we were up against and what needed to be done.

The point is, it's our responsibility to empower others to push forward and defend, simultaneously. Eternal vigilance is necessary for enduring freedom.

### Start with Philosophy

The activation of ambition and empowerment in a protégé is rooted more in teaching them how to think rather than what to think.

Developing an enlightened philosophy hardens the head, meaning one knows what they stand for. They're not bobbing in the ocean of life like a rudderless raft.

Developing skills and intelligence strengthens one's resolve, so that they can set the sails, harness the wind, see beyond obstacles and adapt to external forces.

Developing a sense of empathy softens the heart, meaning they have gratitude and humility and they're predisposed to throwing a lifeline when needed.

One's philosophy must be established as a starting point and strengthened throughout life. How a person sees the world. How they interpret situations. How they interact with people. How they pursue their goals.

Back to the dark forces for a moment, History is basically a story of tyrants, victims, heroes and cowards. History has also shown us that the end game of socialism lies in totalitarianism. In between, it evolves through cronyism – the dealing of favors instead of goods and services, fascism – the conspiring of nefarious corporations with the state, against the best interest of the citizens, communism – value is taken, not created, with complete centralization, and then finally tyrannical Totalitarianism – a brutal, non-viable environment of destruction. The only force that prevents that complete progression is resistance. Unless you want the whole camel in the tent, don't let him stick his nose in – at all. The pitch for their model always starts off romantically with idealistic and emotional notions. Many want to believe, but the utopian descriptions are often delivered by smiling people who are inherently evil.

Marcus Tullius Cicero, a fascinating figure from ancient Rome worthy of studying, said, "though liberty is established by law, we must be vigilant, for liberty to enslave us is always present under that very liberty."

What does that have to do with entrepreneurship? Entrepreneurs are the embodiment of freedom. They create it, they expand it, and by their actions, they nurture and defend it. Business owners employ the most people, generate the most taxes, give more time and money to worthy causes, are the biggest tippers and are the most significant contributors to society - and business will always execute better than government.

We need to attract, encourage and support more people in becoming entrepreneurs. It's an essential counter-force to darkness and it is the best environment to fulfill one's goal of self-actualization.

No other environment is as conducive to those pursuits as capitalism built on the shoulders of entrepreneurs. The counter to that is this position, often attributed to Stalin, "Show me the man and I'll show you the crime." He undoubtedly also said (or at least believed), "It doesn't matter who votes. What matters is who counts the votes." Pure capitalism is too transparent for that level of sinister activity. Dr. Adrian Rogers said you can't multiply wealth by dividing it. Thomas Sowell said you can't take from a producer without producing something yourself.

At the risk of going overboard on the importance of a strong enlightened philosophy, the goal is to emphasize the multifaceted impact entrepreneurs have. It's not just the pursuit of happiness and wealth creation, it's a proactive armor against the forces that resent someone else's pursuit of happiness and wealth creation.

To quote Martin Luther King, "Darkness cannot drive out darkness; only light can do that."

There is a progression to help instill, develop, and stick with an enlightened philosophy. It requires discernment, critical thinking and a rational, fair mind. In *The Gulag Archipelago*, we are reminded to not participate in a lie and always strive to live in a factual reality, but Mark Twain's point bears repeating, "It is easier to fool someone than to convince someone they've been fooled." Strangely, there are some people who don't want the truth, they want what they believe to be the truth. Plato mourned this mindset: "We can easily forgive a child who is afraid of the dark; the real tragedy of life is when men are afraid of the light."

## Consider the Source

We are in an era of intense virtue-signaling. The volume is loud and the tone is harsh. Part of being a mentor is ensuring the protégé considers both sides, no matter how thinly a view is sliced. It's not a great idea to drink water from a toilet or consume food from a dumpster, and we must be as careful before we consume agenda-loaded propaganda for the same reasons.

The generation coming up behind us has been subjected to a degree and velocity of noise and disinformation never before seen. Many of them have had their grit killed by kindness, as well. Nurture/nature is an interesting dynamic. Think about how many generations have gone into a protégé between Socrates and today – it's close to 100.

That's a lot of wars, famines, hardships and wins leading up to that one person, so there is a deep-seated predisposition and many innate abilities in there thanks to DNA. Now combine that with the way many of their generation have been nurtured.

Though unintentional, and with their hearts in the right place, many parents unwittingly create a degree of learned helplessness in their kids. Safety first - of course we can't let our kids be raised by wolves - but often the extreme micromanagement of parenting, and shielding of experiential development, has been like virtual bubble wrap. It's natural to try to step in for our kids to mitigate risk and avoid pain, but they have to "touch the stove" to some degree. Helicopter parents would swoop in to save the day, and that evolved to bulldozer parenting, plowing through any real or perceived injustice. Yes, we want to provide a safety net, just not a hammock where complacency and entitlement can get comfortable. We want our protégés to develop a reputation for action and urgency. When you suggest, for example, they watch a video or read a book, and they do – holding themselves accountable - it's fulfilling knowing that you don't want it more than they do.

Carl Jung said that "The greatest burden a child must bear is the unlived life of its parents." That sentiment can actually work both ways. Tom Stanley in *The Millionaire Next Door* discussed how first generation self-made affluent business owners and professionals – especially the 25-year overnight success stories who fought and scraped to finally break through – often deprive their kids of as much hardship, discomfort, friction, rejection and adversity as possible, "so they don't have to go through what I did." The problem is it was those challenges, and overcoming them, that got them to their level of achievement.

## Not All Heroes ... are Necessary

The urge to intervene and clear a path of less resistance is natural. Sometimes we convince ourselves that it's "easier, faster and higher quality control if I just do it myself," but that undermines the fulfillment of a self-realized outcome. Obviously, everyone is busy and time flies, but there's no rush. We get 18 years +/- to let them make mistakes and then figure them out under our tutelage. We're not checking boxes. External solutions – letting someone else handle it – has its place. Internal solutions, even with misfires, creates skill development, persistence and confidence. The pain fades, but the scar remains and it often takes the shape of wisdom.

## Competing with (or contending with?) Technology

Your mentorship has to navigate through how technology appears to be rewiring brains. The attention span of many seems to be dropping to the level of a hummingbird. Some people, because of their disjointed stream of consciousness, have a tough time finishing a thought as they engage in a real conversation with another person. Some people scroll through and consume the equivalent of 300 pages of information per day from their phones. The virtual reality of the metaverse is surreal. Battery anxiety is a real thing. Tech neck is keeping chiropractors very busy. Fifty people die every year taking selfies. Headphones have radically lowered situational awareness, and rather than being self-aware, many are self-conscious.

All of this is a gentle reminder of what you're dealing with, and to give you the empathy to be patient as you weave in your guidance throughout that maze of distractions.

## So Where Does One Start?

The first step in a long journey like this begins with you. Mentors will often ask themselves, "How can I improve anyone without first asking how to improve myself?" Being an excellent example of well-rounded achievement is far better than providing opinions on how to achieve. We've all met the sanctimonious, who suggest or even mandate something they themselves have no intention of doing. Keep in mind, the goal is to help protégés think for themselves, not prove that you're the smartest guy in the room. In a perfect world of self-discovery, every idea is their idea, not yours. You just led them there. It's like an invention for the betterment of society. You don't need the patent, and you'll just give it away. No praise, no recognition, it's just the right thing to do.

The art is to prompt them with a thought and leave them wanting more – but not necessarily from you. You want them to go and seek it out on their own. Then they come back and tell you the solution that they created that mirrors the advice you were tempted to give them, but you threw a self-directed Heisman and let them figure it out. It's a great skill to allow someone to solve a puzzle with a prompt, and then prepare them to handle the consequences of their decision – good, great or otherwise.

## The Best Advice You Never Gave

Consider an athlete with exceptional ability who hits a rut or a rough patch. As a coach, you can offer advice on what to correct and how to work through it, but before you do, you offer praise. You remind them that they are capable and accomplished. The praise alone might light a fire. Ability feeds off confidence and brings out additional ability. Tell them, "what really impressed me on that last shift was when you..." You can then build on that with an insight, but to a far more predisposed audience. An interesting analogy is this: Photographers have tested a simple approach when taking someone's picture. They will quickly snap a shot of the person as they pose and then immediately tell them they are beautiful. Breaking from the pose, the subject naturally beams from the compliment, and the picture taken at that moment is strikingly superior to the first. Remember, giving advice – especially unsolicited – can imply that the protégé is wrong, at fault or inadequate. The goal of the leader is not to be right, not to find fault and not even to be respected - it's to bring something out in someone else.

## Read the Room

Quality mentors default to respect for the protégé, not superiority. From an intergenerational HR perspective, they show true interest by asking questions. "Tell me about your most meaningful accomplishment." Or "Tell me about the biggest obstacle you ever overcame." Or, "What's the best advice you ever received?" All are very revealing queries. Those who combine confidence with humility will generally talk about the people who have helped them. The resilient will show how they are defined by their comebacks, not their setbacks. They overcome adversity, they are not overcome by it.

## Many Issues are Two or Three Questions Deep

A one-off question can get someone talking. Two or three follow-ups can tell someone you're sincere. One of the biggest drivers of intergenerational communication is respect built on serious interest in the protégé. A poor mentor will not go to the trouble of knowing their audience, and, even worse, will underestimate it. A protégé is wrapped up in their own era and not all that interested in yours, but the moment you show interest in what they are interested in, trust is born. For example, you might discover that your protégé is interested in manga, a graphic novel format originating in Japan and dating back hundreds of years.

You might think to yourself, "Seriously, this guy is still into comics!?!" but you decide to inquire about it with sincere interest. The protégé might be a bit reluctant to open up until you persist with follow-up questions. And through it all, you learn that manga is inspired by almost every genre, sources as disparate as H.P. Lovecraft, the Bible and Grimm's fairy tales, and has in turn inspired many stories including *The Good, the Bad and the Ugly*. The art has deep visceral impact, and the stories have deep allegorical meaning, specifically around morality and the battle between good and evil. When a protégé gives his or her perspective on survival, causality and consequences, you are gaining access to a window into their deeply seated beliefs. You are learning about their core philosophy without saying a word. When they talk metaphorically about destiny and what it means to be human – the pursuit of strength instead of power – you understand what's going through their mind when they are alone with their thoughts, and a deeper connection is made.

You've probably heard the advice that if you want to remember a joke, you only need to remember the punch line. You can reverse engineer and backfill to the beginning. The point is, when you take a protégé to the edge of a breakthrough with your guidance, and then give them the dignity of taking it through the finish line, they come up with the answer themselves.

That brings us to consequences. Sometimes they crush it, and the book-end is to ensure there is humility, shared accomplishment with team members and being understated and gracious in victory. In cases where it goes wrong, you want the support you provide to be interpreted in a way that lets them know you are there for them, but that they have to own it and figure it out. Your job is to ensure they don't overreact, giving the setback too much power. They haven't been shot – or it might just be a flesh wound. It's solvable, but they also can't under-react by putting a Band-Aid on a bullet hole.

In both scenarios, though, the biggest takeaway has to be, "I believe in you!" Virtually no one hears that enough, if at all. The words have to be backed up with eye contact, body language, sincerity and availability.

Over time, as you get the chance to immerse yourself, you can broaden the horizons of things you're trying instill and enhance. It's not a complete list, but all protégés should get your perspective on these essential qualities:

- **Ethics**
- **Responsibility**
- **Resilience**
- **Self-awareness**
- **Diplomacy**
- **Success**

## Ethics

"Falsus in uno, falsus in omnibus" means "false in one thing, false in everything." Insisting your protégés have unwavering honor and airtight honesty in everything and everyone they touch is of massive importance. Being forthright and transparent with clients, being honest with themselves – it all creates a shining example. Dostoevsky wrote, "The man who lies to himself, and listens to his own lie, comes to such a pass that he cannot distinguish the truth within him, or around him, and so loses all respect for himself and for others." It's a gradual, slippery slope that is so corrosive in its subtlety that one hardly notices where it takes them until they're lost.

Race car drivers will clip the apex, not because they're cheating but because it requires skill, will, and saves time. Cutting corners outside racing – and getting away with it – almost universally comes back to haunt, and the reputational damage is done. It has the same effect on the psyche as putting a thumb on the scale to round up a sale.

## Responsibility

We're going to let Jocko Willink and Leif Brebin, two navy seals with immense credibility and intense impact, take care of this department. Their book *Extreme Ownership* is essential reading for mentors and protégés alike because of their incredible take on blaming, complaining, excuses and deflecting. When it comes to self-governance, personal responsibility is non-optional.

A big part of this is making choices and taking action. Admiral William McRaven wrote a simple yet compelling book called *Make Your Bed.* The premise is subtle. By starting the day by making your bed as part of your morning ritual, you've already accomplished something that validates your personal standards. By not making the bed, you're making a choice. Inaction is an action that erodes esteem, even if just slightly. This is a powerful mindset to pass along to the up and coming generation.

## Resilience

Software and technology experts are continually hardening their systems to prevent a breach or hack. The same has to be true for us. The fuel for overcoming adversity includes personal responsibility; never quitting, never giving up. A Japanese proverb says, "Fall seven times, stand up eight." Grit and fortitude are qualities that emerge through trial by fire, support and self-confidence. You can instill in a protégé the urge to never give up, and that even when it seems hopeless, they are still "fourth and inches" and to keep going. The curtain never closes on someone that never throws in the towel.

## Self-awareness

There's an old saying, thunder is scary but lightning is dangerous. You want your protégés to be warriors, not worriers. Humility, respect, confidence and faith are unstoppable. Being self-absorbed or self-conscious creates a self-imposed headwind. Helping someone understand that can be delicate - like diffusing a bomb - but when you disconnect the correct wire, the outcome is incredibly rewarding.

## Success

There are many layers to this, and, while success is more of an achievement than it is a quality, it requires an array of qualities to attain it in a pure form. Just as there is a profound distinction between confidence and arrogance, there is a similar difference between humility and self-doubt, as well as worthiness and entitlement. Through merit, there is no ceiling holding someone back on their version of success, just as there is no limit to the anticlimax that comes with a sense of entitlement. A good decision is often arrived at from a strong position which, in concert, can create a positive outcome.

A significant quality that is associated with success is one's view of money. Is it the primary goal or is it the by-product of achieving one's goal? It's been proven time and time again that money on its own does not make someone valuable. Being rich in life doesn't always mean literal wealth.

That said, the pursuit of affluence – being rich – requires a mindset of what it means to "act rich" -the responsibility, the good fortune and the concept of "earn." We've all seen or read about someone who suddenly became affluent; a young phenomenon in the world of sports or entertainment, who was showered with riches only to see it move through them, never to return. We know of stories of people who won lotteries and were "set for life" – only for the money to disappear like sand in a shopping cart. Then there is the concept of inheritance – the developing avalanche of intergenerational wealth. The numbers, in terms of how much money will be changing hands in the next 10 to 20 years, are staggering. If the first generation that earned the wealth did not prepare the second generation who found the wealth to understand it – to have a mindset for wealth - it could be a burden more than anything else. Again, as described in the books *Beer Money* and *Entitlemania*, they need to think and respect "rich" before it arrives. Otherwise, that family legacy can vaporize.

If the affluent mindset is not built on a strong foundation, after the money changes hands, these are often the outcomes:

- An initial resentment that the amount wasn't big enough.

- They leave the legacy financial professional "because I can take care of it myself."

- The tax man ends up getting more than necessary.

- The shopping spree commences.

- It's gone.

Young people who are taught to be frugal - not cheap, but just appreciative of the value of money - are better suited when the windfall happens. It is often said that the Scottish have deep pockets and short arms (That might have something to do with their history though). When young people are taught to be respectful of others and diplomatic, they create an environment where people feel special, not one where they themselves feel superior. When they are taught to take action – like sending thank-you cards and making phone calls to pay tribute to others who send a birthday gift – they're on a good path. These are learned skills.

Solid stewards of earned wealth have an enlightened approach to the notion of inheritance. They ingrain the concept in the next generation that, whatever it ends up looking like, it will be a bonus - but not one to be counted on. So, to hedge your bets, and for the benefit of personal fulfillment and self-esteem, go and earn your own. You'll take better care of it and do more with it if you earned it. It's your skin in the game.

Don't worry, we're not losing the plot here, drifting off the topic of entrepreneurship, but there are times when being in business can be a bit isolating during decision making. When it comes to putting earned money to work, so that it can make money for you in return – to compete with your business revenues – there are many things to be mindful of. This is knowledge and wisdom you can invest into your protégé.

In *The Millionaire Next Door,* Tom Stanley presented a simple net-worth formula that everyone should be aware of throughout their lives, and especially when the numbers are small. In the spirit of knowing where you stand, and making money your servant, he said to multiply your age by your annual pre-tax income and then divide by ten, and that is about where you should be. Of course, personal net worth is not just about money. Wealth comes in many forms, but being mindful of both the quantitative and qualitative factors that complete the picture creates a checkpoint as the journey is unfolding.

Bull markets (the horns point up) and bear markets (the paw slashes down) are interesting forces that can either contribute to or work against net-worth progression – temporarily at least. There are many fundamentally sound strategies (pay yourself first, dollar cost averaging, diversification and long-term time horizons) that are immune to or can harness market conditions. There are so many ways to show the power of compounding. One of the best is to hold out a sheet of paper, fold it in half, and then ask the protégé how high it would reach if you folded it 42 times. Look it up, it's a jaw dropper on par with the penny that doubles when passing each square on a chess board.

## A Philosophy and a Process – as usual

As your protégé starts earning, their philosophy about money should start with The Rule of 17 – as a beginning minimum, they should immediately save 7%, invest 7% and give away 3% of their income, right off the top. Some go 5/5/7 - whatever moves them, personally. That is just the start. The goal is to keep ratcheting that up as the habit is in place and the income starts growing -ideally to the Rule of 34.

Their savings are dry powder for opportunities that are presented. Their investments will start producing, at which point they can decide to take some off the table as things ebb and flow. Not watching their ice cream melt as markets drop can mean they're positioned to buy more on sale. Good decisions come from strong positions.

The key part of the philosophy is that they pay themselves first, always. If they try to save what's left at the end of the month, there is usually more month left than money. The Rule of 17 can extrapolate further, applying to:

An investor – invest in solid companies and the community with charitable giving.

A saver – lending money to the bank or placed in safe dividend investments.

A spender – Spend what's left on living.

Be sure to convey the difference between an investor and speculator. The concept of volatility is quite the study. In some sectors, market forces can be turbulent, and often it's up like an escalator and down like an elevator. There is a summary of *A Short History of Financial Euphoria* on thebluesquaremethod. com/implementation-resources to learn about the madness of crowd mentality, bubbles and scams.

This is a big factor, especially as it relates to market forces and individual forces. Caveat emptor has to be dialed to 11 in the world of speculating because that's where a lot of the nefarious are lurking. Deception, misrepresentations and manipulation, all cloaked within a too-good-to-be-true but somehow believable pitch, requires immense discernment, critical thinking and judgment. The short story here is that any speculating has to be done with slush. No core capital can be put at risk.

## What to do with it?

With a solid philosophy comes the importance of process. Wealth accumulation is not something someone achieves by winging it. It's not a rodeo where you win by hanging on long enough. Everyone needs an enlightened philosophy, a personalized plan, a sound process and a relationship with a financial professional who can put it all together and continue planning as things progress. This is too important to DIY, and a solid professional will give you the gift of time by liberating you to do what you do best – bring value and make money. This is the message that needs to be relayed to your protégés.

## Prepare Your Heart

As incredibly fulfilling as being a mentor can be, there are times when it can be thankless too. It's not an exact science – so many variables that can support your efforts or conspire against them. Gandhi had an interesting take that at first seems puzzling but then makes sense:

"Whatever you do will be insignificant, but it is very important that you do it."

You'll have some wins, and you'll have some disappointments – at least out of the gate. But expectations need to be tempered or even removed. Mark Twain said it well:

"If you pick up a starving dog and make him prosperous, he will not bite you. This is the principal difference between a dog and a man."

We get his point even if it's a little on the generalized side.

Most people go through life with a "do no harm" philosophy. A smaller percentage adopt the "do some good" approach, which can involve risk. Going out of your way and above and beyond can backfire. Perhaps you've offered a panhandler some money, and offered a few words of sincere encouragement, only to be met with blow back and venom? Your empathy kicked in and you made sense of it quickly, but still...

We strive to become a mentor and contributor to society, not just for what it provides to the world, but also because of what it reveals in us; for what it brings out in us and for what it makes of us. It's an honor and a privilege. You can tell when you're in the presence of someone who deeply understands this. For example, a client of ours in Southern California, Dryden Pence, who, along with his team, runs a complex enterprise serving very sophisticated clients. That alone is impressive, but you'd be hard pressed to have a conversation with Dryden without being moved by his drive to help others, and especially to help others get over the hump in terms of adversity. He is a strong, confident personality with a tender side that is palpable.

Entrepreneurship is not taught in schools, which is odd when you consider the reach and impact it has. Kids aren't taught to be business owners. Where is the glory in that? Astronauts, firefighters, athletes, police officers, rock stars and celebrities are the dream jobs. You don't see a poster on a kid's wall of an owner of an HVAC company. There is no "oohing and awing" in the classroom when a consultant comes in to share a typical day in the life. "Oh look kids, Billy's mum is here. She's a successful fee-for-service professional that helps people look to the future with anticipation." It's all yawns.

But we know. We know what the world looked like before there were entrepreneurs. We know that it's small business owners that create so much income for society to provide services and strengthen the social safety net. When you read the story of a pediatrician that worked tirelessly in 1981 to save a newborn baby, and many years later that pediatrician is in a car crash and gets saved by a paramedic that was – guess who – It hits you right in the heart. Also consider the many quiet, unassuming business owners that created value, wealth and income, all of which contributed to that story in some way.

Thomas Sowell said it so well: Producers are demonized. Non-producers get subsidized. Destroyers get canonized.

History is loaded with examples of non-producers and destroyers, outraged that the producers aren't paying their fair share. (Let's see your financial disclosures and see if you went first and walked your talk, Mr. or Mrs. Non-producer/Destroyer).

## A State of Confucian

"When the student is ready the master will appear" is a classic tip from Confucius, among many others. Let's just focus on what we can control. Helping the next generation find a job? Sure. How about find a leader, and then create a job, and then become a leader?

Expand their thinking along the way. Introduce them to Fibonacci's Golden Ratio. Steer them to the world of Nikola Tesla. Show them Dr. Emoto's Water Experiment, if for no other reason to open their eyes to the wonders of the universe. Skepticism aside, the goal is to make them think as they strive, and in words of a very enlightened mentor Tom Selleck, "We're raising them to let them go."

Again to Gandhi, "The best way to find yourself is to lose yourself in the service of others."

Losing yourself means you ask a lot of questions – and not because you love the sound of your own voice. Every protégé you interact with wants to be heard. When you speak to them they are thinking, "Show some interest in me. Just ask me one question." When you do, it's disarming, engaging and laying the foundation for a terrific exchange.

Many will later come back to you to express their debt of gratitude. Just remember the old saying, "One person's debt is another person's asset." It's an asset to be able - and be invited - to leave a profit in the life of someone else.

It might be the noblest pursuit there is. If you can encourage just one protégé to strive to take over or build a business, so they can find ways to innovate, expend effort, deliver value, develop bravery and enhance their patriotism, you, as a mentor, will have definitely paid more than your fair share.

# Chapter 14:

## *Resources - Translating Relevant Ideas into Measurable Results*

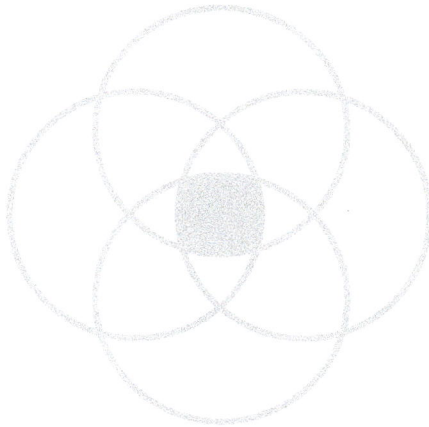

As we mentioned at the beginning of this book, the value of reading The Blue Square Method really begins now that you've reached the end. We've made suggestions and hopefully prompted you to think about refinements, and now you have to make some decisions. The culmination of your investment of effort in reading this book occurs when you take action. To that end, this chapter is designed to be the bridge from intention to implementation. Ideally, you will have made note of six to eight ideas that struck a chord with you in the previous chapters.

The following checklist is mirrored on thebluesquaremethod.com/implementation-resources with active links consisting of:

1. A sequence of overview videos

2. Downloadable and actionable templates

3. Spotlights on supplemental tools

### Chapter 1. The Blue Square: True North

Counter The Law of Diminishing Intent as you bring maximum conversion and convergence to your business.

- Start with the Always ON placeholder

- Learn more about The Blue Square Academy

### Chapter 2. The Origins of Our Approach

Galvanize that your aspirations align with our approach as you move towards the very best version of yourself - personally and professionally.

- Review the Ikigai and Maslow's Hierarchy

- Access our full suggested reading list

### Chapter 3. An Enlightened Philosophy

Differentiate yourself as you consider the relevance of *McNamara's Fallacy* regarding qualitative impact and *Little's Law* regarding your natural capacity.

- Review the C-Suite of Trust and The Rule of 3 checklist

- Learn more about The Blue Square Toolkit for automated process deployment

## Chapter 4. First, Get Clear on Your Gaps

The heavy lifting begins as you clarify your goals, identify your gaps, hold yourself accountable and assess your trajectory and results.

- Kick start your org-chart, playbook, ideal client profile and service matrix.

- Gain absolute clarity and know where you stand with our Practice Management Index.

## Chapter 5. Then, Develop a Branding Strategy

Professional contrast is achieved by articulating your value verbally and demonstrating your value tangibly.

- Build-out your solution stack and frame it with a customized 7 Pillars approach

- Explore our P3 Branding Consulting Approach

## Chapter 6. And Then, Reframe Your Existing Relationships

Direct your initial efforts to your primary addressable audience, your community of long term existing clients, to rejuvenate their appreciation of your value.

- Clarify how you are perceived and then kick-start with The Review Meeting is Obsolete

- Add custom video messaging to your communications

## Chapter 7. ONside - Our Process for Sifting Prospects from Suspects

Attract highly qualified prospective clients rather than chasing them by deploying a professional target marketing strategy.

- Activate advocacy from strategic partners and use an agenda-driven fit process rather than a transactional sales process

- Consider adding podcasting to your one-to-many marketing approach

### Chapter 8. ONboard - Our Process for Fast-Tracking New Clients to Advocate Status

You are at a high level of refer-ability as you transition a new client from their former provider.

- A primer for your client experience service model and matrix
- Add a Personal Organizer/Life in a Book to your onboarding process

### Chapter 9. ONgoing - Our Process for Total Client Engagement

Ensuring expectations are exceeded is achieved by design and ensures that clients feel compelled to empower you as their needs evolve.

- de/serve referrals by deploying your service matrix and positioning your introduction process professionally.
- Deploy tailored strategies with The Greeting Card playbook

### Chapter 10. ONwards - Our Process for Responding to Moments of Truth

Your approach when reacting to the changes that occur in a clients' life can deepen and replicate your best relationships.

- Turn FORM related information into an invaluable intellectual property
- The 10 best books to give to clients after a critical life event

### Chapter 11. Bench Strength - Our Process for Team Development

An enlightened approach and process to human capital can add consistency and enhance the culture within your enterprise.

- Be a serious student of Tuckman's Model and DISC for team formation and harmony
- Learn how C5 Team Dynamics can expand your capacity and add liberation to your life

**Chapter 12. Inflection Point - Our Process for Shifting from Organic to Scalable Growth**

Every investment of effort you make working ON your organic business can be converted to a B2B growth strategy.

- Work through our STRATEGIC Framework to determine your sweet spot between contentment and ambition.

- Learn how to add depth and breadth to your growth model with Level-UP

**Chapter 13. The Torch - Your Legacy and the Mentor-Protege Dynamic**

Few investments are as fulfilling and rewarding as taking someone under your wing and pointing them in the right direction.

- When it comes to human nature, it isn't different this time.

- 7 Essential books for developing your mentor skill set (a sub-list within the bigger list)

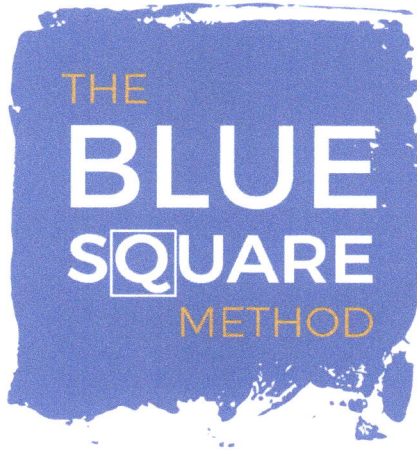

# Our Strategic Partners

# Coaching & Consulting for Elite Financial Professionals

Pareto Systems is an industry-leading business development firm dedicated to the elite professionals and companies within the fee-for-service sector. Duncan and his team of consultants work with professionals in a wide range of fields including Financial Services, Insurance, Accounting, Legal, Mortgage, and Consulting to create predictable, sustainable, and duplicable businesses.

Pareto Systems positions professionals to:

- Build and competitor-proof fiercely loyal advocates
- Run more efficient and profitable practices
- Restore liberation and order to their lives

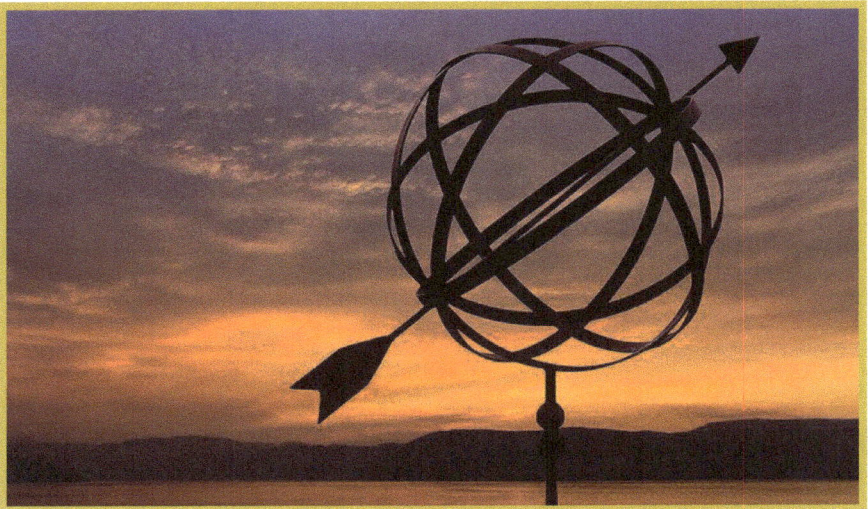

**1.866.593.8020 | paretosystems.com | inquiries@paretosystems.com**

# PMIND⬚⬚X

## Get clear on your opportunity gaps

The Practice Management Index, or the PMI for short, is a multiple choice assessment that explores 18 Focus Areas of your business that are all centered on Practice Management, Relationship Management and Business Planning. Your PMI Score and Report will help you better understand where you stand among your peers, and what action steps you can take now to address your opportunity gaps.

Your free PMI Report includes:

- An overall PMI Score to better understand where you stand in Practice Management

- A breakdown of how you rank in each of the 18 Business Focus Areas

- Specific actionable strategies to address your opportunity gaps

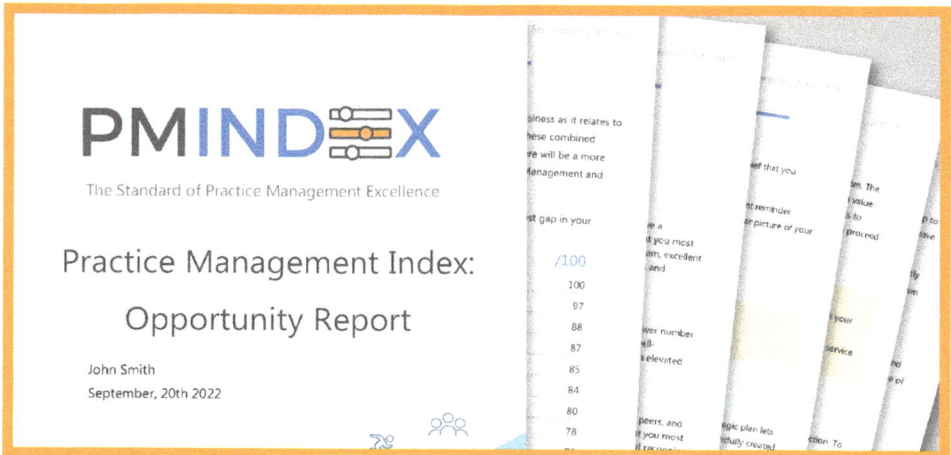

# PMIND⬚⬚X

The Standard of Practice Management Excellence

## Practice Management Index:

### Opportunity Report

John Smith

September, 20th 2022

Take the PMI for FREE today at:

**practicemanagementindex.com**

# Pareto Certified Speakers

In person or virtually, our presentations are not pep-talks or fireside chats; rather our speakers deliver productive, actionable strategies with a clear path for implementation.

The real value begins once the presentation ends. To ensure the audience can translate the ideas and strategies into real results, all of Pareto's Speakers can provide actionable follow-up resources for implementation into their business.

This may include:

- Linked & sequential webinars

- Video & complementary resources

- Articles, scripts, templates and tools

**1.866.593.8020 | speaking@paretosystems.com**
**paretosystems.com/speaking**

# TOOLKIT™
## by Pareto

## The Client Relationship, Simplified

A CRM ideally suited for professionals and teams that want a simple solution that works. Built on the foundational best practices of Pareto Systems.

Become more efficient, consistent and build longer lasting relationships by:

- Collecting F.O.R.M information
- Automating your processes
- Classifying your clients
- Deploying your Service Matrix

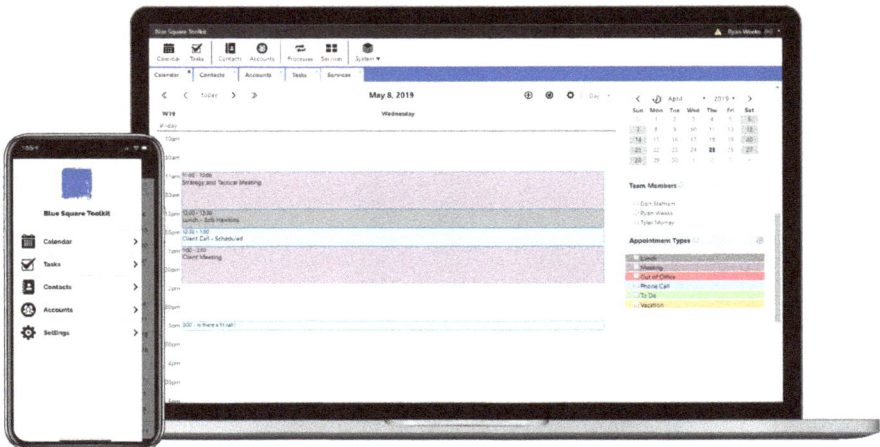

Start your 14-day free trial today!
**bluesquaretoolkit.com**

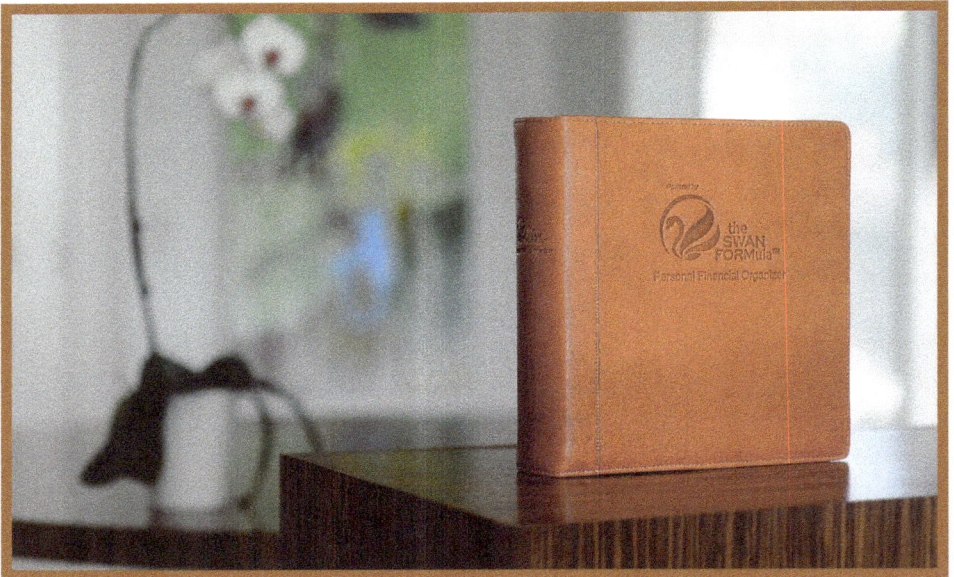

# Professional Branding and Graphic Design

*P3: **People, Practice Process:*** A customized and comprehensive approach for amplifying your professional contrast for upmarket client acquisition by creating a branded identity for your people, your practice and your process.

### Supplemental services include:

- What does your brand say? Brand Communication Development

- How is your brand represented? Brand Design Consultations

- What does your brand look like? Graphic Design Services

**1.877.969.8199**
**P3branding@paretosystems.com**

# Built on Behavioral (DISC) and Motivational Profiling

Culture, Chemistry, Communication, Consistency, Congruency. C5 Team Dynamics is a behavioral and motivational scientific profiling solution designed to build efficiencies and chemistry within your team.

**Understand Team Member Behaviors and Communication Gaps** - Cohesive communication within your team begins with identifying team member's key behavioral makeup, or characteristics that define them, and by understanding the communication gaps that may exist.

**Maximize Efficiencies within your Team** - Further excel your team and adapt to each other in a more meaningful and purposeful way. Is your firm performing to its fullest capacity?

**Enhance Communication** - Knowing the strengths and weaknesses of your team members' communication styles will help you craft focused communication within your team.

Call us to learn more: **1.866.593.8020**
Or Schedule a call: **paretosystems.com/schedule-a-call**

# ELEV▲TED

## Elevated Consulting with Duncan MacPherson

This is a collaborative relationship with Duncan MacPherson. Through one-to-one consultations, Duncan will help to ensure your team is strategically positioned for future growth, can develop multiple income streams, and amplify your intellectual property for increased enterprise value.

Elevated consulting is a highly customized deep dive deliverable for the elite fee-for-service professional who wants to:

- Add scalable growth to their organic growth model
- Develop an intellectual property
- Optimize their team dynamics
- Maximize their enterprise value

Call us to learn more: **1.866.593.8020**
Or Schedule a call: **paretosystems.com/schedule-a-call**

# always ⏻n
*With Duncan MacPherson*

## Podcast with Duncan MacPherson

If you are committed to continually working on yourself and your business, this podcast is for you. Always On is dedicated to and features relentlessly innovative, ambitious and balanced business professionals who are motivated by personal and professional plateau avoidance. Join host Duncan MacPherson as he interviews some of the top business professionals today.

Listen on your favorite podcast channel:

- iTunes
- Spotify
- And many more
- Or watch on YouTube

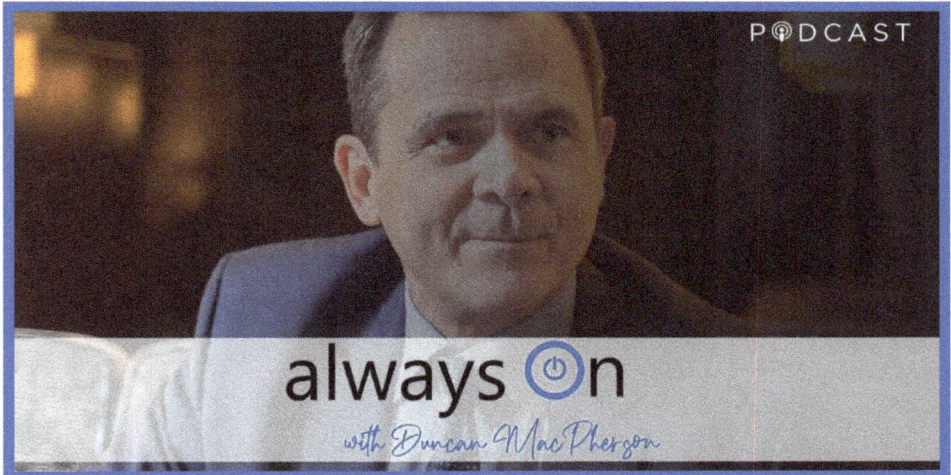

Find all of the podcast links at: **paretosystems.com/podcast**

*All of the Always On podcasts are produced by PROUD MOUTH*

## Podcasting Experts

We help you sell less and advise more by amplifying your influence over a growing audience of magnetically attracted fans who'll chase you down instead. You're already an expert at what you do. We help you become an influencer in your field. The kind of advisor who is actively sought out by clients. Let us help you do what we have done with Duncan MacPherson and his Always On Podcast.

**Be your own loud.**

We help advisors launch a podcast from start to finish:

- Develop your podcast brand
- Set up your studio
- Produce, edit and deliver each podcast

## What Our Influencers Are Saying

"Your team has made this a really easy process for me. All I have to do is think about the guests, topics, and you guys handle everything else. It's been terrific."

Larry Heller, President of Heller Wealth Management

Learn more at:
**proudmouth.com**

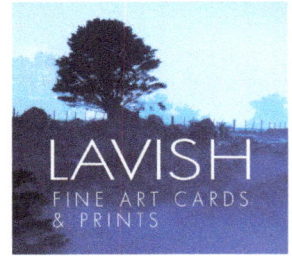

# High Quality Greeting Cards

Our beautiful, gallery-style cards are the perfect way to show your clients that you value their business and, more importantly, you value the relationship. Ordering is simple and the product is exceptional. Call us and find out what sets us apart from other greeting card companies. Personal, one-to-one support from the very first phone call to the successful delivery of your custom cards is a trademark of our business.

Our cards:

- Are handmade to order
- Can be customized with personalized greetings including company logo and name
- All images are printed on high quality photographic paper

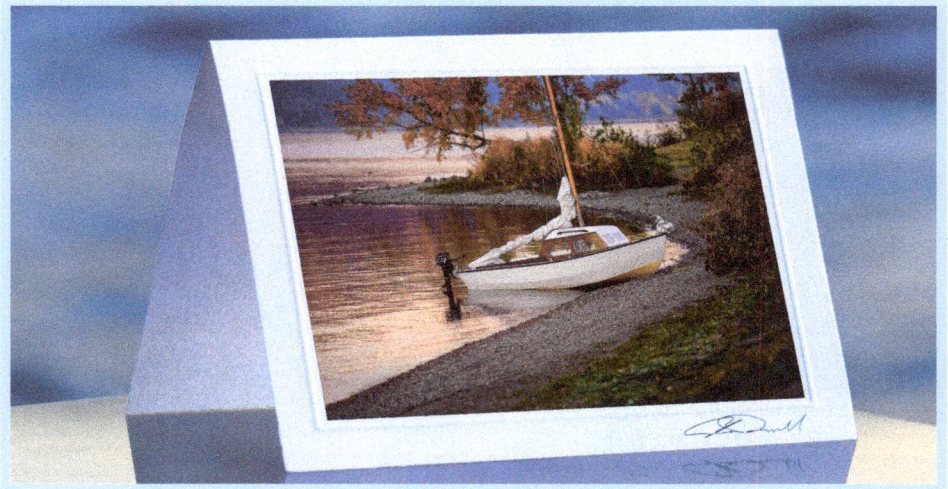

**1.888.599.7599**
**lavishcards.com**

# Grow Your Business with Creative Marketing Videos

The Idea Kit remote video process was built to make it easy. You get a personalized story plan, custom scripts, all the gear you need, live performance coaching in your remote record sessions, and a hands-free editing process. You won't just get videos that get you results, you get more relationships built on trust.

Try 'The Essentials': Pareto Systems Turnkey 2-Video Package

- Experts to help you create two polished videos

- Scripts based on Pareto language

- Step in front of the camera and bring the stories to life

**ideadecanter.com/pareto**

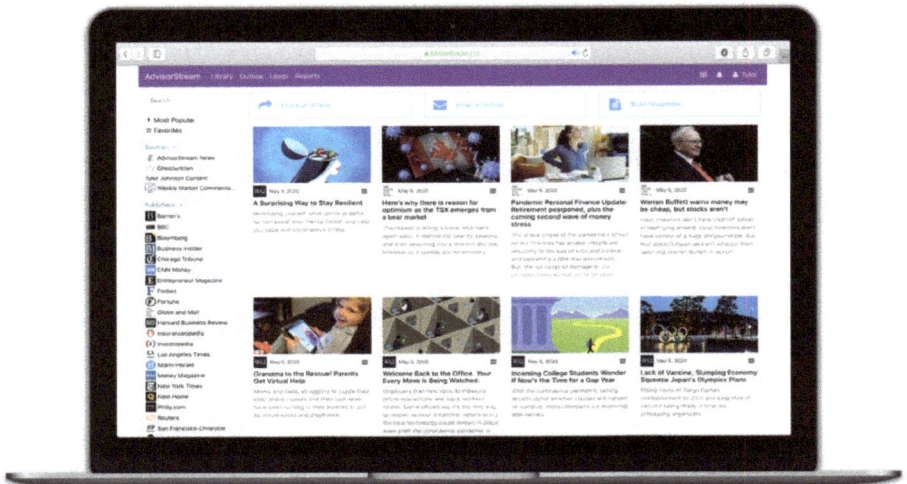

# Have you read all of the books on my list?

I get a lot of credit from people who buy into our philosophy and approach. They applaud me for being creative because of how the processes have been structured and presented. Truth be told, I'm not creative. What I am is a master assimilator. Much of my inspiration has come from the books I have read over the years.

My Reading list includes:

- 10 Best Books: To Give to a Client After a Critical Life Event
- 7 Essential Books: For Developing Your Mentor Skillset
- The books that have inspired me over the years

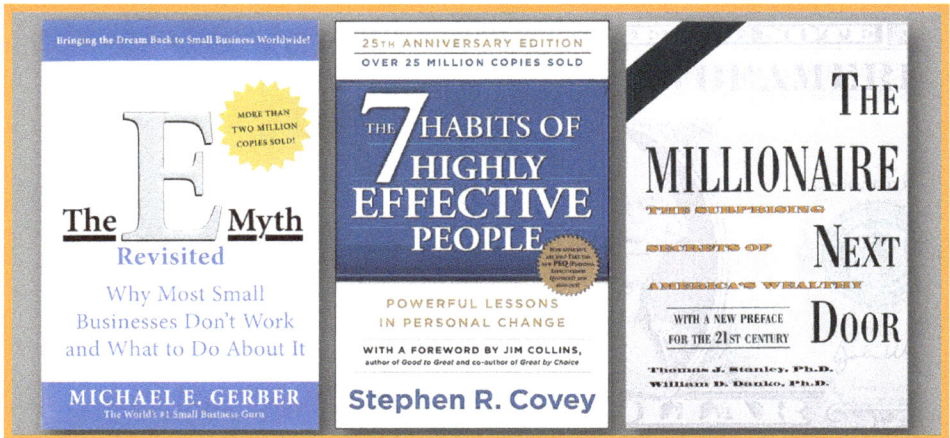

See the full list of books at:
**paretosystems.com/recommended-reading**